BURNING *the* GRASS

BURNING *the* GRASS

AT THE HEART OF CHANGE
IN SOUTH AFRICA, 1990–2011

WOJCIECH JAGIELSKI

Translated by Antonia Lloyd-Jones

SEVEN STORIES PRESS

New York • Oakland

This publication has been subsidized by Instytut Książki—
the ©POLAND Translation Program.

Originally published in Polish by Wydawnictwo Znak
under the title *Wypalanie traw*, 2012.

First English-language edition.

Seven Stories Press
140 Watts Street
New York, NY 10013
www.sevenstories.com

College professors and high school and middle school teachers may order free examina-
tion copies of Seven Stories Press titles. To order, visit www.sevenstories.com/textbook or
send a fax on school letterhead to (212) 226-1411.

Book design by Jon Gilbert

Library of Congress Cataloging-in-Publication Data

Jagielski, Wojciech, 1960- author.
  [Wypalanie traw. English]
  Burning the grass : at the heart of change in South Africa, 1990-2011 / Wojciech Jagiel-
ski ; translated by Antonia Lloyd-Jones.
    pages cm
  Translated from the Polish.
  ISBN 978-1-60980-647-7 (pbk.)
  1. Terre Blanche, Eugène N. 2. Politicians--South Africa--Biography. 3. Afrikaners-
-South Africa--Biography. 4. Racism--South Africa. 5. Apartheid--South Africa. 6.
South Africa--Ethnic relations. I. Lloyd-Jones, Antonia, translator. II. Title.
  DT1949.T47J3413 2015
  968.065--dc23
                              2015017972

Printed in the United States

9 8 7 6 5 4 3 2 1

CONTENTS

I used to have a friend in Ventersdorp, a small Afrikaner town on the veld in Transvaal. She was a journalist for the local newspaper.

When I called to tell her I was going to write about the town, and about Eugène Terre'Blanche, the man who ran it, she hung up and stopped answering my calls.

1

A pale autumn sun had risen over the town and the surrounding veld.

Easter Saturday was dawning, a time of sorrow and uncertainty. The smoke from burning grass, which had clouded the horizon for the past week, had come closer during the night. Driven by the east wind, it had crept up from the farms across the Skoonspruit River, to the very edge of town. It prompted anxiety, as well as thoughts of punishment, remorse, and paybacks yet to be identified.

First to awake, as ever, was Tshing, the black township adjoining white Ventersdorp. It got up as the first rays of sunlight were starting to dispel the darkness and chill of night. As the rooftops gradually loomed out of the dawn mist, smoke from the hearths rose above them, to the sound of hens clucking, gates creaking and then crashing shut.

The streets slowly began to fill with people. Men in navy-blue overalls carefully locked their front doors and gates behind them, then came out onto the road to join others, heading on foot to the white town over the hill.

Black town councillor Benny Tapologo, still half asleep, could imagine the scene taking place around him on all the nearby streets; it was the invariable morning stirring of the black township, heading for the white districts.

Benny, however, had no plans to get up. On Saturdays the town hall was closed. As he lay in bed, basking in the luxurious thought of a day off work, Benny kept delaying the moment when he'd get up, putting off all the pleasures that lay ahead of him that day. He had decided to wash his car that morning, his white Nissan SUV, and that evening he was going to watch a soccer match on television.

Raymond Boardman had got up too early, and reached town too early, long before the bank opened.

He left his car downtown, then, glancing at his watch and calculating how much time he had, he automatically set off along the road, slowly being flooded with cold morning sunlight, that ran toward the black ghetto.

It was so early that he met Tswana women on their way to clean, launder, and iron at the houses in Ventersdorp. He also passed black men in heavy cotton overalls heading for the white town. Some of them were standing at the town limits, near the Caltex gas station, to wait for the farmers who would come here in search of laborers to work on their farms, and would choose the strongest, fittest, and best—the rare few.

As a boy, Raymond had often come here with his father if there was a lack of hands to do the work on their farm or something had to be done that none of their workers could manage. "We need more blacks," his father would then say. "Time to make a trip to the Caltex."

Every time he passed the Caltex gas station in his car, Raymond was reminded of this process of selecting people from among others, all alike, in the same navy-blue or gray overalls and rubber shoes. And the eager way they clambered into the back of the truck. They seemed already on the move before his father had pointed a finger to say you, you, and you. They were in such a state of readiness that they seemed to sense his decision a split second before he did, or perhaps they were trying to force him to make the right choice. Raymond felt relief at the thought that he hadn't had to do that for a long time now. His own blacks were enough for the work on his farm; sometimes there was even a lack of jobs for them to do, and then they were forced to look for work in town.

At the Caltex gas station he stopped and turned back toward the white town. Now he was walking along with the men who hadn't stopped at the gas station. They had jobs in the white houses, and were so intent as they walked ahead that they seemed to be trying to anticipate the white housewives' wishes to do with watering and cutting their lawns, weeding their flowerbeds, and fixing their fences, driveways, and roofs.

There still wasn't a living soul downtown, though usually by this time of day there was plenty of traffic about. In the silence and emptiness, Raymond found a shady bench on a square outside the new town hall, by the triumphal arch. There he sat until late morning, bank opening time, gazing at the wall of the courthouse. In the night, or maybe at dawn, someone had painted some black sevens on it, joined to form a swastika—the emblem of the white brotherhood, a symbol of purity and good, of the never-ending war against the Antichrist.

Ten o'clock had struck when a red delivery truck stopped outside the Blue Crane Tavern, located on the town line. Henk Malan, owner of the bar, watched through the window as the driver got out of his vehicle and walked across the parking lot, nervously looking around him.

"A stranger," thought Henk. He knew why the man had got out of his car. As he unhurriedly dried his hands on a towel, he took a good look at him. "I bet he's not a customer," he decided. Whites only ever dropped in at the Blue Crane to ask the way—how to get to the highway to Coligny without going through the black township. The locals almost never looked in here. They called the Blue Crane a shebeen, a black drinking den, as if it were a disreputable dive, and not a decent bar.

"They avoid me like the plague," thought Henk angrily.

The whites didn't want the blacks to have their own bar in Ventersdorp. They were afraid that by opening a bar on the edge of town Henk would lure them out of the ghetto. And in this town the blacks were meant to stay in their place.

"You're opening a bar for blacks," his mother had said when Henk took her to the Blue Crane for the first time. And it was the last time too, because she'd never set foot there again. "A bar for blacks," she'd kept saying in painful disbelief, as he drove her back to her small cottage under a eucalyptus tree. She thought her son had no idea what he was doing, and that someone had given him bad advice. "Don't you know where we live?" she'd asked, as if he really might not know that. "Don't you know what sort of a place this is?"

But he knew very well what sort of a place it was. And he had a bar for blacks, exactly the kind he wanted.

He thought of his mother as he gazed at the white truck driver, nervously looking around the empty street.

"By now he's probably sorry he got out, or that he stopped here at all. Damn this town," muttered Henk under his breath. "They fear us like the devil fears holy water."

And that had been the case for as long as he could remember. Visitors were just as rare as the rain here. They avoided the town, not only because it was a long way from the main roads, but also because of the sense of threat it inspired in strangers. The young people in town took it worse than the older ones. Henk's stepson Frank, who had spent the morning painting a new signboard in a corner of the bar, cursed out loud at the memory of the previous day, when he'd made a trip to Potchefstroom, a sizeable city not far from here, famous for its university.

"You can't even drive anywhere anymore!" he spat in anger. "A guy lets slip that he's from Ventersdorp, and at once they stare at him as if he's a beast! Maybe we should think about changing the name of this town?"

The white driver from the red pickup got into his vehicle and turned back onto the N14 national road, along which he'd come.

Even more annoyed by this than usual, Henk went outside. Frank set up a ladder and nailed the new sign above the entrance; it had a crane painted in gold, just like the one on the five-cent coins.

"It's crooked! Can't you bloody well see it's crooked?" barked Henk, lighting a cigarette.

Standing in the now deserted street, he gazed at the smoke coming from the veld all the way to the river. That day they had gone outside every hour, to stand in a group with the neighbors, staring at the veld. But this time they were in the street alone, as if everyone else had left.

"It feels deserted," said Frank from the ladder.

The Blue Crane stood in a row of buildings bordering some meadows and the river. Beyond lay the veld, from where the smoke from the burning grassland was drifting toward town.

Sometimes it grew thinner and paler, almost disappearing, blending in with the silvery, livid blue sky, and then it seemed to be off, dispelled by the wind. But now it looked to Malan even closer, denser, almost navy blue, like the storm clouds settled on the far bank of the river.

The blacks had been setting the grass alight for months, sometimes in several places at once, so the town was surrounded by smoke. The whites in Ventersdorp said they were doing it on purpose, so nobody could tell where it came from. Was it just workmen burning the roadside verges, or were they sending another white farm up in smoke? Now the smoke had come so close that it seemed set to engulf the town, lay siege to it, and finally launch the ultimate storm.

"Is that OK?" called Frank from the ladder.

Henk turned his gaze from the smoke on the veld and reluctantly inspected the new sign. To his mind, whatever he painted on it and however much effort he made, there was no way to beat the recession or avert disaster.

"What is there to say?" he muttered. "It's all because of Eugène! Maybe if he weren't here . . . "

But actually Henk wanted Eugène Terre'Blanche in this town.

At noon, Chris Mahlangu arrived at Terre'Blanche's farm, but he didn't find the white farmer there. So he decided to head for town to ask the farmer's wife for money. He knew where she lived—he had sometimes cut the grass for her.

Like everyone in town, Mahlangu knew that Terre'Blanche didn't pay the laborers hired to work on his farm, nor did he even pay for his groceries at the local stores. He bought everything on credit, which the white and Indian storekeepers didn't dare refuse him. He used to pay off all his debts at the end of each month, but in recent years he hadn't been so scrupulous, and at the sight of him the local storekeepers would slip into the back room.

Nor did he pay the blacks whom he would fetch from Tshing to cut his grass or graze his cattle. Like other white farmers, he deducted every last little expense from their promised salaries. He made deductions for the gas he used to transport them from town to his farm, for their overnight accommodation in an old stable, and for electricity. He deducted the cost of every beer or bottle of whisky he bought for them on credit. When payday came, out of the several hundred rand he'd promised, he'd only issue half the money at most to the workmen.

The other white farmers were no better, and visitors were surprised the blacks from Tshing hired themselves out to them at all. As if they had a choice! In the entire neighborhood there was no other work or opportunity to earn money. So they went into service for the farmers, counting on the fact that maybe this time they'd be lucky.

On Easter Saturday Chris Mahlangu already knew he wasn't in luck. When he'd asked Terre'Blanche for money the previous day, Good Friday, the farmer had told him to drive in the herd from pasture and count the cattle in his sight. Chris counted ninety-four head, but Terre'Blanche insisted there should be ninety-seven.

He'd threatened that unless the cows were found, not only was he not going to pay a penny, he was also going to send Chris to prison for theft. The threat to call the police was enough to terrify Mahlangu, who had no documents; if he was arrested, he could be deported back to Zimbabwe, from where he'd brought his family in search of a living.

Terre'Blanche swore and called him a *kaffir*, threatening him with the machete he always carried at the farm. Everybody knew that when he flew into a rage, he lost his self-control. At one point he came up to Mahlangu and seized him by the throat. "You'd better bring me those cows, kaffir," he hissed, raising the machete. "Otherwise there won't be much of you left to clear up."

Mahlangu tore free of the farmer and raced off across the meadow to Dirk Koetze's farm next door. That evening Terre'Blanche sent Patrick, the stable boy, after him, to fetch him back so they could reach an agreement.

They came back together the next day, but Terre'Blanche wasn't on the farm, and his wife in town said she didn't get involved with financial settlements between her husband and the workmen. She called her husband to get him to drive over, and he told them to wait in the street outside.

He arrived in a bright, almost friendly mood. He could be like that, when nothing had made him angry. He told them to get in the car. Without a word, they scrambled into the bed of his pickup truck. The whites in town still transported their black workers or servants that way. They weren't allowed to occupy a seat inside the vehicle. Summoned to the car, they climbed into the back, where shopping, bulk goods, equipment, and other things were put.

On the way to the farm they stopped at the big Overland liquor store at the edge of town. Winking conspiratorially, Terre'Blanche bought thirty small bottles of Savanna Cider, three packs of cigarettes, and some Smirnoff pear vodka for himself. In his typically jovial way, he joked with the store owner's daughter, who'd come to town from university for the holidays, and was helping her father on Easter Saturday. At the farm he proposed that they drink to make it up, and forget about their differences.

But as soon as they mentioned money, he flew into a rage again, and told them to get out, then went into the house, slamming the door behind him.

Mahlangu and Patrick went to Koetze's farm, where they shared the cider with the local workmen. As they smoked, they conferred on what to do. "There's nothing but trouble with that white," they said, shaking their heads. "It would be better for everyone if he were dead."

Late in the afternoon they went back to Terre'Blanche's farm to demand the money from the farmer again. The front door was locked, but they noticed a window left ajar. Chris signaled to Patrick to wait for him, while he went into the stable. Moments later he came back, carrying a heavy metal crowbar.

The shadows were starting to lengthen and the wind was bringing in the smell of smoke and burned grass from out on the veld, far stronger than earlier in the day. In Ventersdorp the white homeowners had begun to take black laborers to their farms outside town by pickup truck. The bright afternoon was slowly changing into a warm, quiet evening.

All afternoon, Martha Terre'Blanche kept trying to call her husband.

Eugène had always led his own, separate life to which she had no access. He was capable of vanishing for days at a time, or shutting himself away in his own thoughts. They even lived separately, he on the farm and she in town. She was accustomed to solitude and silence. She herself was surprised by the alarm that her husband's absence prompted in her that particular day.

With every telephone call he failed to answer it was growing, becoming stifling and incapacitating.

Through the window she had seen some black men waiting by the fence. She had recognized Chris, whom Eugène had hired six months ago to graze the cattle on the farm and to do the gardening at the house in town. He was standing by the gate with a boy whom she had also seen on the farm.

Then Eugène had driven up in his white pickup truck. He had told the blacks to sit in the back, behind the driver's cab, and had gone back to the farm at Ratzegaai, about twelve kilometers out of town. Since when he hadn't been picking up his calls.

Toward evening, now seriously worried, she decided to call the van Zyls, who lived at the neighboring property across the road from the Terre'Blanche farm. Dora, Eugène's beloved sister, answered the phone.

"No, I haven't seen him today," she said. "But he's meant to be dropping by this evening."

That evening, on the Saturday before Easter Day, the feast of Resurrection and Redemption, they were holding a birthday party for their oldest son.

"He's probably gone out on horseback, and left his phone at home," said Dora. "I'll tell Don to go and check what's happening over there."

On the veranda, Don van Zyl glanced at his watch. It was coming up to five.

The shadows were gathering, growing denser in the valley. Don van Zyl sat down on the veranda outside his house to watch the dusk fall.

It wasn't how he usually spent his evenings—he had no time

for such things. But that day he sat down and watched, as if he felt he ought to.

From his house on the hill he had a good view of the dirt road in the green valley and some thick copses growing on the farm located on the opposite slope. It belonged to his brother-in-law, Eugène Terre'Blanche. In recent years Eugène's farm had badly fallen into decline. Van Zyl sat and mused on what was happening to that piece of land. How if you don't have the heart or the head for it, it won't be kind to you, and it'll stop producing.

Eugène lived and breathed major politics. His world consisted of never-ending debates on how appallingly things were going in the country, and how life would get even worse when the blacks finally took over. He would summon his supporters to meetings and marches, and rack his brains over how to deal with the situation, how to prevent the blacks from taking power. Meanwhile, his land had been going to seed.

Eugène's world involved nocturnal rallies with flaming torches. He'd arrive at them on horseback, dressed in his best uniform, and amid fluttering flags he would deliver fiery speeches and threaten war. Could people like him take care of the land?

Eugène was flattered when the newspapers referred to him as a Boer commander, a general, the last defender of the white Afrikaners, the heirs and descendants of the Boers. Although he didn't hold any official post in his hometown of Ventersdorp, he was regarded as its most important citizen—immune, not subject to any laws apart from the ones he established himself. He inspired real terror in the blacks, and the whites dared not oppose him either.

"What a waste," sighed Don van Zyl heavily, as he cast a glance at the Terre'Blanche family farm, which Eugène had inherited from his father. From year to year the weeds had grown to form tall, uncut grass, on which Terre'Blanche's cattle grazed, and here and there on the pastureland clumps of young trees and bushes had sprouted.

Lost in thought, Don van Zyl gazed vacantly at the shifting shadows in the valley. He didn't even shudder when the phone in the living room rang. The ringing stopped, but a little later it rang again, even louder and more insistently.

He heard his wife's voice. Terre'Blanche's wife Martha had called. She didn't live on the farm, but in town. She didn't feel safe at the farm, which was in an isolated place. In the last few years there had been an increasing number of attacks and killings at the farms scattered around the town, and many of the farmers had bought houses for their families in Ventersdorp. Each morning they drove to their farms as if going to the office, and at night they came back to town.

The sun was starting to set, and Don was about to go inside, when from the direction of Terre'Blanche's homestead a black horse appeared on the hill. It crossed the meadow on the hillside, cutting a trail through the tall yellow grass, galloped up to the fence along the dirt road, then turned around and raced back toward the house.

Van Zyl recognized that horse at once, and that was why he immediately knew something awful had happened.

Chris Mahlangu and Patrick crept into the bedroom through the half-open window. The room was shrouded in semi-darkness. The farmer was lying on his back on a large bed, with his arms spread wide, fully clothed, but with his pants undone. He was asleep.

For a while they stood there, staring at the snoring man.

The very first blow, inflicted by Mahlangu with the metal bar, deprived Terre'Blanche of consciousness.

Chris Mahlangu went on hitting, over and over again, putting all his strength, hatred, rage, and fear into every blow as they rained down on the farmer's head, arms, and chest. Mahlangu heard the crunch of breaking bones, and could smell blood in the air.

When he ran out of strength, he handed the bar to Patrick, who was just standing there, watching the killing. Now without a word he took a swing and struck the white man three times on the head and chest. Each blow made Terre'Blanche's body jerk upward, as if bringing it back to life.

It was almost dark and very stuffy in the bedroom. Panting heavily, they stared at the blood-soaked corpse, which looked nothing like the terror-inducing white farmer anymore. Completely smashed, his face was unrecognizable; one of the blows had shattered his jaw, perforating his cheek and tongue. There seemed to be blood everywhere—on the bed, on the pillow and the victim's body, on the walls, ceiling, and floor, on the killers' hands and clothing, on their faces and in their hair.

Chris Mahlangu took a knife from under his belt. He was leaning over the exposed corpse when from the pocket of Terre'Blanche's loosened pants a cell phone and some car keys fell to the floor. The metallic jangle broke the silence alarmingly. Mahlangu shuddered. He glanced at the mutilated face again, but then silently put his knife away in his pants pocket and bent down to pick up the phone and the keys. The moment he touched the phone, it rang. He stuffed it deep into his pocket and signaled to Patrick.

"Let's get out of here."

As they left, they slammed the kitchen door behind them.

Benny Tapologo found out about Terre'Blanche's death before it was announced on the evening radio news. In Tshing that sort of news went round at lightning speed. Once heard, if only by chance, if only in a twisted version, it went out on the grapevine, racing from farmyard to farmyard, and crashing into every small store and bar, now eliciting delight, and now alarm.

On Saturday evenings the townspeople of Tshing retired for the night late, reluctantly, loath to bring an end to their drunken revels, feeling indifferent to the Sunday ahead, which was always worse than the day before. At the end of the week the workers on the local farms received their pay. Others who came back from town in the evening with their week's wages in their pockets included gas station and workshop employees, store assistants, waiters, cleaners and dishwashers from a number of small hostels, bars, and restaurants, and also the domestic staff employed in the white houses.

At home they handed some of the money to their wives and mothers for their keep. With the rest of their earnings, rolled into fat wads of banknotes that pleasantly swelled their pockets, they headed into the darkness to forget the arduous week, and find the strength and faith in themselves to get through the next one, by chatting with friends, enjoying beer and entertainment.

Benny worked at the town hall in the white town, and had such a good living that he didn't need to gather his strength before each new week began. But as in the past, on Saturday evenings he liked to drop in at one of the local bars next to the stores, where they drank beer straight from the bottle, sitting on wooden crates set out on the lawn.

He'd run into friends whose lives hadn't been as successful as his, reminisce about the old days, and ask how they were doing. He didn't want them to think he was getting above himself, like others who'd done well. He'd been lucky, and he had a good life, so good that he could afford a house in Ventersdorp and a school for his children. Any time he liked, he could move out of Tshing.

But he hadn't done that, or even considered it. He couldn't say he liked the township, but he'd grown up here, and was used to thinking of it as his place on earth. To tell the truth, he had thought of leaving, but for Johannesburg, the big city, where anything seemed possible, and your dreams came true all by themselves. Or nearby Potchefstroom, where he could take up studies at one of the local universities, and get a diploma that would help him to build a career. Or at least the provincial capital, Mafikeng.

Benny wanted to break out into the world; with each passing day the feeling was growing that he was suffocating at the town hall, letting the life in which he had so much to achieve trickle through his fingers. Although he longed for change, he didn't regard moving from Tshing to Ventersdorp as any kind of change. "There's nothing going on here," he said. "All over the country everything is changing, but here it's the same as before, as if nothing had happened."

That Easter Saturday night before the Day of Resurrection and Redemption, the only subject on everybody's lips in Tshing was death. But unlike good Christians, they weren't discussing the death of the Savior, but that of Eugène Terre'Blanche, whom they so ardently feared and hated. They held animated debates, like fans after their team has won a match. An inebriated boy came striding down the middle of the main street, one of not many in the township to be lit at night by streetlamps. Imitating the marching pace of a military parade, he was strutting along, singing into the darkness: "Long life the brave guy who killed the white farmer! Now at last we're going to be free too! Hey! Kill the Boer! Kill the farmer! Only cowards are afraid!"

The final words were from a song sung many years earlier by black rebels rising against the white regime. They had finally won and taken power, and yet they were still singing songs about killing the Boers at their public rallies. They said it was out of respect for the past, and that the lyrics shouldn't be taken literally—they weren't singing those words to incite anyone to kill at all. However, the whites saw it as an ominous threat of revenge, and they saw that threat being carried out in the ever more frequent killings of white farmers, brutally murdered at their own farms, scattered about the veld.

Benny, who had also mindlessly sung the song about killing Boers at rallies before now, had no doubts that the white farmers would see Terre'Blanche's death as yet another sign that the blacks' day of vengeance was approaching.

The local white townspeople and farmers may well have seen him as a leader and a hero, but in Tshing nobody was weeping for Terre'Blanche. The blacks, whom he regarded as slaves, genuinely loathed him, and when he died they believed he had finally got what he deserved. But privately Benny thought the man who had killed him had to be an outsider, because although Terre'Blanche treated them like dirt, worse than animals, none of the local blacks would have dared raise a hand to the white master.

The cell phone was still ringing and ringing, driving Chris Mahlangu into helpless rage.

He was sorry he'd taken it—he'd automatically picked it up from the floor along with the car keys, which had slipped out of the white man's pocket. But he hadn't been able to start the pickup truck, and the phone had started ringing almost as soon as it was in his hand, like an alarm, like a call for help. Since then it hadn't shut up.

Chris Mahlangu was not sorry for what he'd done. He'd thought it through long ago, and now he was afraid of nothing—nobody could get in his way. And yet the constantly ringing phone was making him feel anxious, scattering his thoughts.

He had the tart flavor of cider on his lips, and confusion in his head, prompted by alcohol and what they'd done. Patrick was silent as the grave. The field track was narrow, so he was walking a few paces behind, but Chris could feel his mute gaze on his back, as if the boy were trying to penetrate his thoughts, fathom his intentions, and elicit his praise.

He knew Patrick would do as he told him, and wouldn't act without his orders. The boy was sixteen, and had been working at the farm for a month. He slept in the stable. He had performed as he should, if not better. Now they were walking downhill through tall grass toward the dirt road separating Terre'Blanche's land from the neighboring farms belonging to Don van Zyl and Dirk Koetze. There they were going to finish what they had started, just as they'd planned.

Deep in Chris's pocket, the cell phone rang again, loud and insistent. He stopped, took it out, and held it close to his eyes to read the number on the display.

"Again!" he muttered softly, recognizing the same set of figures as before.

The phone stopped ringing, but soon it began again. Mahlangu couldn't bear it any longer. The sound was drilling into his brain, ringing in his head, time after time, again and again.

He tried to prize the back from the phone with a fingernail, and when it sprang off, he picked out the bright SIM card, bit it, and swallowed it. The phone shut up, and silence fell around them, now only disturbed by birds circling the trees in search of shelter for the night.

"Now we'll have to borrow someone's phone to make the call," he heard Patrick say.

Mahlangu just nodded.

When he turned around to look at Koetze and van Zyl's homesteads, visible on the hill, he noticed a black horse running along the fence that separated the farm from the road. It was Terre'Blanche's horse. It looked as if it were seeking a gap, an escape route.

At Buckingham farm, amid maize fields and meadows half an hour's drive from Ventersdorp, the table was being set for supper. Sitting in his study, Raymond Boardman could hear the clink of dishes and smell the aroma of gravy, pumpkin soup, boiled spinach, and potatoes coming from the kitchen.

That day for the first time he had faced the plain fact that he might lose the family farm. It had crossed his mind before now, but he had fended off the thought, convinced it was enough to sit out the trouble and everything would fall into place. Now, however, back from his afternoon round of the fields, as he sat bowed over the table and ran his eye down the columns of figures in the account books, he felt rising despair.

The farm was consuming more and more money. It was like a bottomless well. That morning he'd been into town to talk to his financial adviser, but the bank had refused him credit. Only now did he realize how much he'd been counting on a loan. It would have untied his hands, given him hope and a view ahead. Without it he didn't know what to do.

"There is one way," the bank adviser had said quietly. "Take on a black partner. Then you'll get what you want. Loans, concessions, grants—whatever you like, you see?"

There were two reasons why he couldn't do that. As he sat in his study, he turned them over in his mind again. If he took on a black partner, he'd have to give him a majority share in the farm. His father would never agree to let blacks manage the farm. He was also totally opposed to taking out loans, but refused to transfer the farm to his son. He still regarded him as a loser who'd fritter it away. Raymond was counting on the fact that if he managed to save the farm, the old man might at least agree to transfer it to Raymond's middle son, Mike, who seemed to be a born farmer.

Raymond closed the accounts books, took a deep breath, and went into the dining room. He had decided to tell the family after supper that they were probably going to lose the farm.

His wife Charlene and their son Matthew were waiting for him at table. Charlene asked him to say grace before the meal. They held hands, and in a low, calm voice Raymond thanked the Creator for all that He granted them in His bounty. The words of the prayer and the sight of his family usually filled him with peace, dissolved his fears and uncertainty. It only took a moment for him to feel strong again and recover his faith. But this time he didn't feel relief, the burden didn't grow any lighter. He couldn't gather his thoughts or join in with the lively conversation his wife was having with their son.

He jumped at the sound of the phone.

"It's Malan," he said in surprise, glancing at the number on the display.

Henk Malan, owner of the Blue Crane bar, was in charge of the neighborhood militia that the local farmers had formed.

Since there had started to be robberies and murders on the

farms, the neighbors had been calling each other with news and warning one another of dangers. The police always came too late, and couldn't really do anything. So the Afrikaners in Ventersdorp had recognized that they had no alternative but to take matters into their own hands.

Throughout Transvaal, the white farmers were forming and joining similar neighborhood militias. Armed, in pickup trucks or on horseback, they patrolled the farms and dirt roads, stopped vagrants, and if summoned by phone or via the local radio station, they brought help at lightning speed to farmers who'd been attacked.

Usually retired soldiers and policemen were chosen to lead the militia. Henk Malan had served in the army, and had even been to war, so he was regarded as the right man to command the neighborhood militia; the district entrusted to him included Buckingham farm.

Raymond wasn't fond of Malan, and knew his phone call was unlikely to bring good news. He hadn't joined the local militia, a fact which Malan held against him, as he never failed to remind him.

"Maybe you already know this, but I thought it wouldn't hurt to call you anyway. Eugène Terre'Blanche has been murdered. Probably by some blacks." Like all the Afrikaners in the area, Henk spoke English with a harsh, guttural accent. "I thought you should know. Will you tell Mike, or should I call them?" he added. Mike's wife, Julianna, had once worked at the Blue Crane tavern. She'd resigned when she married Mike and moved with him to a small farmhouse outside town. Malan had often told them they were asking for trouble by living in such a remote place, but as commander of the neighborhood militia he would look after the young couple, like a mother hen tending her chicks. Julianna knew Eugène well. Perhaps she even liked him. If they'd killed someone like him, anything could happen now.

Raymond slowly hung up. To his amazement, rather than alarm and gloom, the news of the murder seemed to prompt a sense of hope in him, a feeling that maybe not everything was lost yet.

If it was true that Terre'Blanche had been murdered, and if blacks had killed him, the government would finally have to take action. Terre'Blanche was not just anyone, not just some van der Merwe, Botha, du Plessis, or Boardman, the response to whose murder on the farm would have been a short note in the newspaper. The murder of Terre'Blanche was an attack, a symbolic blow aimed at all white farmers. Now the government would not only have to guarantee safety for the white farms, but also make sure they didn't collapse. This death might not be in vain. For Raymond Boardman it had come at the best possible moment.

He picked up the phone and selected Mike's number.

The day was reluctant to fade, dragging out its final moments in the crannies of a walnut tree at the western wall of the house. That was where every day ended; Mike was waiting for the last purple glow to vanish from the leaves, and then he could say this one was over too.

He could sense Julianna's presence behind him. She was just standing there, as so often before, waiting for him to bring up the usual issue. Their quarrel had come full circle, bringing them back to the start, to the very same words they had uttered this morning.

Mike watched as the daylight crawled off the foliage, leaving the yard in darkness. He felt disappointment, as if he really had been counting on the darkness to release them from this conversation, as if it would put an end to it in a natural way. But the words remained, just as fresh as in the morning, when he'd said them the first time.

"For people like us Australia is the best place on earth," he said. "It's the only place where you can start over."

"But why start over?" erupted Julianna. "I don't want to start all over again!"

Like him, she wanted to leave the town she'd lived in all her life. She saw no future for herself or for their marriage there. She felt she was suffocating in Ventersdorp, that there was something threatening them, a curse hanging over them, which was bound to come true if they didn't get out in time. Her thoughts were of moving to nearby Potchefstroom, or slightly farther, to Johannesburg, maybe even to Pretoria, but not to the other end of the world. She had never been farther than Cape Town, where the Boardmans had once taken her.

The thought of leaving the country was the only thing giving Mike the strength to carry on. He seemed to think that moving to Australia would solve all their problems, do away with their worries and doubts.

"I can't bear it here any longer! I can't bear it, I tell you! Do you really not understand?"

But no, she didn't.

Even when the news of Terre'Blanche's death reached them, Mike knew that although Julianna could see the threat, she had her own way of judging it. In her imagination it was limited in its destructive force, reduced to something familiar by all the years she had spent in Ventersdorp. Even if Terre'Blanche's death intensified the danger, she still found it less frightening than leaving for Australia. That Mike did understand as he gazed at his wife that evening.

All her life she had been witness to what happened in this town, and yet now she was blind to the fact that matters were going outside the standard frame, changing into an unbridled force that could destroy them. This thought made him even more eager to get away, and at the same time all the more aware of the irreversible nature of such a decision. For the first time he felt scared too, and wanted to remain on familiar ground, just like Julianna. A murder in the neighborhood should have confirmed all his darkest forebodings and fears, but instead of that he felt rising doubts.

"What'll happen now?" asked Julianna.

He shrugged and went out onto the veranda.

When his father called, he was sitting on the steps, smoking a cigarette.

"Have you heard?" asked Raymond.

"Yes," he said.

"Would you and Julianna and the boys like to come here for the night?"

"Drive across the veld on a night like this?"

For a while they both said nothing.

"If they've killed a man like Eugène, I guess nothing's ever going to be the same again, is it?" said Mike at last. "Maybe something's finally going to change around here too?"

The killers came back from Terre'Blanche's place by way of the meadow and the road to Koetze's farm. It was early evening; the shadows were gathering and thickening in the valley. Soaked with blood, they dragged themselves to the outbuildings, where the farmer's black workers lived.

"I've killed Eugène Terre'Blanche, I've killed the white leader," said Chris Mahlangu. "Now I'm gonna be in charge here, I'll be your morena, your leader. I'll be giving the orders, and you're going to obey me now."

They didn't believe him; even when he tried to borrow a phone to call the police and tell them the whole story, they thought he was just bragging. And if it was true, there was all the more reason not to hand him a phone. Finally one of the workmen agreed to let Mahlangu call the police from his phone.

The duty officer told Mahlangu and Patrick to go to the main road and wait there until a patrol car came for them. They were standing on the verge when the police car drove up and took them back to Terre'Blanche's farm.

To the policemen's amazement, the killers didn't even try to run away, nor had they washed the victim's blood off themselves. Calm and reconciled to their fate, they admitted the whole thing, as if believing they had acted rightly, and that the wrong had been done to them. Although they had committed the crime, they were its victims just as much as the man they had killed.

They didn't expect to be punished, but to be rewarded instead.

2

In the fall, the town of Ventersdorp looms out of the fields of maize, sunflowers, and tobacco that tightly surround it. A road surfaced in cracked asphalt leads westward from Johannesburg amid sun-faded crops scattered as far as the horizon, taller than a grown man. Before it gave way to the plantations, waist-high tawny grass used to cover the fields, forming rippling veld on a broad, level, boundless plateau.

Woods and copses are a rarity here. The monotony of the landscape is only broken by solitary, soaring eucalyptus trees, gnarled, bushy acacias, green clumps of fleshy aloes, and grain silos shining silver in the sunlight, betraying the presence of towns and farms that blend in with the veld and the yellowed fields.

In the fall, when the harvest ends, the farmers send people out to burn the stubble and grass. On fine days, when there's mild frost in the mornings, sweet-smelling, gray-blue smoke rises from fire that's invisible from afar. Caught up by the wind, it shoots into the sky and forms trailing clouds that wreathe the fields until dusk. Only when darkness falls can reddish glimmers be seen twinkling close to the ground. People tread them out before nightfall to stop the fire from creeping up to the farmyards.

The earth here is fertile, though the sky has always been sparing with its water. In other parts of the Highveld, which stretches between the banks of the Vaal and the Limpopo Rivers, from the Drakensberg to the Kalahari desert, real treasure has been found. Gold and diamonds were so easily accessible, and in such abundance, that brave souls driven mad by the fever of possessing them were drawn here from all over the world.

Yet in Ventersdorp nobody could be sure of an easy income, and the only treasure here was the rich earth, fit for cultivation and pasture, but demanding effort, patience, and humility. That was what the people who decided to settle and live here had to be like too. They were accustomed to hard work, determined characters who humbly accepted the fate that the good Lord had sent them in his goodness and his inscrutable judgments.

Every time I arrive in Ventersdorp, I feel as if the local citizens are seeing me for the first time.

I have no trouble recognizing the town, which as the years go by hardly changes at all. It's only on the hill separating Ventersdorp from its black township, Tshing, that the veld has now given way to supermarkets and large stores, which have grown up along the highway running between them.

As I slowly drive down the deserted main road across town, I pass the familiar low-rise stores, craftsmen's workshops, and offices. The names of the streets are coming back to me, where they come from and which ones they intersect. I know how to get to a particular address, I know the shortcuts and blind alleys.

It's easy for me to become familiar with the town again, whereas it will never admit to being acquainted with me. Sleepy, sedated by the midday heat, it gives the newcomer the impression of being totally self-absorbed, consumed by its own urgent business. With its back turned, absent, not at all interested, it doesn't answer your greeting; it looks away, like someone you've met before pretending not to remember you.

In fact, it always makes you feel as if nobody's there, as if, arriving unannounced, you haven't found the owner at home. By day it's usually only blacks who trail about the streets. The white citizens are working or keeping out of the sun in bungalows hidden beneath the boughs of old trees exuding greenery. Nor do you see any children. Somehow whenever I'm here, even the schools just happen to be closed.

But any outsider's appearance in this empty town is immediately observed and noted—so are his every movement, every visit, encounter, question, and utterance. You only have to arrive and stay the night, and by next morning the whole town will know that a stranger has appeared. "Have you come to us for long?" asks the owner of the bar next to the gas station, as he brings your coffee. "Have you come far?" asks the bank clerk.

Anywhere else, these questions are friendly, giving you a sense of belonging, but here they are not an invitation at all. Instead they serve quite the opposite purpose: not to welcome the newcomer, but to exclude him, to isolate him. Polite hospitality is a protective layer that prevents strangers from infiltrating, and distracts their attention away from, the real life of the town. It keeps the newcomer at a safe distance, caught in a cobweb of conversations about the weather, politics, or the state of the roads.

Anywhere else, gaining trust, making an acquaintance and having a conversation, would be a permanent enough point to which you could refer or return, or from which you could start the onward journey. In Ventersdorp, each time this road had to be traveled again, each day everything had to be started over.

Each day went by without leaving any facts or words behind it, as if it hadn't happened at all, or were trapped in a time loop, repeating itself over and over.

Four roads from four directions lead across the yellow veld to Ventersdorp. The one that leads from the east, from Johannesburg more than one hundred kilometers away, branches off past a viaduct and, changing from the national N14 into the local R53, then into an ordinary street, it runs on between low buildings straight into town. Before stopping at an intersection in front of a church it passes two gas stations, a car repair shop, several stores, a small boarding house, two bars on opposite sides of the street, one selling sandwiches and the other fried chicken, and a tavern right at the entrance into town.

It used to be called the Blue Crane, and it was run by Henk Malan. In actual fact, the only difference between the tavern and an ordinary liquor store was that here you could drink on the spot. The blacks drank beer, squatting by a stone wall or on the sidewalk outside the tavern. For the whites, who rarely looked in here, Henk had sectioned off a small, smoke-filled room that also served him as an office.

The whole tavern consisted of a chest-high counter made of wooden boards, to which three wobbly bar stools had been added. Henk brought beer or whisky ordered by the customers from the store, set the glasses on the bar, poured the liquor, then screwed the tops on the bottles and stowed them discreetly behind the bar. He only fetched them out to pour the next round.

He watched to make sure the customers didn't have empty glasses, but when they signaled to say that was enough, he didn't urge them to have one for the road, but just wrapped the bottle in a paper bag and handed it to them in parting, like a gift. If anyone drank their bottle dry and still hadn't had enough, he asked if they'd like to try something new. Then, clanking his keys, he'd open the security bars and go into the store for a new bottle of the same old whisky, and then praise its fresh flavor and aroma as he poured it out.

"It's like letting a fox into the henhouse," he'd say. "Since then I haven't had a drop of alcohol. Not even beer. If you want to sell whisky, you can't drink it yourself."

The outsiders who stopped by were lured here by the inn sign with the bar's name on it in black and red letters. Henk Malan thought it was a good location.

"Travelers go past the restaurants after the viaduct because they don't want to stop before driving into town, and are sure they'll come upon something better," he explained to me whenever I went to see him. He usually started the conversation this way, as if we hadn't actually discussed it many times before. He'd pour whisky into a glass, screw the cap on the bottle, and stow it behind the bar. "And my tavern comes into their view at the exact moment when they realize there's no point looking for something else in an unfamiliar town. They also stop to ask the way."

That was how I'd met him. I'd arrived in Ventersdorp in the early evening, too late to go back to Johannesburg for the night. I was planning to stay in town and needed accommodation. I stopped outside Malan's tavern, and he gave me directions to a suburban boarding house owned by a friend of his. Before I left he called to make sure they had a spare room, and to warn them they were going to have a guest.

That day I was the tavern's first and only white customer. Apart from visitors and a few regulars who were dependent on alcohol and Henk Malan's considerate discretion, the local

Afrikaners gave the Blue Crane a wide berth. It wasn't the location that put them off, or the quality of the goods and services on offer, but the blacks, who had taken a liking to the bar on the town line.

They felt more at ease here, on the edge of the white town. The agricultural workers who came into Ventersdorp to shop would drop in at Malan's on the way back to their farms. They'd arrange to meet outside the Blue Crane, and wait there for their employers, the white farmers who dropped them in town and then drove them back again in the beds of their pickups. Eugène Terre'Blanche used to look in at the Blue Crane too, but he used to shop at any place in town where he hadn't yet been refused credit. Malan never refused; Terre'Blanche was too important round here, and the fact that he frequented the Blue Crane served Henk as a defense whenever the local Afrikaners wagged their fingers at him for paying court to blacks.

Toward evening Malan would come out in front to sweep broken glass off the sidewalk.

"I don't stop them from drinking in the bar, but they prefer to go outside—they clearly feel better there. Each creature has his place on earth," he'd mutter, breathing heavily. The cigarettes he was so fond of made him short of breath, and the slightest effort caused him to start gasping, and then coughing. "I've nothing against them, but I can't bloody well understand why they have to smash the beer bottles. I can't make them out, they're so different from us. There's no way you can possibly live with them. Bloody kaffirs."

At the intersection in front of the church the road forks.

The right branch winds around a labyrinth of narrow side streets, lined with modest but well-kept bungalows in perfectly even rows. They're surrounded by shady green fir trees, gnarled, spreading acacias, plane trees, rosewood trees, and wild syringas, whose roots Tswana women use to make potions that relieve toothache.

There are no stores, workshops, or even sidewalks in this part of town; black people rarely come here, and only for work. Eugène Terre'Blanche's house is on one of these streets. It's easy to recognize by the wooden wagon with a thick canvas cover and large wheels that stands on the veranda. It was in wagons like this one that the Boer pioneers first came to Transvaal, driving them thousands of kilometers across wilderness and rivers, through deserts and mountain gorges. On the way they battled against the natives, and fought off wild animals, storms, and drought.

Terre'Blanche loved telling the story of the Great Trek to the Highveld, and talking about the wars and marches of the Boer partisans.

"Our ancestors bore so much sacrifice and suffering," he would say, as he showed guests around the house, with his two German shepherd dogs permanently at his side. "And all so that we could enjoy our own country and place on earth."

Terre'Blanche's town house was like a museum. On all the dressers, cupboards, and shelves there were busts and figurines of horses and soldiers of various sizes, and the walls were draped with the colorful flags of the former Boer republics, old rifles, bandoliers, and cartridge belts. From photographs and paintings Boer heroes looked out, the leaders from the days of the Great Trek to the Highveld, the commanders of partisan armies, and the presidents of the independent Boer republics.

These bearded men with stern faces and expressions, in field uniforms and hats, had been a model for Eugène since childhood. He knew them from the stories told by his grandfather, who would gather his grandsons together each evening to reminisce about past history, the wars, great victories, and heroic deeds, as well as the disasters and martyrdom. Eugène wanted to be just like them—he wanted to be a hero. In his boyhood, that was how he answered the adults whenever they asked who he wanted to be when he grew up.

On the wall of the room where he had set up his office hung a framed photograph of him, dating back to his teenage years when he had served in the war. His tour of the house always included a stop at this photo, showing him dressed in field uniform, staring into the distance while guarding the border. During one of my visits he smiled gratefully when I said he looked like one of the old Boer partisans. As an adult he had let his beard grow and wore khaki shirts and hats, just like the Boer generals.

His family home on Roth Street also housed the office of the political party, or rather brotherhood, which Terre'Blanche had founded to save the Afrikaners from their treacherous leaders, and from the slavery and annihilation to which they had condemned them.

About five hundred families live in the white town. They all know each other, and they all know everything about each other. They have been living here for generations, without changing anything. Nobody new ever moves in, and hardly anybody ever leaves.

The clock on the church tower at the fork in the road shows the same time every day—half-past two. Time has also stopped at another nearby church, made of red bricks, on the main street. The clock there has frozen at ten past four. Nobody can remember when the hands came to a halt and ceased to measure the passage of time, or why no one has ever tried to fix the clockwork and push time forward.

In this town of just under two thousand souls there are as many as eighteen churches; the number of them testifies not only to the godliness of the local Afrikaners, but also to their equally famous tendency to be quarrelsome, and their innate reluctance to yield priority to anyone whatsoever. In the Transvaal towns an old joke goes round about a Boer who is shipwrecked and ends up as a castaway on a desert island. Thirty years later a ship arrives, whose captain has noticed smoke rising above the palm trees. On the beach the sailors find the bearded Boer in rags, and two churches cobbled together from bamboo, palm leaves, and lianas. "How many people live on this island?" asks the captain. "I've been the only inhabitant for the past thirty years," replies the Boer. "What about this church? Whose is it?" asks the captain. "It's mine," answers the Boer. "And what about that one?" says the captain, pointing at the other church. The Boer shrugs and says: "That used to be my church, but I left it, and now I go to the other one."

Before spawning all eighteen places of worship, the town of Ventersdorp grew up around a church built by Johannes H. Venter, a Boer farmer who years earlier had made the journey here, all the way from the Cape of Good Hope. To thank Providence for protecting him as he traveled across this dangerous, boundless region, Venter decided to devote a piece of his land to a church.

News of the fertile land lying fallow to the north of the river, which they called the Vaal, soon attracted other brave souls to the treeless veld. Having occupied the land as a pioneer, Venter sold it to them at a profit. Soon a parish had appeared around the church, and a town had grown up on the farmland; to celebrate the first settler, the townspeople named it Ventersdorp after him.

The church served them not just as a house of prayer, but also as a meeting place where they took the most important decisions and discussed community matters and news from the outside world. They also sent their children to the church to be educated, and held their festivals and even their parties there. Everything that had significance in their lives revolved around the House of God and God's word, as recorded in the Bible, the holy scripture. It was with them throughout their lives, it was their ABC, the encyclopedia in which they sought and found the answers to all the most important questions.

If you turn left at the intersection in front of the church, the road leads into the part of town that serves as a marketplace. Arcades supported by small columns underneath multistory tenements provide shelter from the sun for stores and offices, a clock repair shop and a tailor's, a butcher's and a hairdressing salon. In the corner buildings at the intersection of Carmichael and Vortrekker, three competing banks have set up shop.

On a small square nearby stands the one-story courthouse painted green and white, the police station, and the old town hall, so small and cramped that it looks more like a hunting lodge. The middle of the square is occupied by the new town hall; large and spacious, still smelling of paint and mortar, it is the newest building in the whole town, erected by the new authorities.

Inside it, next to the mayor's chambers, Benny Tapologo had his office. Every morning Benny drove his big pickup into the freshly graveled forecourt outside the new town hall. As a boy he had dreamed of owning a powerful car with big wheels. His dream came true when the blacks were finally allowed to vote and, as the majority, were able to bring their leaders to power in the white town.

The new town hall administrators had rented themselves a fleet of expensive Japanese SUVs of a kind previously only ever seen in this town with white farmers at the wheel. Now, as one of nine town councillors, and later an adviser to the mayor, Benny had been able to select a vehicle for his own use.

He'd chosen a big Nissan pickup truck with a cargo box. Farmers bought this sort of vehicle to transport their workers and agricultural gear along field roads and over rough ground. Benny drove his shiny white truck with leather upholstery to his job at the town hall, just a few kilometers away down a surfaced road. He never had to remove the tarpaulin covering the truck bed.

He was approaching forty, and starting to put on weight. Small, with a shaved head, each morning he sat down at his desk, switched on the computer, and checked over the documents placed on the table the day before. He would open the window, through which he could see his car. He also set the door ajar to be able to see the applicants coming to ask for an audience with the mayor and the town hall officials.

Hardly anyone ever looked in at Benny's office. Nor did he have much to do. When I dropped by, confusing it with the mayor's chambers, Benny was bent over a newspaper, solving the crossword puzzle. Startled by the appearance of an unexpected visitor, he hastily elbowed the newspaper onto the floor in an attempt to hide the evidence of his inactivity and total redundancy.

Although he was an adviser to the mayor, he was rarely asked for advice. The office phone sitting on the desk next to his computer never rang. So Benny spent most of his time looking through the papers and the mail. At noon, like everyone at the town hall, he went into town for the lunch break; on his return he counted the hours until he could lock up his office at four and go home to the black township in his white pickup truck.

Above the shady square next to the town hall rises a marble triumphal arch dedicated to Hendrik Potgieter, built to mark the centenary of the Great Trek, which brought him and the other white Boers—the ancestors of today's Afrikaner citizens of Ventersdorp—from Cape Town across the Vaal River, to the Highveld.

In this part of the country the towns, streets, and squares are named after pioneers and war heroes, and also the political leaders of the old veld republics—van Riebeeck, Potgieter, Pretorius, de la Rey, Kruger, and Botha. And the names of the rivers come from how the newcomers perceived them: Orange, Rooiels (Red), Vaal (Gray), Skoon (Clean), and Modder (Muddy).

The source of water for the Boardman's property, Buckingham farm, is called the Mooi, meaning "Pretty River," while the river on which Ventersdorp lies is the Skoonspruit, meaning "Clean River." If not for the walled developments of bungalows that have grown up on a gentle slope by the river, you could reach it from the marketplace by simply going straight along Voortrekker or Koekemoer Street, downhill, all the way to a meadow, where there's a grove of trees growing by the stream, providing refreshing shade and coolness even in the middle of the hottest summer. The houses on the meadow have separated the river from the town.

New housing developments started to be built in this spot when the blacks took power nationally and locally, and there were more and more incidents of white farmers being murdered at the neighborhood farms. The small houses with little gardens, set in rows, were identical to one another, each surrounded by a fence with a sliding gate and protected by an alarm system; many farmers thought them a safe and comfortable place to come home to for the night after a day on the farm.

One of these houses on the meadow belonged to Raymond Boardman. He bought it with his elderly parents in mind; as they were growing decrepit, he wanted to move them from the farm to town, where he could expect to find care for them more easily.

The road to the housing development runs toward the river along Koekemoer Street, following the dilapidated fence around a soccer pitch belonging to the local elementary school. The first time I came to Ventersdorp the whites were in charge nationally and locally, and the blacks had no rights at all. Rugby matches were played on the pitch, while the students' parents sat watching from wooden stands. Only the white students could play for the school team; in fact only white students attended this school at all. The blacks had their own school, in their own suburban township, Tshing.

When the blacks took over the country and annulled the old system, the public schools couldn't refuse to accept students by reason of their skin color. As the teaching was better at the white schools, black parents began to enroll their children at them, to secure them a better education. The more black students appeared at the public school in Ventersdorp, the more white parents took their children out of it, and sent them to an expensive private school run by a nearby church on the edge of town. The white citizens spared no money on the school, which soon expanded, establishing a high school and preschool too.

Only white children attended them. Black parents didn't even try to enroll their sons and daughters there. Although it was private, the school could not actually refuse to teach blacks, but its owners and head teachers always managed to find a thousand good excuses to explain away the need to limit the number of students.

And so for black children there remained the public school in downtown Ventersdorp. Neglected by the new authorities and deprived of the care of the white citizens, year by year it declined. When I came back to the town again three years after the blacks took power, there was tall grass growing in the formerly well-tended school yard, nobody had replaced the broken panes of glass in the classroom windows, and on the abandoned, vandalized pitch nobody was playing anything anymore—neither white people, nor the new, black owners. It wasn't really their yard or a place where they felt they belonged. They only came here to study, and after school they went back home.

Beyond the town hall and the courthouse, the road runs on past stores selling food and agricultural goods, where the local farmers pull up in their trucks. They lick their fingers and count out banknotes at the tills, while keeping a mistrustful eye on the black store assistants who pack their purchases into paper bags and cardboard boxes, and then load them into their pickups.

At the town line, beyond the Caltex gas station, the street goes past the big Overland liquor store, then becomes the R30 road, and runs on across the empty veld to Tshing, the black township, which, although it has more than ten thousand inhabitants, is still regarded as nothing but a shabby, miserable suburb of white Ventersdorp, population two thousand.

In Tshing the road forks again. One branch turns right and, becoming the N14 national highway again, races on a thousand kilometers all the way to Springbok near the Atlantic coast. On the way it pushes through the towns of Coligny, Delareyville, Vryburg, Upington, and Kuruman, the oasis at the edge of the Kalahari Desert where the Scottish missionaries Dr. David Livingstone and Robert Moffat converted the local Tswana, Hottentots, and Bushmen to Christianity. The farther west, the more the maize fields give way to ash-gray pastures, surrounded by barbed-wire fences, where sheep and ostriches graze, and gangs of mongooses and meerkats appear by the road, anxiously staring at something in the distance.

The other branch of the highway, narrower and humbler, doesn't turn a corner, but bisects highway N14 before leading across the maize fields straight to Klerksdorp. If you follow it, about a dozen kilometers out of Ventersdorp you pass Ratzegaai, where Eugène Terre'Blanche had his farm. It was on this very road that his killers stood waiting for the police.

Although he never held any public office in Ventersdorp, or even ran for one, Terre'Blanche was the king of this town.

His authority over the townspeople was not the result of choice, but simply of his character. For as long as anyone could remember he had always managed to control their minds, to guess what the local Afrikaners were thinking and feeling, their fears and their secret dreams. He was one of them—he had the same desires, thoughts, and fears. But unlike others, he wasn't afraid to express them in public, which assured him unquestioned power over hearts and minds in the white town.

He not only said things that others didn't have the courage to utter aloud, but he also knew how to do it beautifully, how to compose it from the best words, like the poems he also used to write. People listened to him, because whenever he made a speech, they felt as if they were speaking themselves. Terre'Blanche filled them with faith and courage, freed them from their isolation, and gave them a sense of unity and the sort of strength that's carried by the nameless, angry crowd. They blindly and often unwittingly did as he told them. He established the laws and customs in the town; meanwhile he derived his power from the very fact that people saw him as the sort of man he wanted to be taken for, and that he believed himself to be.

The fame of the self-appointed Afrikaner leader from Ventersdorp quickly ran round the whole of Transvaal, and in time the whole country, from Cape Town to Pretoria, and from Durban to Upington. Ministers and presidents knew who he was and took notice of his opinion—both the whites, while they were in power, and the blacks, when they finally took it from them.

Both sides spoke about Terre'Blanche anxiously, calling him a dangerous man, a pretender. They were afraid he would try to transfer his control and his laws from Ventersdorp to all of Transvaal.

To mollify him, they would invite him to the capital for audiences. But he preferred to hold nocturnal rallies there by torchlight, and to make speeches from high tribunes; up there he seemed taller and mightier than in reality, and his powerful, stentorian voice sounded even louder as he menaced the government and threatened the end of the world, a sea of blood and a storm of fire.

He would come to the capital when he chose to, and do as he wished. But when the last white president made a trip to Terre'Blanche's native realm, to persuade the citizens of Ventersdorp that the only way to avoid war with the blacks was to hand power over to them, Terre'Blanche cast him to the four winds.

He never hesitated to provoke a scandal, and each new one brought him even greater fame. The attention and respect he enjoyed confirmed him in the belief that he really was a leader and general for the Afrikaners, like the historical Boer heroes in the old photographs and oil paintings who had guided the white pioneers on their great journey across the African veld, savannas, deserts, and mountains, and led them in wars against African kings, and also against the British, their rivals in the fight for control of southern Africa.

Finally he saw himself as the sort of Afrikaner commander and Boer folk hero he had always wanted to be. He convinced himself he ruled hearts and minds because his own merits entitled him to do so, and so did his birth.

People only came to Ventersdorp because of Eugène Terre'Blanche. The fact that he lived there was the one thing that distinguished the place from other, similar Afrikaner dorpie—settlements on the Transvaal veld plateau.

People came to Ventersdorp because of Terre'Blanche even if he wasn't in town. He merged with it and its citizens into a single figure, which he molded as he wished, giving it his own face. Watching the townspeople or just roaming about the town made you feel as if you were communing with him in person, and with everything people associated with him, admired in him, and found appalling about him. Everything that was tempting and attractive about him, and everything that was shocking and repulsive.

People came to Ventersdorp because of Terre'Blanche, but a trip there was also a strange expedition into the heart of darkness, to look at yourself as reflected in the townspeople, to confront your own fears, prejudices, obsessions, and bigotry, deeply and shamefully hidden beneath a shell of good manners, the ingrained boundaries of good and evil, what's appropriate and what is not, what's permitted and what is not.

By openly expressing something that made everyone feel ashamed, Eugène Terre'Blanche made it less threatening—he domesticated it. He removed the burden of sin and condemnation, but in exchange he made it into a confession of faith imposed on the entire town. He gave justification and a sense of community to those who were relieved to discover a mental affinity with other townspeople. And to those who were shocked at making this discovery, but hadn't the courage to face up to it or admit it, even mentally, he offered the opportunity to condemn in others the evil they wanted to purge from themselves, or otherwise to conceal.

People came to Ventersdorp because of Terre'Blanche, but many of them actually came here purely to perform this shameful ritual of cleansing and atonement.

Remembering her brother, Dora van Zyl always stressed the major, overwhelming effect he had on people. It was particularly evident during the rallies, at which he appeared in dress uniform, amid flaming torches lighting up the night. That was when you could see best what great inner power he had, and how good he was at controlling people's hearts and minds.

"He was a born leader," said Dora. "A leader can only be born. It's not something you can learn. And Eugène was a born leader. Like Adolf Hitler."

Among the Afrikaners in Transvaal the name of the German fascist leader doesn't prompt horror and condemnation the way it does in Europe, where Hitler is the embodiment of pure evil.

Although they were the first white settlers to have landed

there, the Boers lost their fight against the British for control of the Cape of Good Hope. So they traveled north, deep inland, to form their own independent republics on the veld. But one after another, these too were taken from them by the insatiable British.

Finally the whole of South Africa became one of the pearls in the crown of the British Empire. The Boers were the inhabitants of a colony, but they did not regard themselves as its citizens—they regarded the British Crown and its colonial viceroys as alien. They had no sense of community with the new settlers who had come from Great Britain.

The Boers, and the Afrikaners descended from them, always took the side of anyone who was against the British. When, in solidarity with Great Britain, the South African government in Pretoria entered the world war against Germany, the Afrikaners almost incited armed rebellion, and in many Afrikaner towns in Transvaal the German language was added to the school curriculum.

"I compare Eugène to Hitler because whatever you may say about him, Hitler was a born leader," Dora emphasized. "The British say he was a criminal, because he started the war and murdered the Jews in concentration camps. But for us those same British set up concentration camps too, where they starved thousands of Boer women and children to death and sent the whole country up in smoke. Isn't that a crime?"

When they were children, living on the family farm, their grandfather used to tell them about war, heroic deeds and wicked crimes. It was from him that they learned about their great-grandfather, who was taken prisoner, and whom the British soldiers had tied to a locomotive to prevent the partisans from blowing up the railroad. And about the Boer woman, burned alive by the

British because she refused to leave her home, which they set on fire. About the red glow on the veld and the black smoke from burning farms creeping low across the grassland.

Along with thousands of other Boers from the British Cape Colony, Andries Lodewyk Terre'Blanche had come to Transvaal to support his local compatriots in the war the British had declared on them. It was just outside Cape Town that the first of his forebears had settled in the early eighteenth century, Étienne Terre'Blanche from Toulon, France, who, together with other Huguenots persecuted in Europe, had decided to seek freedom and a better life in the south of Africa. His descendant Eugène Terre'Blanche used to stress with pride that in French his surname meant "White Earth," but it could also be understood as "White Land." Or even "the Land of the Whites." Heading off to the war in Transvaal, Eugène's grandfather formed his own unit, with which he joined the Boer partisans and fought under the command of the greatest generals, including Christiaan de Wet and also Jacobus de la Rey, whose military exploits won him immortal fame and made him a folk hero, the subject of Boer songs and legends.

With half the world under its control, it took the British imperial army three long years to conquer the massed ranks of Boers. The British had to bring their best commanders to southern Africa, and were forced to resort to scorched-earth tactics. Prisoners of war were shot, fields and pastureland were destroyed, watering holes and wells were poisoned, and farms, houses, and even whole towns were burned down to deprive the rebels of food supplies, recruits, and every form of support, and to fill their minds with terror, discouragement, and lack of faith. And when even that was too little, the British herded the entire civilian population, old people, women, and children, into concentration camps, where they were forced to remain until the war ended. One of these camps was located near Ventersdorp.

Commandant Andries Lodewyk Terre'Blanche led the local Boers in this vicinity, every single one of whom joined the partisans. After they lost the war, he decided not to go home, to the Cape of Good Hope, but to settle in Transvaal. He bought a house in Ventersdorp, and a farm too, where he raised cattle and grew crops. And there he was finally laid to rest, under a large tree, in a spot he had chosen for the family graveyard.

As a war veteran and hero, he was regarded in the town as its number one citizen, the commandant. His son, De Villebois Marieul, Eugène's father, who was a lieutenant-colonel in the South African army, enjoyed the same respect in Ventersdorp, and after him so did Eugène, who began to assume the role of a Boer leader while still at school, as captain of the rugby team and its best player, and also as founder and president of an organization called the Young Afrikaner Hearts. At its meetings he and his friends discussed the history of the Boers, read Boer books and poetry, and recited their own first poems about their love of their country, nation, and God.

His dream title of Afrikaner leader and hero was brought him by the Afrikaner Weerstandsbeweging—the "Afrikaner Resistance Movement" or AWB—the brotherhood that he established in order to defend the town against any outsiders wanting to impose their rule on it, like the old volunteer force enlisted to fight the British. At AWB rallies and gatherings, Terre'Blanche threatened that he would prefer to incite a new war in the country, cut out a piece of the veld to be the Afrikaners' own, independent state, and resurrect the old Transvaal republic than become a subject of a black government.

Whenever he spoke from the tribune, or from the saddle of

his black horse Attila, in his hat and tawny shirt, he really did look like a Boer general from an old print. He was offered an alliance and all sorts of help by the American Ku Klux Klan.

Members of the brotherhood donned brightly colored armbands featuring a swastika. Worn on top of ordinary shirts or jackets, they made them into uniforms.

"He was accused of using the Nazi symbol as his emblem, but it wasn't a swastika at all, it was just three figure sevens joined together. Three sevens!" To explain the difference more clearly, Dora van Zyl drew a diagram on paper. "Sevens are a sign of purity and goodness! And the war against the Antichrist, whose symbol is three sixes. When the blacks took power and adopted a new flag, Eugène immediately noticed that it features a broken cross, which means the regime of the Antichrist is taking over in our country too.

"Everyone in town respected him and listened to him. Even the officials and the policemen. They received orders from the government in Pretoria, but before carrying them out, they always came to Eugène for advice," she said. "And how can a man like that have been murdered because of a squabble over a few rand?"

The Boardmans came to Africa one hundred years after the Terre'Blanches, but ended up in Transvaal before them.

The first to arrive was William Boardman, a pastor and teacher from Blackburn in the county of Lancashire, who with his wife, nine children, and servant came to Africa with the British settlers. His Royal Majesty's government had sent them to the Cape of Good Hope to impose British order and morals on the Boers who obeyed no authority. Reverend William was assigned to the settlers as a spiritual chaperon and guide.

Two of the pastor's grandsons traveled from the Cape of

Good Hope to Transvaal, brought there by gold fever, and also the promise of diamonds, since the world's richest deposits had been discovered on the Orange and Vaal Rivers. But the Boardmans were not blessed with good luck and failed to find any treasure, or make a vast fortune. However, they never went back to the Cape of Good Hope, but settled in Transvaal. Living among the Afrikaners, the young Boardmans learned their language and customs, and became so like them that with time they almost entirely lost their British character.

One of the brothers, George Herbert, settled in Potchefstroom, where he met the love of his life. After the wedding he moved to Ventersdorp, where he lived for more than fifty years. He was buried in the old town cemetery.

Buckingham farm, half an hour's drive from town, was bought by his son, George Herbert Jr., the first Boardman to be born in Ventersdorp. He made the purchase after the second Boer war, during which British troops had interned the entire Boardman family in a concentration camp along with the Boers.

"The British regarded us as traitors and enemies, because we lived among the Boers," Raymond Boardman told me. "But for the Boers we had never stopped being British, so they took us for the enemy too."

Although the Boers, exhausted by fighting, disease, and hunger, finally surrendered, after the war most of the British who had been living in western Transvaal moved out with the victorious army when the local garrison was withdrawn. Very few remained: a small number of farmers, like the Boardmans, and some tradesmen in town, like the Wrights, emigrants from Scotland.

Douglas Wright was the last of his clan still living in Ventersdorp. Seeing no future here, his children had long since gone abroad.

It was Raymond Boardman who told me about Douglas Wright.

"If you're going to talk to someone in this town about past history, then talk to him and him alone," he said firmly. "And while you're about it, you can ask him what it's like to be a Briton married to an Afrikaner woman in Ventersdorp."

Until Raymond's son Mike married a local, Afrikaner girl called Julianna, the Wrights were the only mixed couple in town.

Ventersdorp was more than two hundred years old, but Douglas Wright was nearly a hundred. The old man had spent almost his entire life in this town, and had been an eyewitness to half its history.

The Wrights had come here straight after the war against the Boers, from Upington in the desert, where they were the owners of the first passenger ferry across the Orange River. In Ventersdorp they had founded a store and built one of the first stone houses. They had singled out a small square by the church, where once every three months the Boers from the local farms gathered for a service conducted by the pastor, where they took Holy Communion.

They came in carts harnessed to horses or oxen, just like the pioneers in the days of the Great Trek from the Cape of Good Hope to the Highveld. They pitched camp on the square, met with the neighbors, made new acquaintances, exchanged news, and did their shopping. The town was only just recovering from the ravages of war, and the local farms still resembled smoking heaps of rubble. The Boers were living hand-to-mouth, still brooding on the wrongs done to them and keeping weapons hidden about their houses, yards, and orchards.

But finally their moment of triumph came. Years on, victorious Great Britain decided to bring together all the territories it had conquered in the south of Africa—the Boer republics, the Zulu, Matabele, and Xhosa kingdoms, the Pedi, Sotho, and Tswana chiefdoms—and create a single colony out of them, stretching from the banks of the Limpopo River to the shores of both oceans and the Cape of Good Hope.

Although they had lost their original republics, in the new, united colony the Boers proved more numerous than the British, who decided to grant South Africa independence. When a free election was announced to choose leaders for the new state from among the white citizens, the Boers took power and exercised it for almost one hundred years. No Briton would ever be the leader of South Africa again.

Douglas Wright was a small boy when one day a large crowd of Boers on horseback gathered in the square outside the church. In the middle of the gathering a well-built man with a bushy mustache made a speech. "That's Louis Botha," his grandfather told him, pointing at the rider.

Botha was one of the bravest Boer generals. After the war he had signed the capitulation and persuaded the Boers to form an alliance with the British; soon after he had become prime minister of South Africa. He had been summoned to Ventersdorp by the local farmers, and above all the tradesmen, who were demanding that he expel the Indian storekeepers from the country, who were treading on their toes, taking away their black customers and their profit.

Botha refused. His successor, another of the Boer generals called Jan Smuts, didn't meet the Transvaal tradesmen's demands either. Not only did he refuse to get rid of the foreigners, he even considered giving the country's colored citizens the same rights as its white ones. He explained that in the long term this was the only way they could continue to exercise power over the blacks.

"These days it turns out he was right. We should have done as he said then, and maybe it wouldn't have come to all this," said Douglas Wright. "But we didn't listen to him. Who'd have thought it then?"

Douglas Wright knew the Boardmans from Buckingham farm. He acknowledged that for some reason the Boers in Ventersdorp had never accepted them. But neither he nor any of his relatives had met with any hostility in this town, maybe because they were Scottish, rather than English. Or maybe because they only came to Transvaal after the war. They were not here when the fighting took place, the farms burned at night, and the British drove the Boers into concentration camps.

Unlike the Boardmans, Wright did not feel like an outsider in Ventersdorp, and had even come to think of himself as one of its most remarkable residents. Not because of the store, but thanks to the game of rugby, of which he had been a champion player, and which the Afrikaners were passionate about. This particular sport required the talents and abilities that they valued the most highly, and that came closest to their idea of perfection: strength, speed, agility, pugnacity, resistance to hardship, and unwavering faith that even the greatest adversity can be overcome. And above all a tie with the community, and harmonious cooperation with it—without that, not just victory but survival was impossible.

Wright had been the best rugby player in town, so good that teams from the bigger, richer cities were always trying to court him. But he'd never left Ventersdorp, even though he might have had a great career, fame, and money ahead of him in another place. He didn't brood on it either, and for years he was perfectly satisfied with the fact that people hailed him in the street like an old friend, greeted him, smiled at him and wished him good day.

He loved to talk about his old tournaments, most of all about the matches he'd played against a team from the British university in Potchefstroom, which was considered the best in all western Transvaal. They rarely won against them, but Ventersdorp celebrated every victory as a great triumph in the war against their hated enemy. Wright was happiest to reminisce about a match that they had lost, but in which he had won all twelve points for his team. On that occasion the British side from Potchefstroom had promised him a handsome reward if he would only join them, but he had refused to change a thing.

If anyone visited him at home, he showed them old photographs of his tournaments. He not only recognized the players in them, but he could remember their first names and surnames without ever making a single mistake. At one time he would recount his memories if somebody asked him to, but then he grew so used to telling his stories that he did it uninvited, to anyone who happened to come along, and sometimes to the same person several times over. By now the whole town knew his tales by heart, and nobody wanted to hear them anymore. But he was oblivious, and never noticed that they avoided his company, got up from the bar when he came and sat down, and said goodbye as soon as he entered.

With age he began to confuse one person for another. The faces, first names, and surnames faded, the old, familiar ones disappeared, and the new ones were alien to him. His visits to the bar became rarer and rarer, and finally old age confined him to a wicker armchair in the yard of his own home, divided from the street by a whitewashed stone wall. He could no longer watch the town, but could just hear the sounds coming from it.

He had very few visitors, and although the townsfolk knew that he existed, the younger ones probably wouldn't have recognized him in the street. He would invite his rare guests to sit in the shade of a eucalyptus tree and offer them lemonade prepared by his wife, tea in old china cups, sweet sponge cake, and above all stories about past rugby matches and residents of Ventersdorp. In these tales he resurrected the world he had lived in, which had gone now, forgetting to take him with it. He said the town hadn't changed much since the days of his youth.

Whenever he received Afrikaners from the neighborhood as guests, the conversation usually got around to the TV serials and competitions in which you could win large prizes, and in which black male dancers embraced white girls, and white ones held on to beautiful black women.

"What sort of parents would allow that?" the ancient Scot and his guests would indignantly agree.

Every Monday a black laborer hired by his wife came to work in the garden, to mow the lawn and tidy up, but old Mr. Wright could never remember his name. He just called him George, the name he gave all the blacks he employed. He said it was a good name, and as it was given to kings, a servant should have no objection to it.

"He's a decent chap, but he's no comparison with the George who came before him," he would say, watching the gardener trim the hedge with a pair of steel shears. "This town has always been full of kaffirs, especially in the daytime, because in the evenings they go home. Maybe things have changed in other towns, but here people know their place."

Before moving into the town hall, councillor Benny Tapologo had no idea about the history of Ventersdorp or about the hostility the Afrikaners felt toward the British. At the school he attended in Tshing, he had learned about the Boer pioneers, the

British generals, and the wars they fought against each other, but he didn't regard their fortunes as part of his own history. It made no difference to him whether a white man was an Afrikaner of Boer descent or British. Even if they had had a falling out, there was one thing they were in total agreement about: a white man can only be a master, and a black man can only be his servant.

All Benny knew about his own ancestors was that they came from the Barolong tribe, one of many which make up the Tswana people, who lived on this land long before the first white settlers appeared and named it Transvaal. He also knew that his family had ended up in Ventersdorp because his father, a mailman, was transferred here from his job at the main post office in Potchefstroom.

The only one of the African kings to feature in the school textbooks was Moshweshwe, the mighty ruler of the Sotho people. Benny learned about the Zulu king Shaka from older boys in the street. Before being conquered by the whites, the African kings had made alliances and pacts with them to oppress their common enemies and increase their own property and importance. The British and the Boers treated the African natives like neighbors on an equal footing while they still had their own kingdoms, which were often more powerful than the white republics and colonies. But once beaten in the wars, they would never enjoy the same rights as their conquerors. "There is no equality between whites and non-whites," it said in the constitution of the Boer Transvaal republic. "Neither in the state nor in the church."

As long as they lived as neighbors, each in his own place, the whites had regarded the Africans as alien creatures, different, but not inferior. They hadn't tried imposing their customs or laws on them, which so far they had only enacted where they were in the majority. Now, although they were the minority, they took control of all southern Africa.

Soon after taking power the whites announced that from now on the greater part of the country would belong to them alone, and that special "reserves" would be created for the blacks. Once the Afrikaners were running the country, they formalized the segregation of the blacks, establishing so-called Bantustans (also known as homelands) on the basis of the reserves, one for each of the individual African peoples, to which the natives were to move immediately. The lands set aside for the Bantu-stans were mainly barren ground with no water, not suitable for fields or pasture.

Natives were only allowed to enter white South Africa with special passes, as outsiders, to be workers and servants, essential in the white homes, on white farms and in white factories and mines. They could only stay in the whites' country in order to work for them. They were never to become its citizens, with civic entitlement to vote in elections—if only because, being in the majority, they would always have been the winners, and would have set up their own government.

The passes regulated the number of blacks entitled to live among the whites, in their towns and on their farms. The aim was to have just the right amount of them—neither too few, so there were enough hands to do the work, nor too many, so they didn't become a threat. A black person not in possession of a special pass could not be sold a railroad ticket—so without a pass he or she could not move from place to place.

Passes were only issued to those who found employment in white towns. Special areas, known as townships, were set aside for them in the suburbs. In Ventersdorp, a settlement called Tshing, situated a few kilometers from the town, served as the township for black servants, store assistants, porters, gardeners, and farm workers.

The pass law was nothing new. The British had introduced it a hundred years earlier, to have control over the white settlers, sailors, soldiers, farmers, and herders. These passes also applied to the reverend William Boardman and the pioneers from Great Britain who came to start a new life in southern Africa. Without special permission issued in writing they were not allowed to leave the locations assigned to them by the colonial authorities as their place of residence.

Before becoming the first member of the Tapologo family to live in Tshing, Benny's grandfather had ended up in a homeland outside Potchefstroom, one of the first to be established by the Boer settlers on the north bank of the Vaal River. His land was taken over by a white farm, whose owner told him to get out. With no plot of land to live off, he went into service for the whites.

Meanwhile the whites needed the blacks, especially to work in the gold mines, which gradually changed the country from a backward, old-fashioned, impoverished land of farmers and herders into an affluent modern state, intent, like the rest of the white world, on an industrial revolution, which would guarantee both progress and profit.

A regular, unimpeded flow of laborers for mines, foundries, factories, and workshops was guaranteed by the new laws. They also imposed an obligation on all African males between the ages of eighteen and sixty-five to pay an annual poll tax, which, along with other local taxes, forced the blacks to look for jobs and accept them. And when that wasn't enough either, penalties were introduced for vagrancy. By this token, all blacks who were living outside the reserves assigned to them, but without permanent employment with whites, were regarded as vagrants. The penalty for vagrancy was a fine, so to get the money to pay it, these people were forced to look for jobs with the whites.

In any case the Africans had no choice. They had lost their land, pastures, and wells. The only thing they had left to sell was their labor. Thus from warriors who inspired terror they had changed into miners, farmhands, servants, and night watchmen.

Blacks could only appear in white towns and districts during working hours, as defined in the passes issued to them. So they had to carry them at all times, and make sure they weren't out of date. Remaining in a white town without a pass was a criminal offense. Meanwhile, not just police officers could demand to see their passes, but any white person, even a child, in whom a black stranger prompted suspicion or anxiety.

That was how Benny Tapologo remembered his first encounter with the system resulting from segregating people according to the color of their skin. One sunny Sunday after the church service in Tshing his father took him to town for ice cream. A white girl stopped them in the street.

"Jim! Show your pass!" she insisted.

Whites addressed blacks by whatever name happened to occur to them. Thus they named them John, Jim, Bob, or—like old Mr. Wright—George. Or quite simply, regardless of age, they called them: "Boy!"

Benny felt a mixture of fear and shame on seeing how the girl admonished his father. At home his father was stern and wouldn't tolerate disobedience. He only had to cast an angry glance or knit his brow to prompt alarm in his wife and children. Summoned by the white girl, he stood at attention before her, smiled ingratiatingly, and carried out her instructions in a disciplined way. To his amazement, little Benny felt ashamed of his father, who had proved so weak.

Benny's father died before the age of forty. He was buried in the black cemetery in Tshing. Throughout the country everything had been divided according to skin color, which established the status quo and marked out your place in life. Even after death.

Blacks were buried in Tshing, and whites in Ventersdorp. Even the handful of Arabs and Indians living in the town had their own ghettos and their own graveyards. There were no mixed-race people in the town, but if there had been any, they would have lived and died separately too.

The white officials, tradesmen, army people, and missionaries who had conquered Africa over the centuries regarded the black natives as an inferior sort of human being, savages to be domesticated, only fit to work on plantations and in mines, as servants or slaves. Black had become the color of man's enslavement. Even in banning slavery, the white conquerors of Africa were guided not so much by the desire to compensate for the harm that had been done, as by calculation. They realized that a passive slave, made into a common tool, is less useful and profitable than a free workman forced to sell his labor.

This system, originally introduced to southern Africa by the British, was convenient for all the white settlers, because it meant that skin color alone guaranteed them a privileged position. Yet just as much as the British sense of superiority over the black Africans came from their arrogance and advantage over those whom they had defeated, so too did the Boers sincerely believe in racial segregation.

They believed it was the will of the Almighty—if he had wished otherwise, he would not have created people so very different from each other. And so they regarded the mixing of races as contrary to God's will; the crossbreeding of species was a deviation from the natural order, a sin leading to nothing but misunderstandings and conflict.

They drew this conviction straight from their unshakeable faith in the Creator and from Biblical parables, which they read and understood as literally as could be. For the Boers who settled in southern Africa the Bible was as sacred as it was universal, often the only book they possessed and knew. They derived their faith from the parables they read in it. It gave them access to God, advice on how to gain salvation, and some guidelines to follow in earthly life. It was also their only primer. Being constantly on the move or scattered about the boundless veld, they taught their children to read and write using the Bible, and derived all their knowledge about the surrounding world from it.

They regarded their presence among the African people as the will of God, which no man should oppose. They believed that the Creator himself had sent them to Africa as a new chosen race, a new people of Israel, a people of faith to rule over the pagans, the descendants of Ham, cursed for disobedience and marked with black skin, "condemned to be the lowest of slaves to his brothers." When the British governing the Cape Colony abolished slavery there, and declared that the blacks would enjoy the same rights as the white settlers, the Boers realized that their only hope of avoiding sin, doom, and destruction was to escape deep into the African interior, as far from the British and their sinful regime as possible. Their journey took them all the way to Transvaal, across the river Vaal. They believed that this was their promised land, where they could live their own way, keeping everything just as God had planned—and so everything was to be kept separate.

When they took over government from the British, they made apartheid, or "being apart," the state system, the law, the custom, and the profession of faith. Apartheid, or forced racial segregation, did not in principle introduce anything new, but merely meticulously organized the actual state of affairs that had been in force for ages. Now its rules came to regulate the tiniest details of every sphere of life—who was to live where, where they were to work, how they were to move about, who was to sit where, and where they were to eat.

Mixed marriages and interracial love affairs were prohibited; separate schools, hospitals, stores, offices, park benches, parks, beaches, restaurants, sports fields, playgrounds, sports competitions, seats on buses and trains, and even bus stops and pedestrian overpasses were introduced. Black medical students were prohibited from dissecting white corpses, and black worshippers were excluded from white churches. Armies of police officers in uniform and plain clothes made sure that racial purity was maintained, and any infringement of the established law was most severely punished. Whites who did not share faith in apartheid raged, and even rebelled against the legislation, but helpless against its omnipotence, most of them eventually became resigned to it and gave up. All the more easily since even as rebels against apartheid, they were still its beneficiaries.

Everything was determined by the National Register, in which officials recorded the country's residents according to their racial status. Which box they ticked for each newborn child determined his or her future destiny and place in life. A child acknowledged to be black was barred entry to the world of whites, and a white child was immediately separated from the non-whites. Your entry in the relevant box in the register and on your ID card was either a pass to a better life or a denial of common rights.

Mistakes did occur. Those completing the register often classified children as colored (in other words, of mixed descent), although their parents were white. Or black. In the case of blacks, being registered as colored meant a promotion, although it caused a lot of trouble. The wrong classification of a white child as colored meant a demotion, condemnation to a worse existence.

A detrimental judgment was entitled to an appeal in court. However, the suit could drag on for years, and its result was never certain. To facilitate matters and secure themselves a favorable settlement, people would approach the registration officials directly, and pay them cash to alter the decisive classification at a single stroke of the pen.

Some people also applied to be demoted, from white to colored, Indian, or even black. This was the only way they could have a relationship with someone of another race without running the risk of prison or a fine. A white man who was reclassified at his own request and officially declared to be black, could love and live with a black woman. However, he could not appear in white towns and districts without the special pass issued to all blacks. Ceasing to be officially white also meant that he could no longer count on his former privileges, or even his job and his salary, because they too were divided according to skin color.

Not all whites could manage, even with the privileges granted by their skin color. Many, especially in Transvaal, became destitute, and the life of the poor white folk was not all that different from the indigence of the blacks. To deal with this and prevent poor whites from living as neighbors to blacks, the government reserved certain professions for them. Situations requiring education inaccessible to the majority of blacks remained open, whereas jobs at least theoretically within the scope of the blacks were set aside for whites.

To protect against this too, one after another, subjects regarded as nonessential for the common laborer, gardener, porter, or servant were withdrawn from the curriculum at schools for black children. "What would be the point and purpose of teaching black children algebra, if they'd never have the opportunity to apply that knowledge later in life? What a waste of money that would be!" explained Hendrik Verwoerd to the white parliament; minister of education and future prime minister, he was a philosopher by education and by nature. "People should be taught what's going to be useful to them in life."

In any case, it was getting harder and harder to find work and earn a living. There weren't enough jobs for everyone, and the whites were insisting that they be kept for them alone, and not given to blacks, even if they were willing to work for free. At the gold mines in Witwatersrand this led to violent disturbances between black and white miners. The government had to send the police to suppress the riots, and even introduced a state of emergency.

In Ventersdorp, where there was neither gold nor diamonds, but just good arable land, it was never easy to find work.

"And in that respect nothing here has changed," said Benny Tapologo. "It's as if time has stood still."

Benny's father, who after moving from Potchefstroom to Ventersdorp connected phone calls at the local post office, had to give up this job to a white man. From then on he was employed mending broken lines, repairing damage, or connecting new phone lines. In fact he never did any of the actual fixing—that was done by his white superior, for whom Benny's father carried tool boxes and heavy rolls of wire and cable. His place at the telephone exchange in the post office was taken by Henk Malan's father, who had just moved with his family from nearby Kloster, where they had been living in poverty.

Henk said he couldn't remember much about those days.

"My mother didn't work, she took care of the house," he said. "My father went to work at the post office each morning. He connected phone calls. He knew all the phone numbers in the area by heart. Nobody ever had to give him the number. They just had to ask to be put through to the Wessels' farm, or to old Viljoen, and my old man dialed the right number."

At home they only just made ends meet, and lived modestly; his father's salary was enough to feed and clothe the family, and also to pay back the bank loan he'd taken out to buy a small bungalow on the edge of town, under a large eucalyptus tree, in the crown of which all the falcons in the district seemed to nest. To amuse the very occasional visitors who came by, Henk would go out onto the porch with a rifle and fire a warning shot. Then dozens, perhaps hundreds, of birds would come soaring out of the eucalyptus tree.

The Malans never had any black servants. In town it was said they couldn't afford a cleaner. But Henk maintained that neither his father nor his mother wanted blacks hanging around the house. They regarded blacks as another species, and wanted nothing to do with them. His mother refused to have blacks bustling about in her kitchen, touching her pots and plates, or the food they'd be preparing for her, her husband, and her sons. She didn't want them entering the bedroom, picking up the sheets and clothes, laundering them, and putting them away in the closets.

Henk's father simply didn't like them, whereas his mother, a very devout woman, often used to say that the pastor at their regular church regarded hiring blacks as servants as displeasing to God. The Terre'Blanches, who lived in the same neighborhood, a few houses along, also attended the same church.

The money he earned at the post office was enough for old Malan to pay for his sons' schooling, but both boys gave up their studies after middle school. Henk went straight into the army, where service was obligatory for all white men. He fought in the war in Angola, which was invaded by South African troops to crush the black rebels hiding there. On his return from the army he found work on the railroad, where the government also reserved most of the jobs for whites who were down on their luck and hadn't succeeded anywhere else.

Henk became an engineer, driving a locomotive that traveled across the Highveld. As he drove the trains from Johannesburg to Mafikeng, he went past the huge grain silos standing on the border of Buckingham farm, the Boardmans' property.

When he was laid off from the telephone exchange, Benny's father lost some of his wages. As a porter and fitter he received a far lower salary than when he was connecting calls. At a time when South Africa was getting rich on gold and enjoying increasing affluence, the blacks were earning less and less. The whites grabbed all the wealth for themselves, even the poor whites, who were making money and living better and better, as well as the middle class in Europe.

Crowded into reservations and townships in the suburbs of white cities, and totally excluded from any sort of decision making, the blacks only did jobs that required almost no qualifications, or else earned several times less than the whites employed in the same positions. As an engineer Henk Malan earned four times more than his black predecessor.

To top up his salary, on his days off from the post office Benny's father would stand out on the main road to Ventersdorp. Every day at dawn the local farmers pulled up there to hire laborers to work on their farms. Sometimes they were looking for permanent workers, sometimes for a day or two, or even just for a few hours. They paid a pittance, but there was no other way to earn extra money. The blacks in Tshing couldn't even open stores or be licensed to sell liquor. The white government had banned these activities, so not only did they have to work for white people to earn a living, but they also had to spend their money at white stores.

Toward the end of his life Benny's father was fired from his job at the post office. He found employment at a metals depot in the suburbs. When he died, Benny was sixteen and was still at high school. He took his end-of-school exams, but there was no question of continuing his studies. He had to earn a living, to maintain the family in his father's place.

They lived in a shabby stone house in the oldest part of Tshing, not far from the sports field, the school, and the only two-story building, which housed the local town hall, and where the township's residents held meetings to discuss matters of particular importance to them. In Benny's house there was a kitchen, a bathroom, and two other rooms, one of which was occupied by the five children. The other served as the living room by day and was his parents' bedroom by night. The house had no ceilings, but the roof, made of gray sheets of fiber-cement bolted together and propped on the walls, acted as a substitute.

Before it became overgrown with shacks cobbled together from plywood, planks, corrugated iron, and blue plastic sheeting, Tshing consisted of just this sort of small, austere building, erected by the government for the blacks. Placed in even rows along the streets, they looked like matchboxes. This impression was enhanced by the site where they were built, in open fields, on a plateau as flat as a tabletop. All around there were no hills, no trees to give even a scrap of shade in summer, almost no landmarks. On cloudy days the wind sprang up and drove yellow balls of tangled grass from the veld along the littered, dusty, rust-red streets.

The days went by steadily, one just like the next, to the same rhythm and in the same order, starting and ending the same way. Everything seemed fixed for good and all. It never even entered people's minds to try to change something, to question or complain about anything. This was how it had always been, and this was how it was always going to be.

"And it looks as if that was exactly right," said Benny Tapologo years later, shaking his head.

Weaving his way through the back streets of Tshing in his big, new-smelling Nissan pickup, every morning on his way to work he passed men in navy-blue overalls sauntering along the roadside verge toward town. Anyone who didn't have a job in Ventersdorp stood at the town line, waiting for the white farmers.

One Saturday, when as usual his father had gone off to the crossroads looking for the chance to earn some money, Benny had raced after him with the midday snack he'd forgotten to take with him. And then he saw his father being pointed at by a white man sitting in the cab of a truck, bowing meekly, with gratitude, before hurriedly scrambling into the truck bed.

Benny didn't run up to hand him the bundle of food. He went home and told his mother that his father was no longer on the road. In his heart he vowed to himself then that he would never, ever climb into the bed of a pickup truck, and if anyone told him to get in a vehicle they'd have to let him sit in the passenger seat.

Armand van Zyl, a young pastor from the Afrikaans Protestant Church, taught that the good Lord assigned a place on earth to each man. Everyone should find his place, and hold on to it.

"Apartheid, segregation, just means being good neighbors," he would say. "The fact that good neighbors live separately, divided by a boundary wall, doesn't have to mean they're enemies, but simply that each of them lives in his own way and is resigned to his own otherness."

In none of his sermons did Reverend van Zyl ever take the liberty of saying anything that could be regarded as placing oneself above others, in praise of contempt or hostility toward one's neighbors. He regarded that as a cardinal sin, which he warned his congregation to avoid.

"The Lord God in his inscrutable wisdom created a world of infinite variety. If he'd wanted to organize it differently, he'd have done so," he would say. "There's no need to improve on the Creator or try to change his works. Since he created lots of different shades, shapes, species, languages, cultures, and races, that was his will, which we can only accept. Blending things together that God intended to be different removes all the world's diversity and beauty, and leads to nothing but unhappiness and the sin of pride.

"Being different doesn't mean being better or worse at all. However great his wish and however hard he tries, a white European is never going to become a black African or a Chinese person, just as an African or a Chinese will never be a European. They are equals, but they are also always going to be different.

"Nobody in his right mind ever debates the fact that there are many colors," explained the pastor in a mild, bashful tone. "We, the Afrikaners, the only white people of Africa, do not wish or intend to be anybody's masters. But nor do we wish to be anybody's servants, or be forced to live according to somebody else's laws and customs."

The pastor often quoted Biblical parables, usually from Genesis, as representing the ultimate proof that his words were right.

"The Tower of Babel displeased the Lord, so he destroyed it," he warned.

Other clerics liked to quote the reference in Genesis to the children of Ham, cursed and marked with black skin, sinners condemned to serve others, by carrying water and chopping wood for them.

"The Bible is a testimony and a source of faith," said Reverend van Zyl. "God gave it to mankind, so that those whom he loved might find their way to him. It doesn't require guides, who by offering help and trying to assist God, actually block the way to him."

He also referred to his mentor, theology professor Carel Boshoff, a eulogist of apartheid who taught that to survive and not disappear, or let their unique qualities go to waste, races and peoples should live in peace, but separately, like good neighbors; they should help each other, but not impose on or exploit each other.

But following the example of the British and other white settlers who came to own southern Africa, the Boers began to regard their distinct nature as superior and deserving priority; they changed the obligation to other races promoted by Boshoff into their own law for using them as their servants.

"From neighbors we became oppressors, exploiting others and refusing them things we demanded for ourselves. We ourselves made living separately hateful," said Reverend van Zyl regretfully. "Greed, pride, and vanity have always led sinful people astray."

Disappointed by his compatriots and their lack of restraint, the scholarly professor Boshoff moved away to the barren, un-inhabited desert on the Orange River, where with a handful of followers he founded a settlement whose residents were to start a new way of life. Only Afrikaners could settle in Orania, as the village in the desert was named, but only they could work there too. No one was allowed to have black nursemaids, cleaners, or gardeners, to avoid becoming dependent on their labor again. For help in the home, garden, or fields the citizens of Orania could only employ their own neighbors.

Reverend van Zyl was from Pretoria, the Afrikaner capital. He trained to be a priest at the theological college there. He chose the church whose teaching seemed closest to him, and that he wanted to serve: the Afrikaans Protestant Church. While other churches, one after another, were moving away from the dogma of racial segregation, this one alone still recognized that by God's will each man had his separate place on earth, and that mixing the races meant disobeying God.

When the citizens of Ventersdorp approached the Church supervisors to send them a new pastor, Reverend van Zyl didn't hesitate for an instant. He didn't know much about the town, apart from the fact that the now nationally famous Eugène Terre'Blanche was from there.

That did nothing to put the young pastor off. He had already served congregations at other places, and accepted each new challenge with humility, and with the joy he derived from serving God.

The citizens of Ventersdorp had started building a new church on the edge of town when the white government announced that the apartheid system could not be maintained. The government ministers explained that although fair in principle, the system based on total racial separation had proved too costly, neither profitable nor productive—just as slavery had in the past too.

With each passing year, more and more money was needed to pay informers, the police, the army, and the courts ensuring that segregation laws were obeyed, and that any infringement was severely punished. Meanwhile, drawn to the big cities to earn a living, the blacks were becoming more numerous, and it was getting harder to supervise them all.

Worse than that, they had begun to rebel, inciting riots; the white government needed even more police and even more troops to suppress them. The street fighting and the arrest of black leaders had also brought global condemnation down on South Africa, a boycott, and painful sanctions.

"Either we must adapt, or we shall all perish," announced prime minister P. W. Botha.

Not long before, he had been shaking a finger at the Americans for accusing him of exploiting and persecuting the black population. He had exclaimed that he wasn't going to be lectured to by people who had arrived as settlers in a new continent, wiped out the native Indian tribes, lived off the labor of black slaves, and maintained a system of racial segregation for years on end.

But now, with the whole world against him, and street war at home, he agreed that representatives of various races could marry each other and have families; he allowed black people to live in white towns and districts, to eat at the same restaurants, and even to apply for jobs formerly reserved for whites only.

"There are more important things than skin color," he explained. "We let black people into our kitchens to prepare our meals and to clean our houses, but we're disgusted when they stand in the same line as us at the post office?"

Rumors went round the country that Botha was holding secret talks with the black rebel leader Nelson Mandela, who was serving a life sentence on a prison island off the Cape of Good Hope.

In the big cities Botha's words and deeds were received with the calm, understanding, and resignation that greet something that's bound to happen. But in towns like Ventersdorp, scattered far and wide across the Highveld, they were regarded as a new form of betrayal and capitulation, a harbinger of dark days and events to come. The old disputes that had erupted after the war with the British flared up again.

Some of the partisan commanders, war heroes such as Jan Smuts, had argued at the time that in view of the numerical advantage of the British there was no alternative but to give them priority, learn from them, and profit from it. Without an alliance with the British, they explained, the white settlers would never keep the black Africans in control. Others regarded their defeat as merely a lost battle and, remaining hostile to the British, continued to wait for an opportunity to resurrect the independent Boer republics. They saw calls for agreement with the British as nothing but low-down treachery.

"Who'd have thought P. W. Botha would turn out to be a traitor too? Of all people! There've always been so many traitors among us! That's our downfall," said Eugène Terre'Blanche's sister Dora indignantly as she brooded on those days. Botha's father had fought against the British in the second Boer war, and he himself had admired Adolf Hitler and sided with the Germans when they tried to conquer Great Britain and the rest of Europe.

Dora's worst curses were aimed at those who had renounced their own traditions and beliefs because they found them a burden in their pursuit of profit. She said it was all the same to them—they were ready to sell their own mothers just to increase their wealth and become more like the rich Britons and Jews from Johannesburg.

"But there weren't any traitors or cowards in our town. Everybody supported Eugène without exception," she said. "The farmers, town hall officials, police, storekeepers—they called him the Lion of Transvaal, like General de la Rey. He never betrayed the Boers or let them down."

By then Terre'Blanche was leading the Afrikaner Resistance Movement, which he had founded, and which was opposed to any kind of change to the apartheid laws and customs. He was also demanding the consent of the government in Pretoria to make part of the South African state into a separate territory, province, or at least a county, where the Afrikaners could create their own republic and live in their own way.

This was his overriding aim, but faced with the threat of apartheid ending, it had had to give way to the struggle to save the old system. Terre'Blanche had decided to devote his entire life to it, as well as his highly promising career as a police officer.

He had signed up for the police force after high school. First he had volunteered for service in South West Africa (now independent Namibia), a former German colony occupied by South Africa. He patrolled the restless Angolan border on horseback, where black rebels were hiding out and making armed raids on South African garrisons. He distinguished himself enough to be chosen from among twenty thousand junior officers and cadets for an elite unit delegated to be an armed escort for presidents, heads of state, and government ministers.

He quit the service because of prime minister John Vorster, the man he was meant to be keeping safe. Terre'Blanche regarded Vorster's predecessor, Hendrik Verwoerd, who as head of state had devised and introduced the rules for racial segregation, as his hero and spiritual guide. But Verwoerd had been murdered by an assassin; his successor and apprentice Vorster, instead of reinforcing apartheid, had begun to dismantle it.

Vorster had started courting the West, and was increasingly often yielding to its demands to allow foreign companies involvement in South African gold, diamond, and platinum mines. Surrendering to Western pressure, Vorster had also sought the friendship of black leaders from other African countries, and was neglecting the heads of the last white governments, the Rhodesians, and the Portuguese in Mozambique and Angola. He lifted racial segregation in sports, got rid of separate park benches, relaxed the pass regulations, and urged whites to consider letting black people attend services at their churches.

Amazed and outraged by Vorster's conduct, Terre'Blanche and the other Transvaal Afrikaners regarded him as yet another *kaffir-boetie* (kaffir lover), of whom there were plenty in the big cities. They warned him not to count on gratitude from the blacks or the West, for whom there could never be enough favors and concessions—it would always be too little.

As they saw it, life proved them right. To win America's approval, Vorster ordered his army to invade Angola, where the Portuguese government was falling. The Americans had promised to join in with the invasion and repay the Afrikaners for their support, but they never sent any troops to Angola. They exposed Vorster who, instead of breaking South Africa's isolation, condemned it to even greater ostracism. At the demand of the African leaders whose favor Vorster was trying to win, South Africa was excluded from the Olympic Games. Deprived of their neighbors' support, one after another the white governments in Angola, Mozambique, and Rhodesia collapsed, and finally South Africa was left, to their way of thinking, as the only white oasis on the "Dark Continent." The blacks in South Africa also repaid him for the concessions he had made with ingratitude. "It's just shifting the furniture about in the same old room," sighed one of their leaders, archbishop Desmond Tutu, who as a child had lived with his parents in Ventersdorp for some time. The young people in Soweto, a black township on the edge of Johannesburg, sparked off a street rebellion that would never die down.

Disappointed by Vorster and his government, Terre'Blanche left the police and returned to the family farm. But he couldn't sit still at the farm, occupying himself with raising cattle or growing maize. He was totally absorbed by national issues and the fate of the Afrikaners, who once again faced a deadly threat. To his mind, the government was leading the nation to perdition, and he alone knew how to save it. One day in the Transvaal town of Heidelberg, along with six friends who shared his views, he founded a brotherhood that he called the Afrikaner Resistance Movement—the AWB—and became its leader.

At the founding session, held in a garage, it was decided that the brotherhood would operate covertly, and the names and faces of its members would remain secret, just like in the Ku Klux Klan, active in the American South. Although thanks to Eugène Terre'Blanche's fame facts that were meant to remain a mystery soon came to light, many Afrikaner politicians, MPs and military personnel preferred to keep their membership of the brotherhood secret.

In those days all the Afrikaner churches took the view that their nation was allied to God with the sort of pact he had once formed with the people of Israel. "Nothing happens without the will of Our Lord," said Dora, who with her husband Don, her brothers, and about a dozen other townsfolk, had founded the new church. Built on the edge of town, in the open fields, it was not just the newest but also one of the biggest in Ventersdorp. From the start the nave was designed to accommodate as many as a thousand people. Unlike the old churches in town, the new one had no clock. "All we can do is thank him every day for showing us special favor. Doesn't our entire fate bear witness to it? The fact that we've ended up here, that we're still alive, and that we've survived so many severe trials and so much suffering? Can better proof be needed that the Creator had clear intentions for us?"

The first vow to God was made in the name of the Boers by Jan van Riebeeck, leader of the settlers who sailed from Europe and landed in Africa, at the Cape of Good Hope. The most important, most sacred pledge of all was made by the Boer pioneers who had travelled all the way to the land of the Zulus—cruel, treacherous warriors—and were surrounded by them on the Ncome River.

Less than five hundred white settlers faced King Dingaan's army, consisting of twenty times as many fearless, seasoned Zulu soldiers. Before the battle, which seemed a foregone conclusion, the pioneers gathered in their camp for prayers. There on the riverbank, their leader, Andries Pretorius, made a vow that if God saved the Boers, just as he had rescued the people of Israel, they would be faithful to him for all time; they would celebrate the day of their salvation as their most sacred holiday, and raise a monument to the Almighty here on the river.

Dora van Zyl believed that on that day the Lord God revealed his will to the Boers. In a violent battle, which lasted for three hours, that small handful of Boers beat and decimated the Zulu troops. So many Zulu warriors were killed that the water in the Ncome River took on the color of blood, and ever since it has been called Blood River. On the Boer side only three people suffered light wounds; moreover, the injured men had disobeyed Pretorius's orders and had not stayed hidden with the others in their fortified camp made from wooden wagons.

In Afrikaner churches and homes the anniversary of this victory was celebrated as the Day of the Vow.

However, not all Afrikaners regarded winning the Battle of Blood River as proof of God's mercy or miraculous salvation. There were those who ascribed the Zulu defeat to the simple fact that the Boers had better weapons. Concealed behind their wagons and shooting from muskets, they never let the Zulu warriors come dangerously close to them. Dora, her brothers, and all the members of their church regarded these people as godless traitors and blasphemers.

This group included a historian who was well known for his liberal views, professor Floris van Jaarsveld of the University of Pretoria. In his lectures he maintained that there was nothing sacred about the victory at Blood River, and there was no reason to celebrate it as a religious holiday. One Sunday when he came to give a talk in Potchefstroom, Eugène Terre'Blanche made the trip from Ventersdorp to attend it, accompanied by a few dozen members of the AWB.

The venerable professor had not yet started his lecture when Terre'Blanche and his associates, armed with whips and riding crops, burst into the crowded auditorium. With all the students watching, they poured a bucket of hot tar over the professor and then showered him with feathers. The old man didn't even try to defend himself. Terre'Blanche then mounted the stage and announced that the scholar had been punished for breaking the oath that the Boers had sworn to the Lord God, and that the Boer patriots would never allow something they held sacred to be desecrated.

For the humiliated Professor van Jaarsveld this was the end of his career. Publishers refused to publish his work anymore, and his history textbooks were withdrawn from schools. He was no longer invited to speak on national radio, though earlier he had presented his own programs there. He was summoned for interview by the secret police, who found his lectures on the history of communism suspicious. People began to move away from him, and soon forgot that he existed.

Whereas the world found out about Terre'Blanche. Newspapers that had previously ignored him now featured him on their front pages, pictures of him were published, and he appeared on national television. From then on, wherever he was going to speak at a rally, the journalists always showed up.

Following the assault on the professor he was brought before a court on a charge of hooliganism. After each hearing, a cheering crowd was waiting for him outside the courthouse, regarding him as a hero and defender of all that the Afrikaners held sacred. Found guilty, he was given a choice of several weeks in jail or a fine, and chose the fine. He paid it with money donated to him by strangers who were pleased by the audacity and cruelty of his raid on the university lecture hall.

So much money came pouring in that Terre'Blanche had to open a special bank account.

Volunteers began coming to Ventersdorp from all over the country to join the AWB. The most welcome were former police officers and soldiers, who were immediately accepted into the ranks of the brotherhood and promoted to lead the paramilitary units called "commandos," just like in the Boer partisan militia. So many of them applied that the government banned policemen and soldiers from joining the brotherhood.

The greater the anxiety prompted among the Afrikaners by the white government's concessions to the blacks, and the closer and more inevitable the end of the apartheid system seemed to be, the more people applied to join the AWB. At its rallies, which drew a larger and larger crowd, Terre'Blanche boasted that his brotherhood numbered a hundred thousand, even a quarter of a million, ready to fulfill every order he gave, and that it was larger and more powerful than the national army. Moreover, he maintained that at the critical moment, when the blacks presented a threat, the white soldiers and policemen would refuse to obey the government, and would stand alongside the representatives of their race.

He threatened that he would sooner incite war and send the whole country up in smoke than allow it to pass into the possession of blacks and those whites who saw nothing indecent in miscegenation.

"Lord God! If necessary, lead us once again to the Battle of Blood River!" he would cry. "With God on our side, we need fear nobody, and we shall conquer any foe!"

He also made speeches in the capital, beneath the Voortrekker Monument, the most sacred site commemorating the history of the Boers and their trek across Africa. Ever since the white government had released the leaders of the black majority from jail and started to negotiate with them, Afrikaners opposed to change would gather beneath the monument to demand that apartheid be kept at any price—even if it meant carving out a new republic for the Afrikaners from part of South Africa.

At one of the rallies below the Voortrekker Monument Terre'Blanche appeared on his black horse, Attila, with an escort of armed riders. Dressed in khaki shirts with the swastika made of sevens on their armbands, holding flags and flaming torches, they lined up in a double row, which Terre'Blanche rode down to reach the platform.

There were others who opposed letting the blacks have any power, or any of the whites' exclusive privileges, and who were also demanding the establishment of an Afrikaner republic. However, nobody spoke with such passion or eloquence as Terre'Blanche. He had a powerful voice, charisma, and a sense of drama, which he had cultivated as a boy, when he had appeared in theatrical performances at school and at church.

On the speakers' tribunes that became his stage, he played the part he had invented for himself, as a Boer general. Once he had finished his performance, people would leave the rally without waiting for the other speakers, because they didn't expect to hear anything quite so stirring from them.

He took care of the most minute details. He gave an interview to one foreign television channel while getting on his horse, then insisted on reciting a poem at the end of the conversation, and made them film him galloping his black steed into the sunset. To be on the safe side, he repeated this final scene four times.

But most of all, being a poet, he knew the right words to use and their power. He knew how to control his audience, how to transport and captivate them. Sometimes he spoke softly and gently, almost in a whisper, to force his listeners to keep quiet and concentrate. Sometimes he would movingly summon up the memory of the pioneers and partisans from the Boer wars, then immediately afterward in a booming voice he would terrify them with the threat of annihilation. Then to finish off, he would almost hysterically pluck at their heartstrings to evoke a sense of injury, rage, and thirst for vengeance. Whenever he called them to arms, as if spellbound, his audience appeared ready to kill and to die.

He didn't hide the fact that he admired Hitler as a leader who had not only helped his nation to rise again after losing a war, saving it from destitution, but had also aroused a fighting spirit in them. In fact, there were plenty of fans of the German fascist leader in the AWB. They held parties to celebrate Hitler's birthday, and when his deputy Rudolf Hess died in Berlin's Spandau prison, they organized a memorial event in his honor at a cemetery in Pretoria, to which they brought flags with fascist swastikas on them. Terre'Blanche's response to the outraged Jewish liberals from Johannesburg was to issue threats.

"By poking your nose into everything, you'll just bring trouble down on yourselves," he warned. "Your homeland is Israel. Why don't you share power with the Arabs there? The Afrikaners have just as much of a right to their own state as the Jews."

Terre'Blanche shared Hitler's beliefs in the power of the nation and in racial purity, as well as his contempt for political parties—he saw them as harmful, unnecessarily dividing the nation, which especially at a time of threat should unite into a single state, into a single brotherhood, under the command of a single leader. It should shut itself in a fortified camp in order to survive the stormy times.

Among the white citizens of wealthy Johannesburg, Cape Town, and even the capital Pretoria, which was regarded as the cradle of the Afrikaners, Terre'Blanche prompted amusement and embarrassment rather than alarm. In the big cities he was mocked for being so fond of pompous gestures and pathos, and seen as a nauseating village tub-thumper and puffed-up megalomaniac.

He was never allowed to forget the fact that at one of his torchlit nocturnal rallies his steed had thrown him off, right in front of the platform, which he had meant to ride up to in a dashing way amid the cheering crowd. And that being ashamed of his meager height, which seemed to him at odds with his image as a hero and leader, he wore shoes with thick soles or heels, and had footstools placed on the platform to make himself look taller. "He's our Mussolini, our little Hitler," people would mock, ridiculing his weakness for uniforms, flags, and torchlit rallies, for parading about with rifles, and even for the fact that his underlings in the brotherhood addressed him as general or chief.

So although he didn't avoid the big cities, he preferred to make his speeches at old battlefields, on the anniversaries of great victories or martyrdom, and also in towns like Ventersdorp, where the people were more strongly attached to the old system.

They couldn't figure out the complexities of politics, they didn't appreciate the outside world, nor were they curious about it. The way they lived suited them, and they couldn't see a reason to change anything. They didn't understand why the leaders in Pretoria were negotiating with the blacks and promising to remove racial segregation as something harmful and outdated.

They didn't want to live under a black government, just as in the past they had refused to be governed by the British. They sensed betrayal, they could feel through their skin that once again they were being led by the nose by outsiders, and by the devious, rich inhabitants of the big cities, people for whom these changes were obviously convenient for some reason.

The Afrikaners from the Transvaal towns believed that everything should stay just as it was. For them, Terre'Blanche galloping on his black horse was like a Boer general from the old prints, bearded, blue eyed, tanned by the sun and the wind on the veld. He had come to their rescue and was telling them what to do, whom to obey, and whom to curse, who was their foe, and who their friend.

In those days accusations of betrayal were cast easily and often, but on Terre'Blanche's lips they virtually had the force of guilty verdicts—they annihilated their opponents, just as they had annihilated the unfortunate professor van Jaarsveld from the University of Pretoria. Terre'Blanche did not hesitate to accuse any Afrikaner politician who had failed to defend apartheid, yielded to the big-city liberals, and negotiated with the blacks.

At the rallies he cursed them as renegades and apostates. He accused journalists, writers, generals, government ministers, and presidents with the same anger and hatred. Even the Afrikaner politicians who shared his desire to maintain apartheid, or at least to resurrect the Boer republics, were afraid of Terre'Blanche's attacks. He demanded that they should abandon their fratricidal fighting and join forces in the face of a common enemy, and if that was too difficult for them, they should step down and recognize his leadership.

"The Lord God has punished us with a government of traitors who have freed Nelson Mandela, the Barabbas of Robben

Island, and want to surrender power to him. I swear I shall never allow that," he raged. "I would sooner incite war and lead my troops against the traitors."

The AWB's units were the armed commandos that Terre'Blanche had established following the example of the old Boer generals. The Iron Guard, in black uniforms, were his bodyguards and an elite shock unit. The Storm Hawks were motorized cavalry, who rode motorbikes instead of horses. The Golden Eagles were farmers who owned light aircraft used for transport and farming, or were into gliding. If war were to break out, the small planes were to serve as bombers. Other commandos were called the Red Falcons and the Black Eagles. There were also units that specialized in training dogs to fight and to patrol. The AWB also formed scout packs, commanded by Terre'Blanche's brother Andries, who had inherited command of the Ventersdorp volunteer force from his father.

Terre'Blanche insisted that he was setting up these units to help the police to keep order, but in reality the uniformed squads, often under his personal leadership, travelled about Transvaal, Orange Free State, and Natal, disturbing conferences where politicians and academics were promoting the need to reach agreement with the blacks and to dismantle the apartheid system.

In Pretoria they invaded a local theater, where the actors were demanding that black spectators be admitted to their performances too, and had collected signatures for a petition to the authorities on the matter. In the street outside the theater, AWB members seized the petition from the actors and tore it up in public view. Liberal writers and academics received letters containing threats that they would end up tarred and feathered, like the traitor van Jaarsveld.

"See you at Johannesburg airport," wrote Terre'Blanche in a telegram to the liberal scholar and politician Frederik van Zyl Slabbert, who was going on a trip to Senegal to talk to black leaders in exile. On his way back from Dakar, just in case, van Zyl decided not to wait for the plane to land in Johannesburg, but got out in Cape Town.

"None of the traitors from the government in Pretoria will speak publicly in Transvaal ever again," warned Terre'Blanche. At the chief's call, supporters of the AWB went to public meetings held by representatives of the government and the ruling party, which had introduced apartheid years ago, but was now promoting its removal. There they cut the microphone cables or mixed in with the crowd, stamping their feet, making a racket, and picking fights, preventing anyone from delivering their speech. At the end of each of these interrupted events Terre'Blanche spoke, presenting the latest incident as a great victory.

In the town of Brits he stopped the deputy minister of information from speaking, and in Nylstroom it was the minister of justice; in Pietersburg he cut short the minister of diplomacy's event by provoking a brawl, and in Veereninging he interrupted the president himself.

There were more and more skirmishes between the AWB and the police, who finally banned members of the brotherhood from attending public meetings with weapons. But the government ministers complained that in Transvaal towns, instead of protecting them from Terre'Blanche's hit squads, the police were actually on his side.

Terre'Blanche got his way. He seemed invincible. None of the ministers or leaders of the ruling party made any more public appearances in Transvaal.

The brotherhood's squads were also making an increasing number of attacks on blacks, threatening to lynch them. Rumors started going round the country that Terre'Blanche and his people were planning acts of sabotage, bomb attacks, and the assassinations of black leaders, and that on their farms they were being trained to shoot, collecting and hiding weapons stolen from government arsenals or covertly bought in neighboring countries.

One such secret cache of weapons was found by the police just outside Ventersdorp in a maize field belonging to Terre'Blanche's brother Andries. Placed under arrest, he boasted in court that the police and the examining magistrate were not treating him like a criminal, but like an honored guest. For hiding illegal weapons a court in Klerksdorp sentenced Eugène Terre'Blanche to two years in jail, but suspended the sentence. The judge conducting the trial said that such a respected citizen did not deserve to be flung in prison.

Not giving a damn about sentences, courts, and police, Terre'Blanche went on amassing pistols, rifles, and ammunition, and forming new units. The secret police, who spied on all the major political parties in the country, received orders to keep an eye on the brotherhood too. The national president warned that if in standing up for apartheid Terre'Blanche broke the law, he would be treated as a subversive and would be punished in just the same way as the black rebel leaders who had spent many years in jail for trying to overthrow apartheid.

On a corkboard above the kitchen table, Henk Malan used to pin pictures of Terre'Blanche cut out of the newspapers, and articles describing his public appearances. After breakfast, as he drank coffee from a large mug, he liked to spread out the old reports on the table in front of him, and would even reread ones that he knew almost word-for-word by now. His favorite was the account of a nighttime rally in Pretoria, which Eugène had arrived at on his black horse.

"South Africa belongs to the Afrikaners. Our ancestors came here to bring civilization to Africa. For thousands of years this land was uninhabited, waiting for God's chosen race to settle here. And it became the image of this earth. Indomitable, pure, and mighty, like the earth. But now those who dream of establishing their control over the entire world want to take it away from us"—silently moving his lips, Henk would read extracts from the speech that Eugène had made outside government headquarters in Pretoria. "We want our place on earth, and no black or white traitor, no Jew, is going to take that right away from us. And there is no force on earth that can stop us! If they want war, they'll get it. And we shall crush them, we shall wipe them from the face of the earth! The time of trial is approaching!"

Like everyone in Ventersdorp, Henk knew Eugène before he became nationally famous. In fact he saw him more often than others—they were neighbors, because Henk's wife Anita had rented the house next door to the Terre'Blanches' property after divorcing her first husband.

Eugène had always been more important in the town than anyone else. Maybe because unlike others, he had his own clear opinion on almost every subject, and knew what had to be done. And he was capable of talking about it in such a way that all you could do was agree with him, admit he was right, accept his view as your own, and do as he said. At any rate, he always made his point in a way that meant it was impossible to disagree with, oppose, or contradict him.

You could be with him or against him, his friend or his enemy. But if any of the townsfolk didn't want to be his friend, they were even less keen to be his enemy, because falling foul of Eugène meant rejecting everything that he took as his creed, his most sacred beliefs. Going against Eugène was tantamount to becoming a proclaimed apostate and traitor, cursed and condemned to ostracism, which made continuing to live in Ventersdorp unbearable.

He had the whole town in the palm of his hand, but that was convenient for it too. He helped it whenever something needed to be said loud and clear, but which others found frightening or shameful. Other people, like Henk, didn't know how to say what they wanted, even if it was bothering, worrying, or upsetting them. Eugène had answers to all questions and doubts— ready diagnoses and remedies.

Like most of the townsfolk, and also the local farmers, Henk Malan attended Terre'Blanche's rallies to hear him cursing the government for wanting to surrender power to the blacks. That made Henk feel as if it was he who was expelling his own stifling rage and fear of the unknown. He could almost hear his own scream.

But although the town was so much at Terre'Blanche's beck and call, not many of the locals joined his brotherhood. Volunteers came down to Terre'Blanche's house from all over the country, but while the townspeople supported, encouraged, listened to, and applauded him, they didn't join his ranks, as if they reckoned it was enough that he, their friend and neighbor, was shouting and swearing, wearing a uniform and threatening war, as if he was doing it in their name. For them.

Henk Malan disliked the local white farmers almost as much as he disliked the blacks. This feeling was partly envy, and partly a sense of inferiority toward people who had done well in life. It made him feel helpless anger, humiliation, and fear. The farmers had nothing to be afraid of, not even a black government. They had money and influence, they knew that any president, black or white, would have to reckon with them. They weren't fighting to survive, but to keep their privileges and profit. Perhaps only the threat that the land they lived off would be taken away from them could make them lose confidence and feel real fear.

Whites like Henk who had achieved nothing and made no money were afraid that if a black government came to power it would deprive them of even the semblance of affluence and security that they owed purely to the color of their skin and to the apartheid system, introduced with the sole aim of protecting them from competition on the part of the blacks.

He had often seen Mandela on television, giving assurances that once he became president he wouldn't take the land, mines, or factories away from the whites, or fire all the army or police officers. In any case the blacks were no threat to the rich, experienced and educated people, economists, engineers, and managers. But Mandela hadn't said a word about engineers, truck drivers, post office or bank clerks, or store assistants. The blacks were suitable for their jobs. They weren't assuming power just to be satisfied with the post of president for Mandela.

Quite apart from the political situation, it was getting harder and harder to find work and earn a living anyway. The current crisis meant not only that blacks couldn't find jobs, but also that more and more whites were losing theirs. As in the years of the major recession in Transvaal, unemployed whites appeared, and soon after, beggars too.

Years ago the government had introduced apartheid to save the poor whites from destitution, at the expense of the blacks.

Now the white president wanted to share power with the blacks. Neither the government nor the rich people in Johannesburg were concerned about the poor white people. But now, hurrying to their aid, came Eugène Terre'Blanche. He organized collections, gathered food, and encouraged the owners of mines and factories to employ whites who were left with no jobs or support, instead of striking black miners and workers. He also persuaded farmers to hire unemployed whites to work in their fields.

They did it reluctantly, dragging their feet, and if they did take them on, it was for the sort of work the blacks used to do. And they were only willing to pay a pittance, just as they had paid the blacks. They preferred to employ blacks because they were cheaper, and they could be treated like farm animals. The famers couldn't take that sort of liberty with the indigent whites, but even so they treated them like representatives of a lower species. Their destitution and unsuccessful lives undermined the conviction that the white race was superior. Even the white post office workers who were called out to the farms to fix the phone lines were only admitted to the kitchen areas, like the black servants.

Henk Malan remembered his father's stories about working at the post office, when he had also gone to the farms to fix phone lines that had been snapped by the wind. He was surprised when old George Boardman at Buckingham farm, whose phone he had come to fix, invited him into the sitting room and asked if he'd like a beer. It was the first time any farmer had let Henk's father enter his home.

Terre'Blanche was different, maybe because although he had land, he wasn't really a farmer. He didn't behave so haughtily, in such a superior way, as they did. Malan liked what he said about the Afrikaner republic, whose establishment he so firmly demanded. From what Eugène said, it was to resemble Ventersdorp, a friendly town, where they all knew each other, where everyone knew their place, and the neighbors treated each other amicably, hurrying to each other's aid. Nobody was to be excluded from the community or made to feel left out. There would be no place in it for the arrogant British, lording it over the Afrikaners and ridiculing their customs, or for the blacks, taking the jobs and wages away from Afrikaner men.

They wouldn't be able to live in the Afrikaner republic—they wouldn't be admitted to it. Henk imagined never having to encounter them in the street or at work. Or in the store where he bought food. He wouldn't have to touch the same door handles or store trolleys. He'd have no contact with them at all.

When the white brotherhood in Ventersdorp announced that it was collecting money for the fine imposed on Eugène for the attack on Professor van Jaarsveld, after some thought, Henk decided to contribute. He had a bit of cash put aside to buy a new television set. It wasn't much, but he decided to pay it all into the AWB's bank account.

"The TV can wait," he told his wife.

He handed the bank clerk a completed money order, and she looked up at him from the document. Although she didn't let it show, Henk was sure she knew perfectly well what cause he was donating the money to. He felt he was doing something important, he felt celebratory, in a festive mood.

From that day on, at Terre-Blanche's rallies he felt better and more self-confident, in his place. He stood closer to the platform and felt he had the right to do so, that now he had a real connection with Terre'Blanche and his brotherhood—now they were comrades-in-arms.

"They want war? Then they'll get it!" Eugène thundered. "They're going to be taught a lesson! Prepare yourselves, for the time of trial is approaching!"

One day, while in Krugersdorp, Henk dropped in at a gun store and bought himself a Beretta pistol, the kind used by the police. He also bought some ammunition and a scope for the hunting rifle he already kept at home.

When he was an engine driver, he used to go through the Boardmans' property, bringing trains in to a railroad halt just outside town, where grain was loaded onto the freight cars from enormous silos. While waiting for permission to drive in, he'd stop his locomotive in the fields and fire his rifle at jackals and quails. The noise of the shots would terrify the black workers at Buckingham farm, and it made Henk laugh to see them cringing and stumbling as they raced off in panic. Sometimes, for fun, to terrify them even more, he'd shoot into the air as they ran away.

They must eventually have complained, because one day, when Henk was looking out for quail in the meadow, he was deafened by the boom of gunfire. He turned round and saw a white man pointing a rifle at him. He automatically threw his shotgun onto the grass and put his hands up.

The man who had him in his sights was Herbert, the oldest of the three Boardman sons, known for his quick temper and for getting into a fight with Eugène Terre'Blanche in town.

"This is my land," he said, without taking his finger off the trigger. "You're on my land."

The astonished Henk said nothing.

"Pick it up!" cried Boardman, indicating the shotgun lying in the grass.

Henk Malan didn't flinch. He felt that if he reached for the gun, Boardman would shoot him. He went on aiming at him, straight at his head, for quite a while longer, and then lowered his rifle.

"This is my land," he repeated.

Henk Malan never fired at the quail on Buckingham farm again. Sometimes, although he tried not to, he ran into Herbert Boardman in town. They would pass each other without a word, without even exchanging glances, like total strangers.

But he rarely met the Boardmans in town. They never came to Eugène's rallies, or to the festivities and fairs organized by the Afrikaners, or the dances. If they showed up among the Afrikaners, it was only at farmers' meetings. And they always slipped away from those too, as soon as the discussion of the rate of loans and grants or purchase prices was over, before the conversation moved on to matters unrelated to crop cultivation or cattle breeding, when the beer and whisky unloosened the Afrikaners' tongues and freed them of their scruples.

"Sooner or later it would end in a brawl," said Raymond Boardman, who after returning to the farm for some time made an effort to take part in the life of the town. "Either someone would tell a joke about the British, or make a sarcastic comment. I always felt like the outsider at a village entertainment whom the locals are baiting for a fight."

By the time Benny Tapologo stood up against apartheid in Ventersdorp, elsewhere in the country the fight had generally come to an end.

One after another the rules and regulations, introduced years earlier to separate the races for good and all and never let them mix, were being repealed. The white government had released Nelson Mandela and other black leaders from jail, and was negotiating with them on sharing power. A date had been agreed for free elections, in which for the first time ever the black vote would count as much as the white, and the numerical advantage of the blacks would mean they would assume power in the country.

While growing up in Tshing, Benny not only knew nothing about politics, but took no interest in it—just like all the other people in the township, who weren't curious about the world beyond the town limits or the county boundary; few of them ever ventured any further.

In the evenings, over a beer after work they would complain of the wrongs and injustices done to them, but none of them ever thought of rebelling, or that the permanent—so it seemed—state of affairs could be changed. They felt disbelief and the sort of dismay prompted by public outrage when they heard the stories about street disturbances, strikes, and imminent revolution told them by the rare visitors who stopped in the town on their way from Johannesburg.

The people of Tshing never uttered the word "rebellion," just as nobody utters a curse that brings bad luck. Opposition to the world around them was not just futile, it was sinful. The schoolteachers and church ministers had taught them that. During the services they were told not to try correcting the Almighty, but to send him their grievances in their prayers and trust in Him to answer them.

"If you're not happy, the door's open!" threatened the white farmers whose land provided the blacks from Tshing with their only source of income. As the Tswana couldn't find employment on the Transvaal farms or in the mines of Johannesburg, the white government had assigned them nearby Bophuthatswana as a homeland, but there was no work there, no future prospects, or even enough room for everyone.

Benny finally discovered that the world did not end on the narrow road to Johannesburg that cut across the maize fields and grassland when he moved from middle school in Tshing to the high school in Khutsong, the black township of nearby Carletonville. Thanks to gold mining, this town was much richer and larger than Ventersdorp. Benny was encouraged to move to Khutsong by an uncle who lived there. He had convinced Benny's father that the boy would be closer to the outside world, would sooner find work in a mine than on a farm, and would earn more, and that the money he sent home would unburden the entire family.

Benny was a good and willing student who never looked for trouble or caused any. His days went by peacefully, without any dramatic incidents or sudden twists of fate, almost like at home in Tshing. He easily reached the final class and was getting ready for his high school graduation exams when disturbances broke out at the school.

He had no idea about it, and that morning, in a clean shirt, calm and confident, he left the house to go and sit the first of his exams. Some way from the school he could already hear shouts coming from it. At the gate into the school yard there was a crowd of students standing in a cloud of black smoke around some burning tires. Benny noticed boys from the junior classes among them. Brandishing machetes and sticks, they were turning back the students on their way to classes.

Benny slowed down, but kept going toward the school. He was already close enough to recognize the faces of the students guarding the gate. Just then somebody tugged him by the arm and pulled him back. He spun around, raising his hands as if to fight.

"Do you want them to kill you?" he heard.

Siphiwe, a boy from the same neighborhood, dragged him into a side street. He was much older than Benny, but he was in a lower class. He had come to Khutsong from Soweto, Johannesburg's black township. He was living with relatives, and according to local rumor he had been in jail for political reasons, and had tried to kill a policeman.

"Get out of here! Go home!" he hissed angrily into Benny's ear. "Are you blind or stupid? Don't you know what they do to people who break the strike?"

Benny heard how during the street riots in Soweto the young men had applied their own justice to black policemen, collaborators, and informers, and had often carried out death sentences by burning their victims alive. They would force a tire filled with petrol over their neck and arms, then set it alight and leave them in the street like a human torch. They called it "necklacing." They also set fire to school buildings, insisting that studying didn't matter until they had won the battle for freedom. Benny had never seen street riots before, barricades made of burning tires, policemen with barking dogs or clouds of white tear gas.

Siphiwe told him that the previous day the students in Khutsong had decided to join the strike declared by the black leaders, to force the white government to release political prisoners. That night the police had tried to arrest one of the organizers of the school strike. Roused in the small hours, only half-awake and terrified, he had tried to escape. When he broke away and raced off down the empty street, the police had shot him. Next day the striking students had announced an armed uprising in Khutsong, and the authorities had sent the police, armed with tear-gas grenades, water cannons, and guns firing live ammunition to suppress it.

Benny had only heard gunfire once before. Two black rebels had once stayed overnight in Tshing. But in a place like that, where everyone knew each other, it was difficult for outsiders to remain hidden. The neighbors quickly found out about the suspicious strangers and sent their children to fetch the police. The rebels had refused to surrender, but before being killed, they had defended themselves for several hours in the shack they had occupied for the night. Since then, nothing unusual had ever happened in Tshing again.

Once the police had crushed the riots in Khutsong and the strike had been called off, Benny took his graduation exams and went home to Tshing. For a while he worked as a schoolteacher, then he and three pals sold illicit sorghum beer at a local shebeen, or unlicensed bar. Finally he got a job at the Engen gas station in the white town.

Eugène Terre'Blanche and his white brotherhood were in charge of Ventersdorp. The owner of the Engen gas station where Benny was employed was a member of the AWB, and so was his son, who owned the Shell station on the other side of the road. In any case, Benny got the impression that all the white men in the town belonged to the brotherhood.

He often encountered Terre'Blanche, who was in the habit of tanking up at the Engen station. He would toss his car keys to one of the black employees, bark an order, and go to the office, where the owner was usually to be found.

One day he stopped at the gas pump manned by Benny. He told him to fill up his car, check the oil and the windshield washer fluid, and clean the windows and mirrors. After carrying out all his wishes, the boy was counting on a tip. Benny hadn't been back in Ventersdorp for long; he didn't know Terre'Blanche well, or that round here he bought everything on credit.

"You goddamn miser," he muttered in the Tswana language after Terre'Blanche, who had taken the keys without a word and was heading for his pickup. "I hope you choke on your money."

Terre'Blanche stopped and turned round.

"You're new here, eh?" he replied, also in Tswana. "You'll have time to learn. Unless you're stupid, but there's nothing you can do about that."

Amazed and terrified, Benny just stared in silence.

"We'll be seeing each other again," quipped Terre'Blanche as he fired up the engine. "We'll be seeing each other often."

A week later Benny was beaten up by members of the AWB.

Trying to earn a bit of extra cash, he and a few friends used to sell beer by the road from Ventersdorp to Tshing. They didn't have a license for the stall or to sell alcohol, but the business did well. It wasn't just blacks on their way to town to work or shop who bought beer from them, but also white farmers driving along the road.

So when a pickup truck stopped at the stall and several white men got out, Benny didn't sense anything wrong. They were young, not much older than he was. But they hadn't come for beer, or at least not to buy any.

The one who looked like the leader came up to the stall, and without saying a word threw a punch at Benny. He aimed at his face, but missed, and that infuriated him. Struck on the temple, Benny reeled and fell onto the dusty road. The men immediately surrounded him, punching his head and kicking his thighs and belly. He curled up, trying to protect his head with his hands as he took the kicks and punches.

"Fucking kaffir! Black bastard!"

Suddenly they stopped beating him and started destroying the beer stall and smashing the bottles. Busy with the stall, they didn't notice Benny leaping up and racing off into the waste-land along the road. They tried to chase him, but he had van-ished into the long grass. They went back to the road, loaded the crates of beer bottles that they hadn't managed to smash into their car, and yelling at the tops of their voices drove off toward town.

The blacks from Tshing steered clear of the white youths who went cruising around the neighborhood in farm trucks. Noisy, often half-drunk, they thought it fun to accost black girls on their way home from work, insulting them and provoking rows. The blacks in town were afraid of the whites and kept out of their way to avoid squabbles.

The white teenagers in cars would hunt down the black winos who spent their days begging or looking for an opportunity for a free drink. When the white boys called them over, tempting them with alcohol, they would shakily clamber into the back of the pickup truck, which would drive off with tires squealing.

Usually the white boys drove them out into the veld, got them drunk, and laughed at their clumsiness. Sometimes, for fun, they beat up the gibbering drunks. But sometimes they were drunk too, and then the fun and games were over.

When he returned to Tshing, Benny found his old friends again. His contemporary, Kaizer Jesile, had just come back from studying in Randfontein, and Kabelo Mashi, who was younger than them, was still at school in Tshing. They would meet up in the evenings, wander the streets of the township drowning in waste matter and refuse, or sit until late at night in the tall grass on the veld surrounding the town.

Benny told them about the riots in Khutsong and about the Soweto uprising, which he had heard about from Siphi-we. Kaizer Jesile would talk at length about Nelson Mandela, whom he'd seen at a public meeting in Johannesburg. Kabelo Mashi mainly listened; if he did speak, it was just to say that nothing had changed while they were away, except for the fact that it wasn't really the white mayor and his officials who exercised power in Ventersdorp, but Eugène Terre'Blanche and his brotherhood.

Busy with national affairs, Terre'Blanche was rarely in Ventersdorp, which during his absence sank into idle somnolence, but nervously awoke whenever he came home and summoned the citizens to a nocturnal rally. On those days pickup trucks would cruise around the town from early morning, fitted with loudspeakers through which the brotherhood would warn the blacks to get out of town before "the General" began to speak.

Benny and his friends were baffled by the fact that while there was a revolution under way throughout the country, turning the old order upside down, in their town everything was just as before and nothing was changing. As he listened to his friends' grievances, Benny remembered Siphiwe's parting words in Khutsong: "So you've decided to go back there?" There was mockery in his tone. "It's the right choice, you'll be a good kaffir, like all you people out there in the countryside."

The whites in the town had called Benny's father a good kaffir when they wanted to praise him or persuade him to do something for them. "You're a good kaffir," they'd say, patting him on the back. "Not like the others." So Benny decided never to be like his father. He didn't want to be a good kaffir.

One day, on the dot of noon, some white policemen drove up to the local black cemetery with a man's corpse wrapped in a blue plastic bag. Nobody from Tshing recognized him; he couldn't have lived here. In a town where nothing ever happened, the police turning up with a dead body caused a stir. The small cemetery was soon full of people.

In Khutsong Benny had heard that it was in dumps like Ventersdorp that at night the white police secretly buried the bodies of black activists tortured to death during interrogation, or simply shot dead during arrest. On hearing that some policemen had brought a corpse to the cemetery, he and his friends hurried there.

They had no trouble inciting the people gathered at the cemetery gate to crowd round the policemen and insist that they didn't want this man buried in their cemetery, when nobody knew how he had died or where he was from. The police explained that they had found him on the road outside town, run over, probably by a truck, and that he had no ID on him, so they didn't know who he was, where he lived, or where he'd been heading.

Benny and his friends demanded to be shown the corpse. The policemen uncovered it. It was the first time Benny had ever seen a dead person. His head was smashed, and it looked as if someone had ripped off the top of his skull. They refused to let the body be buried in the cemetery at Tshing, so the police drove away with it to Ventersdorp.

A few days later they came back. Before anyone had time to notice, they buried the body, which nobody now had the courage to exhume. A couple of weeks later another freshly dug, unmarked grave appeared at the cemetery.

At this point Benny and his friends banded together with some other young people for a secret nocturnal conference at the soccer field. They decided to demand a meeting with the black authorities in Tshing, and to threaten that if they didn't explain the matter of the secret burials, and generally do something to change the course of events in this town, the young people would organize an uprising.

Next day they were stopped in the street by Naledi Rampa, who though only just thirty was one of the richest people in Tshing. He had made his money running a store that the white authorities had allowed him to open in the black township. His mother was on the town council in Tshing, and had arranged it for him.

Naledi must have been aware that the youth in Soweto and other black suburbs of Johannesburg regarded black officials like his mother as traitors and collaborators. When street riots erupted there, those people's houses, stalls, and stores were the first to be set on fire. And sometimes they were dragged outside, humiliated and beaten, or even burned alive. Naledi must have known that, because he came up to them in the street and promised to take care of all their requests, as long as they didn't incite a riot.

They agreed, and for several weeks peace reigned. Until one night some white policemen brought another corpse to the cemetery and buried it there. Next day Benny and his friends went to Naledi's store and informed him that they were going to take matters into their own hands by declaring an uprising in Tshing.

They had no trouble persuading the students to stop going to school. The adults, however, refused to obey their calls to join the strike. Each morning, they set off as usual along the road to town to work for the whites—compliantly, obediently, as tame as farm animals. There were too few young rebels to stand in their way, stop them, and rouse them from their lethargy. They let them go off to town, only demanding that they pay a tax for the revolution.

But there were enough rebels to post guards at the boundaries of Tshing to make sure everyone observed the ban issued by the insurgents on buying things from the whites in town. Each evening they would stop the people coming back from work and search their bags and bundles; if they found anything bought in Ventersdorp they destroyed it on the road, as a lesson to others. They trampled flour and sugar into the ground and smashed bottles of milk and olive oil.

Their elders saw them as hooligans. They hurled abuse at them, and it often came to scuffles and blows. But the young people took the upper hand, not because they were stronger, but because they were acting as a group. Knowing there were plenty of them gave them courage and audacity. Singly, they would never have dared to do the things they found it so easy to do together.

The adults were always on their own, and were always the losers. They were even alone in a crowd—although they came back from the white town after work in large numbers, nobody came to the defense of those whose shopping the young people seized from them. They were against the uprising, they didn't like what the youths were doing, and were sure it would all end badly. They felt contempt and hostility toward the young people, but they were incapable of teaming up to restrain them when they took control of Tshing, where their entire world was located.

The white police from Ventersdorp didn't immediately appear in the black township, as if they didn't know what was happening there, although news of the uprising was even broadcast on television. Benny Tapologo saw himself on the evening news, and one of the reporters named him as a leader of the uprising. Next day Benny quit his job at the Engen gas station. He was scared of the whites from Ventersdorp, and realized he couldn't set foot there anymore.

After a week, when the uprising had started to die down, Benny and his friends organized a march of demonstrators and led them to the square outside the building housing the township's authorities. Most of the local officials were blacks from Tshing, such as Naledi Rampa's mother. But their bosses were three white people, who came here to work from Ventersdorp each day.

As he led the insurgents in front of the town hall, Benny had no plan, and certainly wasn't intending to storm it. He was hoping to breathe some new life into the uprising, to save it from fatigue and doubt. He didn't even notice who threw the first petrol bomb at the building. Bright flames engulfed the facade. Stones flew through the air, smashing the glass in the window panes. Someone set fire to a car parked outside the building.

One of the white men trapped inside had a pistol. Benny saw him stretch a hand out of a gap in the front door and fire blindly into the crowd, which, growing more aggressive by the minute, full of hatred and angry, was moving closer to the burning building.

They failed to burn it down. Summoned to help, the police and the fire brigade drove down to Tshing. While the firefighters put out the blaze, the policemen marched on the demonstrators in line formation. A white cloud of tear gas rose over the square. By evening it was all over. The uprising had been crushed.

At once the arrests began. As in Khutsong, the police came in the middle of the night, banging their fists on the door and shining flashlights in people's eyes. They knew the names and addresses of the rebel leaders, they knew everything. They came for Benny too, but they didn't find him. He'd spent the night with friends next door, in the attic just in case.

Next day at dawn he set off on foot along the road to Klerksdorp. He was already far from town when a police car passed him. The white policemen probably took him for a laborer on his way to work at a white farm. But the black informers sitting in the backseat recognized him—Benny clearly saw them pointing him out to the uniformed officers. The car turned round. Benny felt his legs go as heavy as lead from fear. He didn't even try to run away, or to break free when they tied his hands and pushed him into the trunk.

That night, the white police and their black informers had caught about fifty people who had led or taken part in the uprising. The jail in Ventersdorp was too small to house them all. Benny was transferred to Potchefstroom, where the interrogations were conducted by two black officers, April and Vente.

All the blacks in the area knew these names by hearsay, and prayed never to fall into their hands. At his first interrogation, before asking any questions, they battered Benny in silence with their fists and sticks. The second day was the same. Only on the third day, when the pain and terror were no longer preventing him from thinking, Benny realized that they kept hitting him on the right jaw and temple. That side of his head was so painful and swollen that it didn't seem connected with the left. And every time they dragged him back to the cell and threw him onto the concrete floor, locking the bars behind him, they said: "You'll come to like it here, you'll come to love it."

After three weeks of interrogation Benny went deaf in his right ear. He never regained his hearing.

The trial was held in Ventersdorp. Of the fifty defendants, a dozen were sentenced to several months in prison for hooliganism, starting fights, and destroying property. Benny was released.

"So how did you enjoy your stay with us?" quipped April as a parting shot.

Their experiences of the uprising in Ventersdorp—disobedience, the power of the crowd, hatred, and freedom to do violence, but also paralyzing fear, pain, humiliation, and a sense of defeat— changed everyone who had taken part in the street rebellion.

After his release from jail, Kaizer Jesile never got involved in politics again. His meetings with Benny Tapologo and Kabelo Mashi became increasingly rare, their conversations wouldn't take off anymore, and they had less and less in common. Finally they lost touch. Although they still lived in Tshing, where everybody knew all about everyone else, Benny couldn't say what his friend was doing or how he was getting on.

For Benny, and for Kabelo Mashi too, the Tshing rebellion and their time being tortured in jail didn't mean breaking with politics, but bonding with it for good. After his release, Benny was driven by the desire for revenge on those who had humiliated him and made him suffer. He was still talking it about it many years later, with the same determination and cold calculation. He wanted to pay them back in the same token, but for that he needed strength or power.

He knew it was pointless to count on the residents of Tshing. Brought up in fear and compliance to be good kaffirs, they had opposed the uprising, and after its suppression they would never join another rebellion. No, the blacks in Tshing wouldn't even hear of revolution.

But the Ventersdorp revolt was reported nationwide, because it had erupted in the Transvaal town made famous by Eugène

Terre'Blanche, on his home ground, the stronghold of his white brotherhood, which was threatening war if the blacks assumed power in the country.

Emissaries of the African National Congress—or ANC—started coming to Ventersdorp. The ANC was the country's biggest black party, which once apartheid was abolished was planning to establish a new government of its own under the leadership of Nelson Mandela. It had started life before the First World War as the South African Native National Congress, founded to protect the rights of blacks in direct response to government-sanctioned injustice. Some forty years later, the ANC was a mass resistance movement, which persisted and survived despite endless government efforts to block its activities and imprison its leaders.

Even in the days when its activity was banned by the white government, the ANC had underground offices and supporters in almost every black township in the country. In Ventersdorp nobody belonged to the ANC, not even once it had been legalized and Mandela was negotiating with the white government and preparing to be the country's first black president.

Now ANC envoys were coming from Johannesburg to take part in meetings at the township community center in Tshing, to encourage people to join the ANC and to vote for it in the forthcoming elections. They spoke of an imminent change of power, of justice, and of compensation for past injuries. And also of a black president in Pretoria, and a black mayor of Ventersdorp.

The older residents of the township listened to the visitors in silence and disbelief. Perplexed, they cast hesitant glances at their neighbors as they wondered how to refuse the guests without offending them. Only once did they liven up—they snorted with laughter at the idea of a black mayor for the white town.

The envoys from Johannesburg were disappointed and annoyed. They waited outside the community center for the car that was to take them away. Benny and his friends had been at the meeting too, but hadn't spoken up in the presence of the older people. They stood on the other side of the road, staring at the visitors from the big city, scrutinizing their clothes, behavior, and attitude. They only went up to them when one of the envoys beckoned them over.

He asked what was wrong with the people in Tshing. When white rule was coming to an end in the rest of the country, and the blacks were about to have their moment, why were they so terrified of everything? Why were they so opposed to any change? Kabelo Mashi, the boldest, replied that it wasn't worth wasting time on the older people here, but that they, the younger ones, who had incited an uprising, could also join the ANC and establish an office for it in Tshing.

The visitors nodded, and asked if they had heard about the rally the ANC had held in Church Square, in Pretoria. Once the white government had repealed its ban on the ANC's activities, released its leaders from jail, and allowed them to return from exile, at first the blacks had held rallies in their own townships. With time, as further rules concerning racial segregation were abolished, they had held torchlit marches to the very center of Johannesburg and other white districts previously closed to them.

Finally they had demanded official consent to hold a rally in Church Square in Pretoria, one of the Boers' most sacred sites. Here stood the building where the parliament of the independent Boer Transvaal republic had assembled, and near this spot its founder and first president, Paul Kruger, had once lived. His grateful compatriots had erected a monument to him in

Church Square. It was also the site of the courthouse where Nelson Mandela had been sentenced to life imprisonment.

For the blacks, the rally in Church Square was to be a show of strength, proof of the new era that would change the country for ever. For the whites, a black march at the heart of Pretoria was confirmation of their worst fears. Although the government had given the ANC permission to hold the rally, that day members of the AWB—the Afrikaner Resistance Movement—had gathered around the square as well, to prevent their sacred site from being desecrated by the blacks.

When black demonstrators climbed onto Kruger's statue and hung ANC banners and red Communist Party flags around his neck, members of the AWB broke through the police cordons and burst into the square, crying, "Hang Mandela!" Even though the ANC rally ended in a street brawl, for the blacks it meant breaking through yet another formerly impenetrable barrier.

The envoys from Johannesburg asked Benny if he and his friends would dare to do something similar—to convoke a rally or organize a march, not in the black township, but in white Ventersdorp, right under the noses of Terre'Blanche and his brotherhood.

Benny shrugged and replied that he wasn't afraid of anything—he'd gladly hold a rally right outside police headquarters. And if the party, which he was joining, won the elections and took power, he wouldn't hesitate to move into the white town hall as well.

Raymond Boardman was not in Ventersdorp at the time. He had got away from his hometown at the same age as his son, Mike. And just like Mike, he had kept saying that if he didn't get out of this damned place in time he'd become just like its other citizens, locked forever in the small circle of what they'd always known and understood. He had felt he had to escape from under the invisible dome that seemed to cover the town, the surrounding farms and bush, giving them an illusion of secure permanence.

It was if time had stopped in Ventersdorp, and the past was still here in the present day. Here the Afrikaners were still waging their old war against the British, which elsewhere was just a memory by now. But here they had never forgotten the injuries and suffering inflicted on them, and they dreamed of having their own state on the veld, a state for them alone, where they would live according to their own laws and preferences, where nobody would impose anything on them or interfere in their affairs.

In Ventersdorp the British were regarded as oppressors and enemies. The Boardmans of Buckingham farm sent their sons to the local school, to study with the Afrikaners. They only sent them to the British high school in Potchefstroom for further education because they regarded it as better than its Afrikaner competitor. Every morning, as Raymond took a shortcut across the neighboring farms on his way to the stop where the school bus picked him up, the Afrikaner boys, his schoolmates, threw stones at him and set dogs on him. Later on the same thing happened to his sons, and before that it had happened to his father when he attended the local school.

The swarthy Afrikaner boys would tease the British ones for having pale skin that went red in the sun, calling them "beetroots," and as the British spoke of themselves as a cut above the rest, the salt of the earth, they also called them "pickled pricks." Raymond Boardman couldn't understand the Afrikaners' animosity. He felt the pain of rejection rising in him, and a sense of totally undeserved injustice. He realized that the Afrikaners had never forgotten losing the war to his compatriots, or the persecution and miseries they had suffered in the concentration camps. But after all, Raymond's grandfather George Boardman and his entire family had been thrown into a camp by British soldiers too. They had shared the fate of the Boers, and had suffered as they did. And his maternal grandfather, Willem van Rensburg, was one of the Boer pioneers, and had even served as president of their republic, Transvaal.

Raymond got the impression that whatever he did, there was no changing the fact that the local Afrikaners would always be against him, if only because they always had been. Provoked by their Afrikaner contemporaries, the Boardman boys often had to fight with their fists. Raymond's father and brothers regarded this as perfectly obvious, as natural as the seasons, the established, permanent state of affairs.

In this part of the country violence had always been an ordinary way of settling disputes, enforcing subservience, or achieving precedence. The blacks fought among themselves, and so did the whites. The white farmers beat their black workers and servants. Intimidated and humiliated, the blacks dreamed of the day when they could get their own back on the whites.

Raymond didn't fight. He wasn't capable of it, and in any case, inflicting violence, as well as being on the receiving end of it, made him feel alarmed and insecure. He wasn't afraid of pain, but of the temptation presented by the freedom to inflict violence and the general license to do so.

He was different. The local Afrikaners would beat their black workers for any offense or disobedience, almost regarding it as their duty, just like the imperative to bring up your children strictly. They meted out punishments without mercy, but for the good of those on the receiving end. They regarded violence as the simplest, surest, failsafe method for setting the rules and limits.

This made Raymond feel confused and ashamed. He refused to be like that, but he felt that if he remained in this town too long, it would suck him in as well, and never release its grip— never again would he find the strength to break away from it. He would be the loser, and the defeat he would have to acknowledge would also mean voluntary renunciation of his right to have a choice and be different.

He didn't regard himself as a racist. His childhood playmates were black boys, the sons of the workers permitted to live on the farm. Together they played soccer, tracked jackals in the bush, and flushed out quails, which whirred into the air when the boys threw stones at them. Thanks to these friendships he became fluent in Afrikaans. He and his black pals were on very friendly terms, and so it remained, even when he grew up and took over the farm, becoming their employer and boss.

By contrast with his father, he did not regard black people as inferior creatures, destined to be servants. But he was convinced that they were not suited to the same things as white people. He accepted this as fact, and didn't stop to consider the reasons for this state of affairs. Besides, since leaving to study in Johannesburg, he had almost entirely lost contact with black people.

Like most of his fellow students at Witwatersrand University, where he enrolled for courses in bookkeeping and management, he was not in favor of apartheid. The university was a liberal one, and its students and lecturers regarded the system of enforced racial segregation, and also the Afrikaner politicians who introduced it, as an embarrassing, onerous burden.

Onerous, because the petty rules about racial separation made life difficult, restricted freedom, and condemned the public to constant deference toward officials, policemen, and informers. And troublesome, because they earned South Africa the contempt of the rest of the white world, which, though not free of racial prejudice either, at least didn't flaunt it.

The well-off, educated, worldly whites from the big cities, mainly descended from British settlers, regarded apartheid as an unreasonable and totally unnecessary system. They didn't seek the reasons for their affluence and privileged position over people of another skin color in the apartheid system, but in natural advantages arising from the cultural legacy inherited from generation to generation.

They mocked the Afrikaners for their obsession with racial purity. They reminded them that it was the Boer men, the first white settlers, who had spawned so many bastards with black women that finally they had had to regard them as a separate race of colored people. However, they tried not to ridicule the absurdities of apartheid for fear of inflaming the Afrikaners and giving them an excuse for further complaints of being persecuted by the arrogant British.

Another reason why the young people in well-heeled Johannesburg didn't attach much weight to the issue of racial separation was because they didn't really have much to do with people from other racial groups. As they didn't work together, they didn't go out for a beer or a whisky after work together either. The apartheid laws didn't allow either of these options anyway. Nor did people from different racial groups make social visits to each others' houses—that was forbidden by law too.

As they never went to the black townships in the suburbs, they had no idea how the blacks lived. The topic wasn't described in the censored, white newspapers or featured on state television. Keeping to the districts assigned them by the authorities, and complying with the prescribed separation, they stopped knowing anything about the blacks, and then ceased to take any notice of their existence or needs.

The blacks whom they encountered on a daily basis in the streets, stores, banks, and offices or while at work only featured in their lives when they handed them change or tanked up their cars. Those were the only moments when blacks and whites came into contact. Seconds later, each would vanish to their own side of the invisible barrier dividing their worlds.

Raymond was not in favor of apartheid, but nor did he rebel against it either. Just as he didn't rebel against the rainy weather in the fall, or the fact that in winter the sun sets earlier. He didn't like it, but there was no helping it. He didn't even try to fight against it. He never felt the need, nor did he believe that the accepted order could ever change.

Another reason why he didn't worry about it was that the life away from Ventersdorp on which he was now embarking, impatiently and avidly, was totally absorbing, and the opportunities it promised him were making his head spin. Never before or after did the world seem so bright, friendly, and good to him.

South Africa was enjoying its best years. Gold and diamonds were bringing it wealth it had never known before. The favorable upturn, supported by hard work and enterprise, had made it one of the most affluent and best-endowed countries in the entire world. Foreigners admired South Africa's roads, hospitals, and schools, the wealth of its stores and the splendor of its residences. Their general delight was only marred by the thought that the exclusive owners of this land of plenty—some of the richest people on earth—were its white-skinned citizens.

Their extended houses in the hills, equipped with swimming pools and tennis courts, were steeped in shady greenery and flowers. They drove to the downtown areas, where most of them worked, in the costliest, newest cars, along tree-lined avenues. The positions they held guaranteed them excellent salaries and good retirement packages. The courts and police, tasked with maintaining security and order, did their job so efficiently that nobody had to lock their houses.

Better yet, there was never the smallest cloud on the horizon to herald the end of the idyll. Every revolt by the blacks was instantly and ruthlessly suppressed, their political parties were made illegal, and their leaders thrown into jail or driven out of the country. The image of a paradise on earth was completed by nature—here there was wide-open space giving a sense of boundless freedom and opportunity, bright sunshine almost all year round, and air as pure and transparent as in the mountains.

Regarding this abundance of gifts as further proof of God's special benevolence toward the white tribe of Africa, its members joyfully increased their wealth and took full advantage of life.

Raymond Boardman took advantage of life too, enjoying his first taste of freedom since escaping from his hometown and the watchful eye of his strict father. In the downtown districts of Hillbrow and Melville, the Johannesburg equivalents of Greenwich Village, Montparnasse, or London's Soho, the city never slept. The streets were never empty, at the clubs the music never stopped, and the buzz of conversation never died down.

There he met Charlene, his future wife. She was a white girl from Zambia, daughter of a famous boxer called James Badrian. She often came to Johannesburg to visit her numerous relatives. She had mixed blood inherited from just about all the white settlers whom fate had put ashore in southern Africa—the Boers, the British, French, and Portuguese, and even the Jews who came from the cold Baltic shore.

After college, Raymond only ever changed jobs for a better one and a higher salary. Charlene bore him three sons, whom he sent to the best schools. From Johannesburg they moved to Cape Town, held to be the loveliest and richest part of the country, where they lived in a house by the ocean.

In Cape Town, as well as in Johannesburg, Witbank, and Pretoria, where they finally settled down, they lived in large houses or apartments in the smartest, most expensive districts. They ate at the best restaurants and stayed at the best hotels. They spent their vacations on the beach in Cape Town or Durban, or on a wild-animal safari in one of the national parks. They were rich and happy, their dreams had come true, and they felt secure and calm about the future.

Raymond's hometown of Ventersdorp on the Transvaal veld seemed so far away as to be unreal. He was amazed by the very memory, the very thought that he was part of it. And that at one time he might have remained there forever.

Whenever he went home for a vacation or to help his aging father on the farm, he felt as if he were in another country, a remote and alien world. Everything was still familiar, still instantly recognizable, and yet so distant and different from what constituted his new life, as if made of a different fabric.

Whenever he showed his sons the place their family came from, just as before, the small world defined by the town borders seemed overstated, loud, and full of itself. Like the garish artificial flowers the Transvaal women liked to decorate their homes with, and the kitsch paintings they so loved, featuring blood-red sunsets or wild animals at watering holes.

In fact, everything here was more abrupt, more extreme and exaggerated—the conversations and the way they were held, the words used, and the quarrels, which led to fights at lightning speed. The summers were hotter, and the spring storms over the veld were like biblical tempests. Even the time of day changed differently here; day changed into night so suddenly that there seemed to be nothing between light and dark. Just as there was nothing between love and hate, friendship and enmity, or peace and war.

The country's new wealth improved life for all whites. The poor whites, although they were still called that, stopped being poor. Life in the countryside improved too. Raymond's father became a wealthy man. He extended the modest old farmhouse into a large, spacious residence, with a wonderful living room, a study, and guest rooms. He bought agricultural machinery and modernized the farm. Other local farmers, who had led a modest, austere life until now, had also made money cultivating crops and raising stock, and above all thanks to purchases prices that were guaranteed by the government; they too were developing their farmhouses and buying expensive cars in which they drove to church and to visit their neighbors.

Raymond Boardman was tall and powerfully built with hair the color of straw and a pale complexion, so susceptible to the sun that during his army service he'd contracted skin cancer. Whenever he came to the farm on vacation he stopped shaving so that the stubble would protect his face from the sun. When he went back to Pretoria, tanned and with a beard grown over the summer, his big-city friends would be delighted. Shaking their heads in disbelief, they'd say he looked like a Boer partisan general. His workmates at his job in marketing would ask him not to shave and so, bearded, wild, and uncouth, looking like a Boer, he would come to business meetings and events with foreign clients.

"What a face they'll make at the sight of you," they'd insist. "Doesn't Raymond look like a typical Boer from Transvaal? The spitting image of Eugène Terre'Blanche!"

Like most of the country's white citizens, Raymond Boardman wasn't involved in politics. He browsed the newspapers at work, and listened to the news on the radio in his car, but he didn't attach major importance to it. He was happy with himself, certain that everything he had achieved he owed to himself alone, his abilities and hard work. And that the way a person's life turns out depends on him and him alone.

He reckoned that those who'd done well had no need for politics. It was needed by people who wanted change, people who'd been unlucky, who were disadvantaged or hopeless. Raymond Boardman had nothing to complain about.

But even without taking an interest in political matters, he couldn't help noticing that they had started to take a new and disturbing turn. The black townships were in turmoil. There were constant riots, which the police and army were sent to crush. Black union leaders were declaring strike after strike. The authorities were warning that the black rebels were communist subversives who didn't believe in God and wanted to destroy everything. They reminded the public about the consequences of the black uprisings that had occurred in Angola, Mozambique, and Zimbabwe, right next door, as well as in other African countries where the assumption of power by the natives had ended in war, the massacre of the white settlers and colonists, and economic collapse.

Anxiety was creeping into the minds of the whites. Though

they had never had to protect their houses before, they began to install sophisticated alarms, bought weapons, and furtively transferred their savings out of the country and into foreign bank accounts. Many of Boardman's compatriots, descended as he was from British settlers, got themselves British passports. They said it was just in case. "For Judgment Day," they joked.

It seemed as if that day had come when, in his annual address to parliament, president F. W. de Klerk announced that he had ordered the abolition of all the apartheid laws, and the release of black leader Nelson Mandela from jail, where he was serving a life sentence.

On the day when Mandela was to be set free, all South Africa sat down in front of their television sets. For the blacks he was a hero, for the whites he was the embodiment of their worst fears. Nobody knew what he looked like. The newspapers had been forbidden to publish his photograph, or even to mention his name. He had spent more than twenty-five years in jails and at stone quarries. When he was locked away he was a tall, well-built forty-four-year-old. He was coming out of prison as an old man.

Everyone wanted to see if he still resembled the resolute fighter of the past—even in his defense summation before the court in Pretoria he had proudly declared that he was ready to give up his life for the cause he regarded as sacred. And they wanted to see if he would live up to his own legend; shut up in prison, he hadn't had much influence over its development. There were rumors going round the country that he was old and sickly, and had finally broken down and agreed to renounce everything he believed in, if he could only live out his days in freedom, with his family.

At the offices of the corporation where Raymond Boardman

worked, everyone had been watching the television since early that morning. During the long run-up to Mandela's appearance the worried, mustachioed journalist had run out of stories to fill in the waiting time.

Until finally the prison gates opened, and a tall, thin black man with graying hair, dressed in a gray suit, appeared. With a raised fist, he walked down the rows of cheering people, smiling, but as if overawed or bewildered.

"And here he is . . . " cried the television reporter. "Nelson Mandela is free!"

In Boardman's office silence reigned, as everyone watched the broadcast without saying a word. From the street came shouts of joy. Raymond leaned out of the window. On the sidewalk a group of black office workers was staring through the glass at a TV set that had been switched on in the front window of an electronics store.

It was a late, hot summer afternoon. As usual at this time of day, laden with shopping, the blacks were slowly walking to the stops where the microbuses dropped them each morning for work in the city, and picked them up each evening to return to their ghettos in the suburbs. Everything looked the same as usual, as if nothing special had happened that day.

And yet as he watched the people in the streets, Raymond felt that in their figures, their voices, in their way of behaving he could sense a weight and a strength he had never seen before; suddenly their movements had acquired direction and purpose. And suddenly he felt a stabbing, wistful envy. He realized that it was a very long time since he had felt bright, joyful confidence in the choices he had made, or a firm belief in his own unique qualities and his own exceptional role in life.

Once again he asked himself the question that had been mentally recurring for some time now. Was what he was doing what he really wanted? Was his life really meant to be like this, and only like this? Was this his entire destiny? He remembered a saying he had heard or read somewhere: each man has his own place in life, and he should find it. Where exactly was his place, and was he looking for it? And did he really need it?

He remembered Reverend William, thanks to whom the Boardmans had ended up in Africa. He had been brought here by a sense of mission and the duty to serve God and others. Had he fulfilled his purpose? And what about Raymond himself? What was his destiny, his place in life, and his purpose?

He was approaching forty. Although he was doing better than ever, and had more than enough reasons to be satisfied with life, there was something missing. More and more often he found himself telling his wife and friends that he wanted to make his mark in life, and he wanted it to be more than just a bank account number, or an address in a well-off district.

In those days he and his family were living in Pretoria. Encouraged by one of their neighbors, for some time they had been attending communal gatherings of people describing themselves as Christians who were rediscovering God. Supported by a pastor, they were exploring their own faith and thinking about their lives, endeavoring to give them proper meaning.

Not long after Mandela's release, at a gathering of this group of converts, Raymond had a revelation. He understood his vocation and could clearly see what he wanted from life. He decided to go back to the family farm, to the town he had escaped from when he couldn't bear the life there or its citizens, trapped under the invisible dome of never-changing endurance. Now he felt no fear, just strength. He felt that not only would he refuse to yield to the town, but he would also succeed in changing it.

Goedgevonden farm, situated near Ventersdorp, was government property. The authorities had taken this land over years ago, appropriating it from the natives. Those who were needed for labor could move to Tshing. Those with no occupation of use to the whites had to move to nearby Bophuthatswana, created as a homeland for the Tswana.

When the white government released Mandela and abolished apartheid, many blacks assumed they could go back to the places they had been expelled from, and demand the return of property taken from them years ago. They were being encouraged to do this by the priests at church services and by the black leaders at public meetings, who said they were due compensation for the wrongs done to them, and that as soon as Mandela became president they would get it.

Once the passes and laws separating districts had been removed, there was nothing to stop those blacks who could afford to—a surprising number of township residents had managed to make real fortunes—and those who had enough courage from moving into districts previously reserved for whites only, and living alongside them, right next door, shopping at the same stores, sending their children to the same schools, and walking in the same parks.

In the big cities, where people were strangers to each other, it happened more rapidly and more boldly. The bohemians from the Johannesburg district of Hillbrow had let the blacks move in some time before it was permitted. Once apartheid was lifted, Hillbrow instantly became the first downtown black district, and the musicians, poets, and dancers were displaced by shady characters selling guns and drugs.

In towns like Ventersdorp, where everyone knew each other, the changes took place very slowly and apprehensively. Nothing ever happened here without being noticed, no action escaped attention, and the perpetrator was known by face, name, and address.

That may have been the reason why the blacks who came to Goedgevonden farm to demand restitution of their land pitched camp by night, under the cover of darkness. By the time the sun came up, a settlement had appeared on the pastureland, consisting of about a dozen shacks cobbled together from cardboard, planks, and corrugated iron. That same day, before dusk, some white men arrived from the town to order the blacks to get out the next morning.

But not only did they not get out, Benny Tapologo and his friends from Tshing came to their defense too. By now they were official members of the ANC, and were running the party organization in the township. Since the days of the street riots life in Tshing had continued at its usual, monotonous pace, day after day, each just the same as the one before. Finally, by setting up camp at the state farm, the newcomers had disturbed the hypnotic order and shattered the peace. Benny and his colleagues saw it as a new opportunity to shake up the town and rouse it from its trance.

So they went to the occupied farm and provided the newcomers with food and clothing. They declared that from now on Goedgevonden farm would have its old, African name, Khaya, and they encouraged them to stick it out and not be afraid of the white farmers. They also promised to come to their defense, should the need arise.

For the local whites were now insisting that the police should evict the people squatting at the farm. The farmers had been to the police station in Ventersdorp to make an official complaint that the blacks at Goedgevonden were stealing cattle from their pastures, making a mess, and getting drunk. They had also taken their grievances to the AWB, which had transferred its office from Pretoria to Eugène Terre'Blanche's house in town. One day, Terre'Blanche came to the town hall and warned the mayor and the chief of police that if they didn't do something about the black squatters at the farm, he and his people would restore order there themselves.

On hearing of these threats, the young ANC activists from Tshing decided to post guards at the occupied farm, and also to send Benny Tapologo to Mandela himself for advice. It was the first time he had ever been to Johannesburg—never before had he seen such a large city.

By some miracle he had managed to get hold of Mandela's home phone number. The call was answered by his wife Winnie. At the time they were still living in their old home in Soweto. She said that Nelson was asleep and couldn't be disturbed. She asked what he was calling about, and when Benny explained the reason for his call, she advised him to contact a lawyer friend of hers in Johannesburg, and in Ventersdorp to insist that the police should protect the squatters at the farm against Terre'Blanche's people.

He was dismayed, because in their town the blacks didn't trust the local police, believing that they covertly supported the white brotherhood, and that many of them had even secretly joined it. However, when he got home, he went straight to the police station, where he was told that without a direct order from the capital the police weren't going to worry about the blacks at the farm. That evening in Tshing he learned that during the night someone had painted large white crosses on the doors of the houses where the young ANC activists lived.

Finally, one night in May, a group of white men on horseback rode down to the occupied farm. Led by Eugène Terre'Blanche, they charged the place, trampling the squatters' miserable shacks and demolishing them with sticks. The police were summoned to help, and when they arrived at the farm, the attackers withdrew. But an hour later they were back, in far greater numbers, not just on horseback this time, but also in pickup trucks.

There must have been about a thousand of them. Car headlights glared from every direction, illuminating the night to make it as bright as day. Some of the attackers had their faces covered with scarves or knitted balaclava helmets, but most of them hadn't bothered to hide their identity. Benny, who had rushed to the farm with his friends to help the occupiers, thought he recognized the owner of the butcher shop on the marketplace, and Kobus, one of the sons of the man who owned the Engen gas station where he used to work. He also saw Eugène Terre'Blanche on his black horse, leading the raid.

There turned out to be too few policemen to stop it. Especially as not all of them were defending the blacks against the raiders. While the police officers brought in from Potchefstroom and Krugersdorp fired at the attackers, and even wounded some of them, to an equal extent the local police deliberately got out of their way.

At high speed, the farm pickups broke through the police cordon, and before further reinforcements could reach Goedgevonden, the squatters' camp had been razed to the ground. To save themselves from carnage, the blacks had scattered in the darkness on the veld.

Just before dawn, the white brotherhood had attacked Tshing. The deserted township was pitch dark and paralyzed by fear as they toured it in convoys of pickup trucks, firing into the air, and smashing the streetlamps, stalls, and cars left out on the street. They stopped outside the houses marked with white crosses whose residents had not yet managed to wipe them off the door or the gate, jumped out of their trucks, and threw stones at the windows, breaking the glass.

At the time Benny was living with his mother in the oldest part of Tshing, not far from the soccer field. When he got home at dawn, there was no sign of the brotherhood attackers anymore. There was almost no trace left of the events that had played out during the night. As the new day dawned, everything slipped back into the old, familiar, well-worn ruts.

On the night when the white brotherhood carried out its raid on the occupied farm, Henk Malan was awoken by noises in the road outside his house. Someone was shouting his name.

"Who the hell is that in the middle of the night?" he cursed under his breath, crashing into the furniture in the dark.

He looked out of the window. In the lamplit street outside stood two pickup trucks, with their headlights on. There were white men sitting in the cabs and in the truck beds. Someone waved to him from the car in front, calling: "Henk! Malan!"

He recognized Hendrik, the guy from the agricultural equipment store, whom he had met at a recent rally of Eugène Terre'Blanche's in town. Henk went to all the public events organized by the white brotherhood in Ventersdorp. They weren't very frequent, because Eugène spent his time travelling about the country in search of supporters rather than making speeches to the neighbors, on whose support he could rely.

Henk never went to rallies in other towns, not even to Pretoria, although the white brotherhood organized real spectacles there. He was badly paid at the railroad, and he couldn't afford trips about the country, travel, hotels, and boozy dinners. To tell the truth, he didn't like being away from this town, where he felt at his best. Strange places intimidated him, and strange people made him feel awkward.

Unlike Henk, who hadn't enrolled in the AWB, Hendrik was a member. At the rally they had informally agreed that if the brotherhood organized anything locally, Hendrik would let Henk know and take him along. Now he was urging him to get in the bed of the pickup truck.

"Come on, man! How long can we wait?"

The car pulled away abruptly as Henk was scrambling on board, making him wobble and almost fall to the ground. Supported by the men in the back, he recovered his balance. Only then did he get a look at the other passengers. Besides Hendrik there were two others, whom Henk had never seen before, but in those days plenty of brotherhood supporters would come in response to Terre'Blanche's call from near and far.

They turned into the main street, which was completely lifeless in the foggy orange glow of the streetlamps. Driving down the middle of the road, they raced toward the Caltex gas station and the black township.

"Are we going to Tshing?" Henk called out to Hendrik, shouting over the roar of the engine and the wind.

"Paying an unexpected visit," confirmed Hendrik.

The two other men in the truck bed laughed out loud. One of them pulled a bottle of whisky from his jacket pocket.

"Better warm up before things get hot," he said, handing round the bottle.

Beyond the town it was pitch dark, and Henk couldn't even see his companions' faces. They slowed down on a hill. Below them the lights of Tshing were shining. In the darkness it looked even bigger than in the daytime, tidier, more like a big city than fast-asleep Ventersdorp. Despite the time of night, it was still brightly lit and seemed to be vibrant with life, heedless of tiredness or the late hour. But when they came closer, once they had driven down the hill and were looking straight at it, the township no longer resembled a glittering urban center.

The musty stench of refuse hit them. By the road, bright flames flickered from heaps of burning trash. Kindled by day, but left there all night, as if set at liberty, they were feeding on their power over the human settlements, which they could destroy at any moment.

They passed the soccer field in the oldest part of the township, the only place Henk could have reached on his own. He didn't know Tshing, he had rarely been here, and always got lost in the treeless labyrinth of nameless streets, alleys, and paths running between the same sort of numberless low shacks and similar small yards divided from the road by chicken-wire fences. He couldn't understand how the blacks found the right address or reached their destination. Tshing reminded him of an anthill, and its residents were like the insects that in childhood he used to spend hours examining, trying to discover the logic and the rules governing their lives, labor, and wanderings.

The trucks drove through the township quickly and confidently, turning corners without hesitation. At some point it occurred to Henk that the men driving their vehicles must be police officers, as they were the only local whites who knew Tshing well.

They suddenly stopped in a small street in total darkness, without switching off their engines. The drivers positioned the vehicles so that four bright beams shone from the headlamps, lighting up a shack that had a white cross painted on the door.

When Henk jumped down from the truck bed, he thought he saw a black face flash past in the shack. He wasn't sure—a man or a woman? Or maybe it was a child?

"Hey! Kaffir! Come on out here!" cried one of the drivers.

"So you got a fancy for living with whites, eh? Then come on out!" shouted another. "Or bring us your old woman out here."

He picked up a stone and threw it at the illuminated door. More stones, hurled by the white men, broke the window panes with a loud crash. Around them, total silence reigned. In the next-door shacks nobody put on a light, nobody looked out at the road, or came to help the neighbors under attack. Nor did they show any sign of life either.

The white men continued to throw stones at the house for a while, hurling abuse and insults too. After smashing all the windows, their noiseless strikes at the door and walls brought no further destruction or the sound of breaking glass, but merely dampened their ardor, disheartened, depressed, and irritated them.

Suddenly one of the whites noticed a car parked by the fence, an old white Toyota Corolla.

"Just look at this!" he cried. "Look how well the kaffir's doing!"

At close range, he threw a stone at the front windshield, which dented it, changing it from a mirror into a cobweb of cracked glass.

The other whites joined in, hurling stones at the windows and kicking the bodywork.

Henk stood aside and watched, smoking a cigarette. Earlier

he had thrown two stones, both of which hit the wall of the house.

"*Alles sal regkom*, it'll all be OK," said Hendrik with an encouraging smile. "The kaffirs are afraid, they're simply dying of fear."

He'd been watching Henk, as if trying to gauge whether he was disappointed by the adventure and the fun he had promised him. Now he was waving at him, calling him over to the car by the fence.

"Got a lighter?" he asked.

Dragging on his cigarette, Henk said yes.

"Then set it alight!" said Hendrik enthusiastically.

There was an acrid smell of petrol coming from the car's broken windows. On its dented hood stood a yellow plastic canister, the kind the blacks used to carry water.

"Well, go on!" urged Hendrik.

Henk took a fresh cigarette from the pack and lit it. He took a deep drag, then another, to get it to take light, then tossed it through the broken window onto the car seat. The fire flared across the upholstery, jumped over to the bodywork, and spilled onto the ground.

Henk felt emptiness instead of his previous uncertainty and fears, and then at once the clarity and ease he had felt in the army, in the Angolan bush.

"What does a monkey need a Toyota for?" he said, scrambling into the bed of the pickup truck. "He'll only do someone harm with it."

He had fought in a war, where the rules were familiar to everyone taking part. He who kills must also know that he can be killed too. He did as he was told, which meant it wasn't just permitted, it was also legitimate.

More and more attacks like the one at Goedgevonden farm were happening all over the country. The newspapers featured them on their front pages, right next to their reports about the negotiations the white government was conducting with Mandela and his comrades at the World Trade Center building in Johannesburg.

During the talks, disputes kept erupting, or even rows, and both sides kept threatening to break off the negotiations. This usually occurred when unknown attackers organized nighttime shooting and carnage in the black suburbs scattered around Johannesburg. Mandela accused the white government of sending out masked killers to incite war and interrupt the talks. The whites charged Mandela with failing to control his supporters, who were organizing fratricidal murders. But although the negotiators were hurling accusations at each other, eventually they always came back to the talks, and finally struck a bargain, establishing the terms on which the blacks would take power.

But in Ventersdorp, where Terre'Blanche's brotherhood held sway, everything stayed the same as ever. As before, the blacks weren't allowed to enter the banks and stores—they were served on the street, through a special little window. The store assistants brought the goods they requested out to them on the sidewalk. They could buy bread or meat, but the choice was made for them by the retailers.

Despite the abolition of passes and the curfew, in Ventersdorp and other towns in Transvaal "white nights" were still in force. After dark, AWB squads would set out on patrol in cars or on horseback, making sure no black people stayed overnight in the white part of town. Any black whom they found there at night was detained and deported.

George Nkomane was stopped by a brotherhood patrol in the town of Belfast. Beaten, tied up, and tossed in the back of a pickup truck, he was driven out of town and dumped on the road. Just as drunk as the white thugs who caught him, he insisted he was going back to the town. The white men battered him until he stopped moving. In court they swore they had only wanted to frighten him, to teach him a lesson. But not kill him.

Soon after the white farmers' raid on the occupied Goedgevonden farm, nine members of the brotherhood stopped two cars with black passengers at the limits of Ventersdorp on the road to Randfontein. The whites were dressed in field uniforms, so the drivers pulled over on the verge, thinking it was a police patrol stopping them. The passengers obediently followed the order to get out of the cars and kneel by the road.

All the attackers were from Ventersdorp. They were drunk. As they beat the blacks and shone flashlights in their faces, they shouted at them to confess freely that they belonged to the rebels, and to show where they hid their weapons. The victims' pleas for mercy only made the whites even angrier. Finally the man in command of the attackers took out a pistol and shot one of the blacks in the head.

"We must kill them all!" he cried.

More shots rang out. Next day the police found two bodies on the road. The third victim was alive, but badly wounded; the attackers had cut off his ears and abandoned him. It was dawn before an ambulance came for him, summoned by the survivors of the attack. He was taken to the hospital, but died of blood loss.

On the road outside Carltonville, five members of the white brotherhood tortured a black laborer whom they had stopped to question about two blacks wanted for theft. The man swore he knew nothing and hadn't seen anyone. Beaten almost to death, he lost his sight, and the doctors at the hospital in Carltonville had to amputate his shattered leg.

Bombs planted by members of the AWB exploded at schools that agreed to take black children, and at restaurants and hotels that served black guests. Attackers fired from the windows of speeding cars at black people waiting in line at bus stops. In Johannesburg unknown perpetrators blew up the local bohemians' favorite movie theater, which was due to show a movie called *How To Make Love To A Negro Without Getting Tired.*

To the very last, Eugène Terre'Blanche never believed the Afrikaners and other whites would put up with the loss of power that President de Klerk was persuading them to accept, claiming that it was for their good that he'd released Mandela from jail, and that as a result he'd be able to bargain with him for the best terms for their capitulation.

At first Terre'Blanche thought the white president was conducting some elaborate intrigue, incomprehensible to those less expert in the craft of politics. It never occurred to him that de Klerk had let himself be frightened by foreigners and rich whites from Johannesburg and Cape Town, for whom racial division was an obstacle to business that lowered their profits. But evidently de Klerk had caved in to them, in breach of the oath he had sworn as the country's leader.

Terre'Blanche hated de Klerk. He regarded him as a fool, a coward, and a traitor, just like the old Boer generals who had surrendered to the British and agreed to their regime, renouncing everything they believed in. He was convinced that his negative opinion of the president was shared by other Afrikaners who didn't want change and saw no reason to give away everything they had fought so hard to achieve. Terre'Blanche could see it in their eyes and faces when they came to hear him speak in public. They cheered him, patted him on the back appreciatively, and cried: "Lead on! We're right behind you!"

He had no doubt that in coming to terms with the blacks de Klerk was digging his own grave, and that his government was bound to be ousted by the whites whom he had let down. His power was visibly waning. Nobody was listening to him, and nobody respected him. For the blacks, to whom he had given way, he was still a white oppressor, and for the whites he was a turncoat who had betrayed them. Already buzzing with depressing rumors and predictions, the country was being shaken by rioting and strikes; the violent clashes in the black suburbs seemed to herald the apocalypse. Instead of preventing it from happening, the president and his ministers were bringing it down on their compatriots.

"What good can come of making deals with the blacks?" cried Terre'Blanche at his rallies. "What on earth can Mandela give us? Maybe just his wife's wig for de Klerk's brainless bald pate."

He was convinced that taking power away from de Klerk would present no difficulty, because that was exactly what the Afrikaners wanted. They may have lacked determination and not known how to oppose de Klerk, but Terre'Blanche was in no doubt that they would stand solidly behind the man bold enough to cast the president a challenge.

Terre'Blanche wasn't afraid of de Klerk because he despised him, and thought him a disgrace to the office entrusted to him. When de Klerk was still a government minister and head of the ruling party in Transvaal, Terre'Blanche had sent squads of his brotherhood to break up the public meetings where he was trying to persuade the Afrikaners they had no alternative but to live with the blacks and share everything with them.

Terre'Blanche could sense instinctively that de Klerk feared him, his physical strength and his violent temper.

When Terre'Blanche demanded an audience with de Klerk, to insist in the name of the Afrikaners that he agree to carve a new Afrikaner republic out of part of the country, de Klerk did not respond. He only agreed to receive him at the urgent insistence of the civil servants in his office, who asserted that avoiding a confrontation with Terre'Blanche would expose him to charges of being afraid of the man.

On the appointed day, at the presidential palace in Pretoria, the AWB delegation handed the president a petition in which they demanded the restoration of the old Boer republic of Transvaal, if only on similar principles to those on which the white government had created the Bantustans for the Zulus, Xhosa, and Tswana during apartheid. De Klerk refused point-blank. He didn't even try to hide his loathing for the brotherhood and its leader.

The delegates lost their tempers, and the audience turned into a violent quarrel.

"What if the Zulus came to ask you for land for their own state?" cried the delegates. "What answer would you give them?"

"I'd be sure to give it to them!" replied the president.

"And in what way are we Afrikaners inferior to the Zulus?"

De Klerk replied that nobody had entitled them to act in the name of the Afrikaners and that he wasn't going to waste his time on futile conversations. He got up from the table, and his officials signaled to say the audience was over.

Soon after, de Klerk announced that he intended to go to Ventersdorp to convince its citizens that the abolition of apartheid could not be stopped, and to tell them how much they were letting themselves be deluded by their fellow townsman, the leader of the white brotherhood. Terre'Blanche regarded this as a declaration of war, a gauntlet thrown down before him.

That evening in Ventersdorp, long after nightfall, nobody was getting ready for bed. The townspeople were expecting unusual events, and had gathered downtown to watch them. Dusk had fallen, but on the streets there was still no sense of threat or even anxiety, just curiosity about the show that would soon begin. The men sipped at bottles of beer and smoked cigarettes. Some of them set up portable cast-iron braziers on the sidewalks with cooking grids on which they grilled sausages and cuts of meat.

Since afternoon, in answer to Terre'Blanche's call, members of the brotherhood had been gathering in Ventersdorp. They came in their thousands. Dressed in black uniforms and fawn-colored shirts with armbands carrying the swastika made of sevens, they came from all over Transvaal, from Natal, Orange Free State, Cape of Good Hope province, and even from Namibia, the former German colony, which de Klerk had just handed back to the blacks. Many of them had hunting rifles and pistols.

At least the same number of policemen had come down from all over the country too. They had surrounded the building where the president was to speak with barbed-wire entanglements and sandbags, set up checkpoints on the main streets, and posted armored cars equipped with small bore cannons at the town limits. They had also tried unsuccessfully to set up a cordon on the access roads into Ventersdorp, to stop the AWB members from entering the town. Toward evening there were twice as many policemen and AWB members in the town as citizens.

De Klerk had been planning to fly in to Ventersdorp by helicopter, but at the last moment the police had dissuaded him, warning that the vehicle could be shot down over the town. Too late, the president decided to travel by car, and the audience assembled in the hall had to wait a good hour for him to get there.

The townspeople gathered outside a hotel on Carmichael Street, near the town hall and the marketplace. Henk Malan was in the crowd outside the hotel too. By the time Terre'Blanche finished his rally it was dark, and the town was now only lit by streetlamps. He had come out to the people gathered in front of the hotel and announced that he was going to hand de Klerk a petition. The crowd moved after him.

At the head of the procession, right behind their leader, marched members of the brotherhood. Rowdy and overbearing, in this town they felt at home. They paraded down the streets and across the marketplace like gunslingers, confident of victory in the imminent duel. The police were distinctly tense and nervous. Henk, who since the days of his military service in Angola regarded himself as an expert on everything to do with violence, reckoned they were inexperienced and terrified.

As the procession moved forward, Henk remained slightly behind. He couldn't see the line of policemen blocking the brotherhood's way. The first scuffles and fistfights occurred. The police threw tear-gas grenades into the crowd, but the AWB members broke through the cordon and headed toward the marketplace. Suddenly, in the deserted main street a small bus full of black passengers appeared. Nobody knew where it had come from. According to the white brotherhood's orders, blacks were not allowed to be in town after dark at all. At the sight of the crowd striding down the pavement toward it, the bus didn't stop or turn, but accelerated, as if wanting to force its way through the procession.

Reckoning that the black driver was trying to run them down, the demonstrators started shooting at the bus, which at the last moment turned into a small square in front of the police station and collided with a police car parked outside the entrance. And then, without warning, the lights went off all over town. It later transpired that one of the town hall employees had switched them off, taking his own personal action to disrupt the president's speech.

Then, with the town plunged into total darkness, violent gunfire erupted. Everyone who had a gun, brotherhood members and police alike, was firing it blindly, at anything that moved, at people and cars, whose bright headlamps were the only definite target.

When the lights went off and the shots rang out, Henk tripped and fell over, becoming disoriented. Feeling his way in the dark, he crawled behind a wall. It took a little while for him to realize he was sitting behind the brick wall surrounding a church.

It was Terre'Blanche who put a stop to the gunfire.

"Hold fire!" he shouted in his booming voice, walking in among the men who were shooting. "I repeat! Let's stop firing!"

Gradually it died down, though the crack of an occasional shot still echoed in the darkness. Until finally silence reigned, and the streetlamps flared on again.

In the chaotic nighttime shooting, later dubbed the Battle of Ventersdorp, three members of the white brotherhood were killed. Two were run over by a car speeding along in the dark, and the third was hit by a stray police bullet. About fifty people were wounded, including policemen, members of the AWB, ordinary bystanders, and about a dozen passengers from the bus, which had been targeted by brotherhood members.

That same night Terre'Blanche went to the local police station and persuaded the police chief to release AWB members who had been taken into custody during the unrest. Terre'Blanche gave his word of honor that they would stand trial before a court.

He was there with them on the defendants' bench, once again on a charge of hooliganism. During the trial he persuaded the court that the president was to blame for the rioting and the street battle.

"It's de Klerk who has abused his power, bringing an army of police officers with him out of fear of the people, and using our tax money to pay for it," he explained. "They were the ones who started it. We just wanted to have a talk."

Once again his penalty was a fine, though everyone in Ventersdorp was sure he wouldn't wriggle out of a jail sentence this time. When the trial was over, he put up a monument to the three brotherhood members killed during the nocturnal Battle of Ventersdorp. It was a black granite obelisk with the names of the dead inscribed on it, erected in the square opposite the courthouse, right next to the triumphal arch dedicated to the Boer heroes.

While the town was in a hail of gunfire, President de Klerk slipped away under cover of darkness, guarded by policemen armed to the teeth. The expedition to Ventersdorp hadn't brought him humiliation, but nor had it provided a sense of triumph or certainty that he'd proved his argument and strength to the people. He still didn't know if they trusted him and continued to regard him as their leader, or whether they would follow him down the road into the unknown, where he was going to lead them.

Although he didn't like bravado and was known as a cautious procrastinator, he resolved on a risky step that might mean the end of his leadership. He decided to hold a referendum, asking the Afrikaners directly whom they would rather follow—him, who saw no alternative but to abolish racial differences, live together, and share everything, or people like Eugène Terre'Blanche.

Terre'Blanche was totally convinced that in the public poll the Afrikaners would finally turn away from de Klerk and his like, and would declare themselves in favor of maintaining apartheid, and ultimately of recreating the old, independent Boer republics. But when it came to the secret ballot, all those people who came to his rallies, cheered him, said he was right, and assured him of their support, changed their minds. When the time came, they voted for exactly what he had been publicly opposing and warning against.

As a result he lost all the elections in which he stood, and every public poll, including the one announced by de Klerk for handing over power to the blacks. Only in northern Transvaal did the Afrikaners declare themselves in favor of keeping apartheid. In Pretoria, Johannesburg, Durban, Cape Town, and Bloemfontein, the vast majority voted in support of coming to terms with the blacks.

Terre'Blanche's explanation for his defeat in the referendum was that the question that de Klerk put to the public was formulated in an underhand way. The voters were asked whether they supported further negotiations with the blacks, and not about the obvious consequences of holding those talks. The Afrikaners were not asked if they wanted to have a black government and live alongside blacks. "If the question had been put like that," Terre'Blanche told the journalists, "the result of the poll would have been completely different." He also added that many of the whites had been terrified by Mandela, who had announced before the voting that if those opposed to negotiations were victorious, violent fighting would erupt and the blacks would take power by force.

The power bargaining was conducted in the glass skyscraper housing the World Trade Center, near the airport, in the Johannesburg district of Kempton Park. Once it had been a white area, but as police enforcement of the apartheid rules relaxed, more and more colored people had moved in. In time, they had become just as numerous there as the whites.

Each morning since de Klerk had won the referendum, white government representatives and black leaders had met here to establish the terms and conditions for dismantling the old order and creating a new one. The negotiations were now proceeding quickly and peacefully. By now a date had been set for free elections, in which blacks and whites would have the same rights to vote for their new leaders. And as this time everybody's vote would have the same value, the next president of South Africa was bound to be Mandela. Only the details of the surrender of power were still being agreed.

Terre'Blanche, however, had no intention of laying down his weapons. Like many other Afrikaner political parties who didn't agree with the handover of power to Mandela, his brotherhood was not involved in the negotiations with the blacks. They were still making demands for an Afrikaner state to be resurrected on part of the Transvaal veld, as compensation for the loss of the entire white dominion.

A year before the free elections, supporters of the Afrikaner republic came to the World Trade Center building to appeal to the conferring government representatives and black leaders, by formally delivering a petition in which they demanded the right to their own state for the Afrikaners.

On a sunny morning, when the next day of negotiations was underway in the glass tower, the Afrikaners camped on the lawn outside the main entrance. They had come by car from all over the country, several thousand of them in all. Some had brought their entire families, and immediately set about organizing picnics on the grass in front of the building.

The idyllic autumnal atmosphere was interrupted by the appearance of Eugène Terre'Blanche and his personal escort, armed with pistols, in the black uniforms of the Iron Guard. They had brought an armored car with them, the sort of vehicle used by bank security guards to transport money. Terre'Blanche climbed onto it to command the Afrikaners from there.

Gathered in front of the main entrance, they accosted late-coming delegates by thumping their fists on the roofs of their cars as they slowly forced their way through the growing, ever more insistent and hostile crowd. Step by step, the police officers guarding the building began to retreat under the pressure of the encircling protestors as their numbers and spirits rose. Finally they broke through the police cordon and forced their way inside. At the head of the crowd storming the building rode Eugène Terre'Blanche on his armored car.

General Constand Viljoen, retired commander of the South African army and war hero whom the Afrikaners had chosen as leader of their new great trek, tried in vain to restrain the pressing crowd. He promised them that he would persuade Mandela to agree to the creation of a small Afrikaner state, and above all that no fighting would be necessary for that. Now, when along with Terre'Blanche, whom he loathed, and the other Afrikaner leaders, he was meant to be handing the petition to Mandela and de Klerk, his own supporters were not obeying his orders or listening to his pleas.

Instead, Terre'Blanche was fully in command. The armored car broke through the glazed door of the skyscraper, only coming to a stop in the lobby, into which the terrified police and security guards had fled. Amid the crunch of breaking glass, hundreds of AWB supporters forced their way into the building. They raced down corridors and up staircases in search of the conference room where the negotiators were drawing up the new constitution.

But all they found were empty rooms. At news of the white brotherhood's raid, the delegates had taken to their heels, hiding in the building's familiar labyrinth of corridors, offices, conference rooms, bars, and restaurants. In their panic, they had even left behind their leather briefcases and documents, which the raiders now turned upside down.

For several hours they had total control of the place where the future fate, order, and shape of the country was being decided. Disappointed that the negotiators had managed to escape, they helped themselves to the sandwiches, coffee, and other refreshments prepared for them, smeared the brotherhood emblem on the walls and furniture, and painted messages insulting the government and betrayers of apartheid.

As the delegates were gone, the Afrikaner leaders found no one to hand their petition to. General Viljoen vowed never to forgive Terre'Blanche for the humiliation. Other Afrikaner leaders too, who had long been afraid of Terre'Blanche's violent temper, started muttering that maybe it would be better to avoid him and have nothing to do with him. Yet seeing the admiration and delight that the AWB leader invariably inspired, they stifled their anger, shook his hand, and congratulated him on his audacity and triumph.

Meanwhile, he called on his supporters to leave the captured building calmly and quietly. He promised that none of them would be bothered by the police. They obeyed him without a word of protest. They said prayers together, sang the anthem of the apartheid state, then formed a marching column and left, without looking back at the vandalized World Trade Center.

Next day, without waiting for the cleaners to wash the paint from the walls and sweep up the broken glass, or the glaziers to repair the smashed front entrance, the white government representatives and the black leaders resumed their interrupted discussion of the new order that was soon to prevail in the country.

Benny Tapologo couldn't understand why the police had allowed it to happen. Why hadn't they driven out the attackers with their batons, thrown tear-gas grenades at them, set dogs on them, fired warning shots, or arrested anyone? In Khutsong, and later in Tshing, he had seen for himself how tough the police had been on the black demonstrators. Why was it that in Johannesburg they had just stood there with their arms folded?

Nor had they done anything to stop the increasingly violent war that was raging in Johannesburg's black suburbs between Mandela's supporters and the Zulus from the workers' hotels who had come there to earn a living. Not a week went by without nighttime shooting, lynching, arson, or punch-ups in one of the townships. The number of corpses was in the hundreds, and it looked as if the blacks, with power within their reach, instead of finally taking it, were at each other's throats, at war over the spoils. They were fighting each other more ferociously than they had ever fought against the white regime.

Mandela was pressuring de Klerk, asking accusingly if the police were incapable of maintaining order, or if they didn't actually want to. And whether they would be equally inactive if it were the blood of whites, not blacks, that was being shed. The black activists in the Johannesburg suburbs had no doubt the police were not just taking sides with the Zulus and protecting them from vengeance, but were also training and arming them, inciting them to fight against Mandela's supporters.

At dusk Benny and his friends would meet up at the gates of the soccer pitch, then until late at night they would wander the alleyways full of puddles, refuse, and foul air. They had nowhere to go—there were no bars or taverns in Tshing, and they hadn't the courage for a nocturnal expedition to Ventersdorp.

In the evenings the young people of Tshing simply went out and aimlessly trailed along the streets of the township, knowing that sooner or later they would bump into friends, acquaintances, or simply people of the same age group, driven out of the house by boredom and despair. As they roamed the alleys or the veld covered in tall grass, they would discuss the latest events and news.

Benny couldn't stop wondering why Mandela was being so slow to take power from the whites. A thousand days had passed since he came out of jail, and he was still negotiating with the white president, who was dragging out the talks, setting more and more new conditions and piling up the obstacles.

The young people couldn't understand Mandela's patience. Where did he get it from? And what was the point? The only explanation was his venerable age. He was an old man, sagacious, dignified, and sedate, and that must have been how he perceived time and the whole world around him. He must have understood it differently from the young people. Benny even found it comical that Mandela could recommend patience so highly at the age of eighty, as if he had umpteen years left to live—while the young, with their entire lives ahead of them, refused to do any waiting at all.

In these days of suspense, doubt, and lack of faith, when it looked as if the changes would never come but had got lost along the way, amid the pushing and shoving, prolonged talks, bargaining, and negotiations, Benny thought back to the time he had spent in jail more often than before.

Idleness was merely intensifying his wish to be active, refreshing his memory of past suffering and humiliation, and inflaming his desire for revenge. As if he wanted to make sure that there was still something left from that time of struggle, the simple signposts and clear divisions into friend and foe; that not everything would be erased without leaving any distinct trace of itself, any mark; that not everything would be wasted.

The party leaders in Johannesburg were telling people to forgive, forget, and never go back to what had happened in the past. They were saying it should be done in the name of reconciliation, and in exchange for the fact that the whites were giving up power voluntarily. That was meant to be adequate reward for their suffering and sacrifice.

Whereas Benny wanted at least to preserve his hatred, his experience at the hands of his oppressors, and what they had taught him. He didn't regard hatred as a bad thing—he even enjoyed feeling it. But that certainly didn't mean he surrendered to it, allowed it to control him or push him into violence. He just wanted to remember it, to be able to summon it up, because it came back with the proud memory of the only important thing he had ever done in his life. Although he had taken action at almost the final moment, he had stood up for the right cause at a time when that still demanded courage and sacrifice. His suffering was in no way inferior to that of others, including Mandela himself. But anyway, how could you measure fear or pain, or how much anyone had been through? He refused to renounce or diminish the one act that distinguished him, in which he had been better than others.

He had no intention of conforming to the magnanimity recommended by Mandela, and even if he were to be reconciled with his enemies, he would never consider loving them. He also thought it fair for injuries to be requited, and that you can only absolve someone from blame once they have personally suffered the injustice they have inflicted on others. "First let them see what it's like, before we forgive each other and throw our arms around each other," he would say.

He was being eaten away by impatience. What was the point of negotiating with the whites? If they didn't want to hand over power voluntarily, it should be taken from them by force! He couldn't see any other way, if things were going to change in his life, or the life of the town where he lived. The satisfaction he felt whenever they called Mandela the future president on television evaporated like smoke every time he encountered Eugène Terre'Blanche and white brotherhood members in his hometown. At such moments Benny's thoughts were never of patience and forgiveness, but the quickest way to pay them back in their own coin.

At the thought of the imminent lifting of apartheid forecast by the government and the end of white rule in Africa, Raymond Boardman felt both anxiety and relief.

His anxiety came from the fact that the future under black governments was indeterminate and unpredictable, removing his sense of security and the privilege of being able to proceed with a positive mindset, make plans, or even have dreams. He was to lose the certainty—illusory, but necessary to each person—of having full control of his own destiny. From now on his fate would depend on how the blacks coped with running the country.

He believed, he hoped, they would cope. He trusted Mandela, his calm, common sense, and moderation. Mandela plainly didn't want revenge on the enemies who had deprived him of freedom and half his adult life. "What happened is in the past," he was known to say. He was promising that under his administration there would be room in this country for everyone, white and black—they would all need each other, so it was better to try to live in harmony.

Raymond liked to think that once the blacks had taken over, although they hated the whites, they would need them, their skills and experience, and that even if vengeance were justified, they wouldn't be able to take the liberty.

And yet his relief was stronger than his fears. Like many whites, Raymond could tell that abolition and condemnation of the apartheid system would remove his sense of guilt for the evil he hadn't opposed. Like it or not, he had after all taken advantage of the benefits that came with his privileged skin color.

The death of apartheid would release him from the stigma represented by his white skin and passport abroad. It was enough to say where he was from, and people who had no idea who he was or what he thought would back off and watch what they said to him. He prompted similar suspicion in Johannesburg or Cape Town when he turned out to be from Ventersdorp.

Just as when slavery was abolished in America, the end of apartheid meant the promise of release from guilt and shame, it meant absolution and exculpation. No white person would have to apologize for his or her skin color anymore. They would be rid of their pangs of conscience, and finally feel innocent and free.

Raymond was prepared to give a great deal for that.

His return to Buckingham farm had now acquired extra significance. He had decided to abandon the life he'd been living and go back to the countryside, as a way of making his mark and leaving something behind him. It didn't strike him as pretentious to think or say he needed to be in contact with the soil, to smell it and touch it, and that he wanted to rediscover his roots and return to them, because only in the place where a man grew up did he truly belong, only there could he really be himself.

He wanted to maintain the farm, take over and preserve the family property and legacy, passed from generation to generation, and one day hand it down to one of his sons. The middle boy, Mike, was best suited to inherit the farm. He suffered from a congenital eye complaint and wasn't as good a student as James or Matthew. But he loved the farm and enjoyed every vacation they spent there. He was always happy to go to the countryside, as if returning to his proper place, which is so hard to find and recognize in adult life.

Now that the old order was collapsing, Raymond Boardman saw a chance for atonement in going back to the farm. He wanted to share all his achievements and capabilities, everything that mattered to him—just as Mandela was encouraging people to do. To give and share with others, to help each other, to build a community, to change and improve life and the world.

The Boardmans were proud of the fact that compared with other white farmers in Ventersdorp they treated their black workers well. They let them live on their land, paid them decently, and on time. Raymond wanted to teach them how to run a farm for themselves. He was even considering parceling off a piece of land from the farm and giving it to the black workers as their property. He reckoned they deserved a better life, and he wanted to help them achieve it. Deep down, he was also counting on the fact that they would repay him for his good deeds in kind, would gratefully accept the gift he was making them, and wouldn't try to grab all his property or take away the farm and land, as Eugène Terre'Blanche was predicting to frighten the white farmers.

During the preparations to move, while traveling to and fro between Pretoria and Ventersdorp, Raymond felt as if he were moving between two worlds divided by an invisible but extremely palpable boundary. While he had been coming to Ventersdorp as a visitor, he had hardly noticed it. But he knew that once he settled on the farm, crossing to the other side would stop being quite so easy.

He felt as if he were leading two separate lives. We sometimes have this impression of a parallel existence, and of passing from one life to another on trips to faraway countries, into worlds so different from our own that being there feels like being in a different incarnation, like a migration of souls. It ends the day we go home, back to our old role, and the abandoned traveling persona freezes until the day it's reanimated.

When the date of the elections was announced, Raymond decided that on that same day, which would mark the start of the new order, he would be in Ventersdorp, not in Pretoria, and would cast his vote along with the blacks at the polling station set up in a school for black children.

With only a month to go until the election that Boardman was so eagerly anticipating, Eugène Terre'Blanche finally triggered the war he had been threatening to start for so long. When all else had failed, war remained the final solution.

He couldn't believe his compatriots' blindness, as like a flock of sheep they meekly let themselves be led by de Klerk to certain perdition. But he believed it was still possible for them to come to their senses. By now he had cast off the illusion that all the Afrikaners, acting as one man, were ready to make sacrifices as long as they could have their own state. Yet he was in no doubt that even set at odds and indolent, they would awaken and summon up the strength to survive when lethal danger was staring them in the eyes—when the blacks attacked them.

Terre'Blanche was sure that when this war broke out, the white army and police, who so far had carried out de Klerk's orders without a murmur, would declare allegiance to him and side with their compatriots. Racial solidarity would triumph over blind obedience enforced by hierarchy, and no white soldier or police officer would stand by and watch as the blacks murdered his compatriots. And once the army and police had come over to the white camp, they'd have won the war of the races. All the talk about living together and mixing the races in a single state would be cut short for good and all, and the country would be divided up into republics and kingdoms of Afrikaners, Zulus, Tswana, and Xhosa.

Terre'Blanche and his supporters were not the only ones who weren't thrilled about living under a black administration. The leaders of the black Bantustans—the tribal homelands that the white government had declared to be independent states with their own president, parliament, army, and police—were not keen either. Not wanting to come under Mandela's rule, the Zulus from the KwaZulu Bantustan were demanding their own kingdom. The authorities in Ciskei, the Xhosa homeland, were refusing to hand over Joshua Oupa Gqozo, a former prison guard and diamond smuggler, who had organized a coup d'état and declared himself president. Hoping to revive their own Transvaal republic, Viljoen's and Terre'Blanche's Afrikaners had decided to form an alliance with them. They were also joined by the Tswana leader Lucas Mangope, who did not want to part with his realm of Bophuthatswana either.

Not far from Ventersdorp, the Tswana homeland consisted of seven enclaves, scattered across three different national provinces. The farthest apart were almost five hundred kilometers from each other. The land here was stony and barren, as in all the black homelands, but it concealed one of the world's richest seams of platinum. Its mines, belonging to foreign mining companies, secured one quarter of the homeland's earnings. Half of its income was money transferred by the white government in Pretoria, which was happy to support the Bantustans and pay their leaders, as long as they testified to the validity and superiority of the apartheid system.

As their diplomatic ministers or administrators, it was white people from Pretoria who advised the presidents of the Bantustans, and trained and commanded the local army and police force. They pandered to all the whims of the Bantustan rulers. In Bophuthatswana they built a whole new town, Mmabatho, to be President Mangope's capital, with a university and a soccer stadium for one hundred thousand spectators, twice the population of the capital.

The rest of the budget consisted of profits from the casinos, nightclubs, and brothels that the whites from Transvaal built there, so that just across the border, little more than a hundred kilometers from devoutly religious Pretoria, they could abandon themselves to gambling and enjoy the erotic charms of black girls, forbidden in the land of apartheid.

Scenting a profit, cunning entrepreneurs from Johannesburg had built an entire town full of casinos, hotels, and nightclubs in the desert. They called it Sun City, but its bad reputation soon earned it a new name, or rather nickname, Sin City, where in a single night the guests were capable of blowing more money than the average inhabitant of Bophuthatswana earned in an entire year.

Although Sin City was built inside a homeland, not many blacks could afford to make use of the facilities—bathe in the artificial lake, eat at the smart restaurants, play a round of golf, seek their fortune at roulette or poker, watch a beauty contest, or dance until dawn at parties where the best, most famous musicians used to play. In fact there was some trouble with them, because in protest against the apartheid regime in South Africa, many musicians refused to perform in Sin City, and even turned down lavish fees.

Whereas the homeland's ruler, Lucas Mangope, was very fond of Sin City, and held the national Independence Day celebrations there. Here he could be sure of good fun and a sophisticated atmosphere, while in his own capital his subjects could easily change a festive parade into a street riot.

They regarded him as a greedy traitor. Not much younger than Mandela, who had preferred to go to jail rather than kowtow to the whites, Mangope was their lackey, enjoying liberty, power, and wealth in exchange. If Bophuthatswana had really been an independent state, its president wouldn't have been very different from the other African leaders of his generation, who regarded their countries as their personal property, and the citizens as their subjects.

Now he had declared that Bophuthatswana was autonomous, and that he wasn't going to organize any elections there. He ordered his policemen not to let Mandela cross the border at all. But when Mandela decided to travel to Bophuthatswana so its residents could meet their future leader, the security guards joined his convoy.

"I don't need to ask permission to travel about my own country," said Mandela. "But explaining that to Mangope is a waste of breath."

Mandela's supporters announced that if Mangope didn't give up power, they'd come to his capital and drag him out of it by force, after which they'd knock down the border posts sanctifying his state's separate identity.

The terrified Mangope joined the Freedom Front with the Afrikaners and Zulus, who were also unwilling to come under Mandela's rule. He couldn't count on the South African army, which the white government had formerly been accustomed to send to its rescue in times of trouble. Now the white president, just like Mandela, was ordering him to hand over power and dissolve his state.

When riots began in the Bophuthatswanan capital Mmabatho, Mangope told his secretaries to find the home phone number of Eugène Terre'Blanche in nearby Ventersdorp.

He made the call for help in person.

Terre'Blanche took the call in his study, which acted as the head office of the AWB.

"Things are taking a really bad turn," said Mangope. "I'm afraid I can't cope on my own."

For three days, there had been rioting in Bophuthatswana, started by Mandela's supporters. More and more common criminals were joining in, taking advantage of the general chaos to rob and set fire to stores, houses, and cars. The police and army were incapable of restoring order, and as Mangope admitted, many of the soldiers and police officers were clearly on Mandela's side. He was afraid that without help he would never hold on to power.

"We won't abandon you," promised Terre'Blanche.

Fearing not just for his power but for his life too, Mangope pressed further.

"My people won't fight if they realize they're in the losing position," he said.

"I'm going straight to Pretoria," Terre'Blanche assured him. "Please don't worry. We'll teach them a lesson."

Before setting off for the capital, he called General Viljoen and other leaders of the Freedom Front, telling them to meet the next day for an urgent conference. He also issued a call to arms to his brotherhood commandants, to be ready for war.

Next day, a cold March dawn, a convoy of farmers' pickups drove into Mmabatho and nearby Mafikeng, carrying a thousand Afrikaner volunteers, the decided majority of whom were members of the AWB. There were plenty of willing participants in the military expedition, not just because Bophuthatswana's seven oases were scattered across Transvaal. The Afrikaners were not afraid of war against the blacks, and felt sure of winning. The black rebels didn't know how to fight, and although they'd grabbed hold of weapons and were threatening the whites with war, they had never won a single battle. The only thing they were capable of doing was planting bombs in churches or restaurants. So large numbers of Afrikaner volunteers had readily responded to the call, coming from Witbank and Rustenburg, Vryburg and Krugersdorp, to avoid missing a certain and easy victory over those to whom de Klerk was planning to surrender everything without a fight.

On arriving in Bophuthatswana, the volunteers headed first for the districts where the whites lived. Greeted as saviors from the black rebels and thieves, they set up guard posts and sent out patrols. Intoxicated by this initial success, they headed farther into the city to restore order and crush the riots.

While the Afrikaners who did not belong to the AWB did their best to exercise restraint, by contrast Terre'Blanche's commandos toured the streets of Mmabatho and Mafikeng in their pickup trucks, firing at every black person they regarded as suspicious. Shots rang out all over the town. The riots changed into an effort to hunt down blacks. The Afrikaners fired pistols and rifles at anyone taking part in the disturbances, at thieves, accidental passersby, and onlookers. Even at local policemen and soldiers. The streets were soon littered with the dead and wounded.

The shooting was in full swing when Terre'Blanche was informed that instead of supporting the intervening volunteers, the local army and police had renounced allegiance to Mangope and were on the side of the demonstrators, and that the South African army had been called in from Pretoria to suppress the riots and the shooting.

Fearing that his men would be surrounded and wiped out or imprisoned, Terre'Blanche ordered a retreat. He told the brotherhood members to assemble at the airport, form a convoy, and take off their armbands carrying swastikas, which distinguished them from all the other volunteers, before leaving the Bantustan.

A crowd was gathering around a sky-blue car standing on a sandy road just before an intersection. On the ground, with his face in the sand, lay a dead white man. A second, leaning against the open door on the driver's side, was begging for his life. A third was hanging out of the backseat.

The Afrikaners were fleeing Bophuthatswana in a tight convoy of pickup trucks and passenger cars along a road where the local soldiers and police had set up ambushes. The Afrikaner volunteers were shooting back in response to their gunfire. Abandoning vehicles that were immobilized by bullets, quick as a flash they were scrambling into the beds of other pickups. Though outnumbered and not as well armed, they had hardly suffered any casualties. About a dozen of them were wounded, but none had been killed. Meanwhile, in the street shooting that day they had left more than a hundred blacks dead, and wounded about five hundred. At the very sight of the vehicles full of white volunteers, the blacks had panicked and run off as fast as they could, without even trying to fight.

The blue Mercedes must have got detached from the convoy. Maybe it had run out of gas and driven off the main road to find a gas station in the deserted town? Or perhaps it broke away from the column to explore the neighborhood and look for withdrawal routes? The men travelling in the car were AWB commandants. One had the rank of general, another was a *veldkornet* (or field cornet). Even the driver was a colonel.

They fell into an ambush before a police checkpoint. Machine-gun bullets strafed the car. One of the whites, hit in the neck, was dying. The two others, who were wounded, pushed him out of the car onto the sandy road, and then, with the last of their strength, they crawled out too. The man from the backseat lost consciousness. The bearded driver, on his knees and raising his hands in supplication, asked for his life to be spared.

"Call an ambulance . . . please . . . get a doctor."

He was wounded in the arm and paralyzed with fear. The crowd gathering around the car was threatening and insulting him. Journalists were taking pictures, coming right up close to catch every detail—the frantic eyes and the blue lips muttering pleas for help.

"A doctor . . . call an ambulance . . . for God's sake . . . help us . . ."

"They're going to take care of you," put in one of the journalists. "They're arresting you, then they'll get you a doctor."

"Aren't you sorry you came here now?" asked another, pulling a notepad from his pants pocket. "Aren't you sorry for what you've done here?"

The crowd parted to let a black policeman through.

"I'm arresting you," he said. "Hand over your gun and lie face down."

The white man obediently did as he was told. And then a second policeman came up. He raised his gun, and without a word aimed at the white prisoners at close range. The dry crack of a shot rang out, then another. Then four more, two bullets for each man. The force of the bullets made the lifeless bodies jolt upward as they lay sprawling on the sand.

Next day in Ventersdorp Eugène Terre'Blanche invited the journalists to his house for a press conference. He announced that his people had carried off a glorious victory in Bophuthatswana, but it had been stolen from them by treacherous politicians.

"We were cheated and blood was shed," he said on the lawn in front of his house. "I cannot get over the fact that we weren't allowed to remain in Bophuthatswana and finish the job."

He called the three brotherhood members shot dead in Mmabatho heroes, and six months later he added their names to the monument outside the town hall in Ventersdorp. One of the widows invited to the unveiling of the obelisk said that her husband's death had not been in vain.

Several days after the riots in Bophuthatswana Nelson Mandela drove down to the disbanded homeland. Filled to bursting, the stadium for one hundred thousand went mad with delight when he greeted them in the Tswana language.

"Greetings, my people!" he said in a husky voice.

Among the spectators yelling at the top of their voices was Benny Tapologo. He would never have missed the opportunity to see Mandela with his own eyes. He and his friends had set off from Tshing in a borrowed car when the sky was still gray, and the cold fall dawn was only just breaking. They'd decided to leave early enough to get there before Mandela, and also to avoid meeting any local police or AWB patrols on the highway.

They took the same road to Mmabatho through Coligny and Lichtenburg that a week ago the white brotherhood commandos had taken on their way back from their military sortie. Not all of them had gone straight home. Many had stopped in town. The day before, Benny had seen bearded strangers in tawny shirts and shorts, drinking beer at the hotel or wandering aimlessly along the main street. They weren't in a hurry to return to everyday life, but were lingering, waiting for Terre'Blanche to give them new orders.

Despite Terre'Blanche's swaggering, it was clear to Benny that he hadn't carried off a victory in Bophuthatswana at all, but on the contrary, he had suffered a crushing defeat, maybe his last. Benny sensed that Eugène and his men were perfectly aware of that themselves, even if they weren't yet ready to admit it. He preferred to avoid encountering them on the road to Mmabatho, where he was heading for Mandela's triumphal rally, which would put the seal on their loss.

They reached Mmabatho without any trouble. There was still plenty of evidence of last week's riots. In the streets downtown there were smashed paving stones lying about, and old tires from the recent barricades. On the sidewalks glass from smashed store windows crunched underfoot. Stores gutted by looters exuded the smell of a recent blaze.

Mandela was delayed, but at the stadium nobody was complaining. They'd been waiting for him for such a long time that a few more hours in the hot sunshine made no difference. And when he finally appeared, came out onto the platform, and raised his clenched fist in a gesture of victory, even the weariest spectators felt strengthened by an extraordinary force.

"The fact that I am standing here before you means that you too have been set free," said Mandela, prompting applause. "It's not the white government in Pretoria that has overthrown the tyrant. You did it yourselves, by raising a popular insurgency against him."

People began to clap when he mentioned the three Afrikaners shot dead in Mmabatho by a local policeman.

"Those who sent them here have been taught a lesson they'll never forget!" he cried.

But when he stopped talking about revolution and liberty and, wagging a finger, reminded them about the looting that had accompanied the riots, the stadium fell silent, and some people even started to leave.

The day of the election was fine and warm. It was nothing like the end of the world predicted by Eugène Terre'Blanche.

At the Ventersdorp town limits, opposite the gas station, a notice board had been stuck into the red earth informing visitors

that they were crossing into the territory of an Afrikaner republic. "Here starts the Volkstaat," announced the sign. The Volkstaat
was the Afrikaners' name for their state, their fatherland.

A week before the election, Ventersdorp had still been in the
possession of the bearded men from the white brotherhood,
who patrolled the town with guns in their hands, and kept
guard outside Terre'Blanche's house. They had reinforced their
guard posts with sand bags and barbed-wire entanglements.
The town had been gearing up for war, and its residents had
been hastily buying up candles and canned food.

But when election day finally came, Terre'Blanche and his soldiers had disappeared, and their fortified posts had gone with
them. According to the newspapers he had lost, and his downfall had been decided by the defeat in Bophuthatswana. There for
the first time it had turned out that white soldiers and policemen
placed the orders of their superiors above blood ties and skin color.

Just before the election, and also on the actual day, in a final act
of desperation members of the white brotherhood had planted
a number of bombs in Johannesburg and Pretoria, and had also
fired from speeding cars at stops where black people were waiting for their microbuses. They had killed more than twenty, and
wounded almost a hundred, but they had failed to disrupt the
election. Years on, when all the attackers had been caught and
brought to trial, the judge sentenced their leaders to as many
years in jail as Mandela had served for fighting against apartheid.

Although the election was being held on a weekday, in town
the streets were empty, and half the stores were closed. It felt
like a Sunday, except that there were no church services.

On election Wednesday, a day off work, Benny Tapologo did
everything unhurriedly, reluctantly, with an unconcealed lack

of enthusiasm. He got up late, and took his time eating the oatmeal his mother had made him for breakfast.

"Aren't you going to vote?" she asked as he ate.

"I'll get there," he muttered, gazing out of the window.

She shrugged, and brushed some crumbs off the waxed tablecloth with her apron.

Outside he could see the street, dressed for election day in the yellow, green and black colors of Mandela's party, the African National Congress. There were posters with his likeness and the slogan "One Man—One Vote" hanging on the chicken-wire fences and plastering the walls, telegraph poles, and even the cars.

With each day that brought him closer to the long-awaited election Benny felt all the joy and impatience slipping out of him. Rebellion and struggle had defined his life, given it meaning, and distinguished him from others. But now it was all coming to an end, just like that. People only had to cast their votes into the ballot boxes, and the victory he had fought for would belong to everyone. Including those who had never made any demands at all, but had just acquiesced in every way, like good kaffirs.

As he gazed out of the window, Benny had no sense of joy, just emptiness. It was spoiling the festive mood for him, and making him feel irritated. By the time he left the house and headed for the polling station, the sun was high in the sky. The street was fairly deserted, as on a Sunday, but at the intersection with the main, surfaced road there was a large crowd of people. Dressed up for the occasion, they were standing in a long line, waiting patiently to cast their votes.

Some of them had lined up before dawn. There were old men in hats and worn-out jackets with ragged sleeves, and women wrapped in blankets against the cold. Although the government had set aside several days for the election and had given assurances that everybody would have their chance to participate, the old people preferred to vote as soon as possible, the moment the polling stations opened, as if afraid that at the last moment something would go wrong, the miracle wouldn't happen, and the election, in which they would cast their vote for the first time ever, would be cancelled.

And so they were standing patiently in line, in solemn meditation, like the congregation in church waiting to take Holy Communion.

Benny noticed Samuel Zuma in the line, who had been a friend of his father's and who often dropped in at their home. He recognized the old man standing just behind him was Jeremiah Kgotla, known locally as "the cripple," because he was lame in the left leg, which he had broken, falling under a tractor on a white farm. Also in line with them was Walter, the former night watchman at the town hall.

Afraid of missing anything, or letting an unnecessary word disturb the great moment, they were keeping quiet. In their pensive mood, they nervously patted their pockets to check if the documents entitling them to vote were still safely in there. Formal and erect, one after another they went up to the ballot boxes to throw in their vote, testimony to the first free election in their lives.

Everything was going to change.

Henk Malan only watched the voting. He went out in the morning and walked about the town. Although he knew it like the back of his hand, that day it seemed different somehow, as if he were looking at it from the other side. The whole town seemed lifeless and deserted, like an expensive mock-up in a design studio, closed for the night under a glass dome so that no one should tinker with it, make any changes without the architect's knowledge, or spoil anything.

Henk didn't see anybody going to vote in Ventersdorp. He walked past several polling stations, but they were as deserted as the streets. However, when the results were announced, it turned out that plenty of white citizens in Ventersdorp had cast their votes for the Afrikaner politicians who were reasoning that as they couldn't prevent the collapse of the old world, they should join in with forming the new one—if only in order to have some sort of influence on it, and to be able to change it if it proved intolerable.

They also firmly believed that Mandela would allow them to establish their own, separate country, or at least a separate province. Desperately afraid of war and wanting to avoid it at any cost, they were ascribing words to him that he had never uttered. To dissuade the Afrikaners from inciting civil war, Mandela had only promised to consider their demands, not to fulfill them.

In the square outside the town hall thick, white, acrid smoke was rising. "They've set something on fire again," thought Henk, spitting, to clear the stench from his lungs. There was smoldering trash lying around behind the stores on the main street. He couldn't understand the blacks' habit of burning all those things, trash, refuse, and old tires.

"One day they'll send the whole town up in smoke," he muttered to himself.

Henk didn't vote, because he figured it had nothing to do with him. It was the blacks' election, and he saw mixing in with the blacks as evil and sinful. The day before, he and his wife Anita had been talking about it after supper. They had known each other for years before becoming a couple. Anita and her first husband, Anton, had lived on the same street as Henk's mother, but when they divorced she'd moved out and rented the house next door to the Terre'Blanches' place in town. Once she and Henk were married, they'd come back to her old stamping ground, settling opposite her first husband's house. Living across the road from each other, sometimes the two men got on, and sometimes they fell out. The hot-tempered Henk was just as quick on the draw as Anton.

At the time they were on good terms, and the day before the election they had invited Anton to supper. As they ate, they watched a TV program encouraging people to go and vote.

"Mark my words. It'll come to everybody mixing with everybody else, everyone's going to mate with everyone else," said Henk. "And finally there'll be nothing but half-caste bastards. There won't be any more whites or blacks or yellows. And nobody will know who's who."

"That's what they want," added Anton.

"That, meaning what exactly?" asked Anita.

"They don't want things the way the Lord God made them," explained Anton. "They want to live contrary to his will."

After the election broadcast a multicolored rainbow appeared on the TV screen. Ever since Mandela and his people had made it the symbol of the new world, where all races would live together as equals, in the Afrikaner towns in Transvaal it was regarded as a bad omen. For the white citizens, the good times weren't beginning, but ending.

"Half-castes are the worst," said Henk. "You don't know who they are, just who they're not. You see a guy like that and at once you know how badly they've sinned against God. They're the children of Cain."

For Sunday worship Henk usually went to the small church under a large eucalyptus tree right near his house. The congregation there was called the true Israelites, the true Sons of Israel. Henk liked the fact that they believed that the Creator's chosen race, the one He loved best, were the white Europeans, and not the Jews, who had distorted everything at Satan's behest. The true Israelites could cite dozens of verses of the Old Testament to prove their legitimacy. They also claimed that the Creator Himself had sent His chosen race to Africa, and had given them the lands to the south of the rivers of Ethiopia as their kingdom, but had told them that under no circumstances were they to mix with the natives.

Henk headed home. The church under the eucalyptus tree was closed. In any case, it almost always looked idle and abandoned. He passed Terre'Blanche's house, but there wasn't a living soul there either. Henk was just approaching the way into his own yard when at the end of the empty street he noticed a car, from which somebody was waving to him. He stopped at the gate. A farm pickup truck was slowly pulling over onto the verge. Its registration plate wasn't local. Both the driver and the passenger were solidly built white men.

"Apparently Eugène Terre'Blanche's house is somewhere round here?" asked the passenger in Afrikaans through the window. "How do we get there?"

"You turn right and drive on a few meters," replied Henk. "But the bell at the gate doesn't work. I can show you the way."

The visitors were pleased and invited him into the car.

"Come far?" asked Henk.

"From Ermelo, eastern Transvaal," said the driver, changing gear.

"So you've come to see Eugène?" asked Henk.

"Yeah, to see Eugène, to see Eugène," said the passenger,

nodding. "But it looks as if we've come in vain. The kaffirs have evidently done their voting here anyway."

"Bloody kaffirs," growled the driver, turning the corner.

Raymond Boardman came from Pretoria for the election, with his wife and sons, as if on vacation. It was a fine day, perfect for a drive to the countryside. Warm, damp fall air pushed its way in through the open window, scented with the chill of earth cooling after the summer, the fragrance of wildflowers, and smoke from the grass the blacks were burning before winter.

They turned off the highway down a country road across the fields and pastures, then onto a bumpy track, rutted by the rain, which led slightly uphill, but it was a straight run to Buckingham farm. The house was almost hidden beneath the spreading boughs of acacia and eucalyptus trees. Only as they drove into the sandy yard could they see the low, squat building steeped in shade.

First to run out to meet them were the dogs—there were always several here. Then the black workers came out of the farm buildings adjoining the house. They lived with their families just across the road.

"Raymond's here! Raymie!" They spoke English the way the Afrikaners did, and loved using all sorts of diminutives.

They laughed out loud, patted each other on the back, and squeezed Raymond's hand. They greeted him like a relative they hadn't seen for ages. He returned their embraces, and greeted each of them by name to show them he remembered, and thus to show them his respect.

"Jomo! Harry! Tsepe! Petrus!"

Petrus was the same age as Raymond, and they'd grown up

together on the farm, playing games, tracking cranes, and hunting jackals.

He was filled with the carefree joy he had felt as a boy when he went tearing across the veld, through grasses and wildflowers that came up to his arms. The sight of the wildflowers rippling on the veld always reminded him of childhood.

He was happy to stop the car in the fields to let Charlene pick some to put in a vase. She loved cosmos, with their tall, strong stems, long leaves, and purple, red, pink, or white flowers similar to asters. The farmers often sowed them along the roadside to decorate their border fences. Apparently these flowers had come to the Transvaal veld all the way from Mexico, imported as fodder for British cavalry horses fighting against the Boer partisans. It was also said that wherever they grew the British had spilled Boer blood.

For the voting, he and Charlene took their sons and drove to the school for the black workers' children, which had been built on the grounds of Buckingham farm but served black people from the entire district. A polling station had been set up there. Raymond felt that he wanted to cast his vote right here, and not in the white town, so he stood in line with the blacks. He was the only white man to vote at the farm.

On the way home, he passed lots of blacks on the road, heading somewhere on foot. Most of them were people he had never seen before. As usual, they were ignoring the warning signs put up by white farmers to prohibit trespassing on their land. The blacks treated the white farms as their shortcuts, and nothing could ever change that.

Raymond's father complained that lately there had been a lot of strangers hanging around the neighborhood.

"There are all sorts of vagrants drifting around the farms, nobody knows anything about them, but they seem to get wind of everything," grumbled old Boardman. "One of these days there's going to be trouble."

But that day Raymond wasn't taking any notice of his father's usual grouching and acerbity.

"You've brought weeds in again," he muttered when Charlene came into the house with a bunch of wildflowers. "Their place is in the meadow, not in the living room."

Raymond just smiled. He felt lighthearted, like someone emerging from the confessional. Guilt-free and pure, full of positive ideas and resolutions, as well as faith in himself and in the fact that from now on everything was always going to be all right. This day was exactly as he'd hoped it would be. It hadn't brought any disappointment, but was like a dream come true. Now, with impatience and curiosity, he was looking forward to the changes to come.

3

The night of the election, which had threatened to be so restless, had gone by without any trouble, disturbance, brawling, or mugging. Only when the sunrise was gently starting to dispel the night were the policemen at the local station roused by thumping at the door.

"Who the devil's that?" muttered the duty officer, tidying his uniform.

Henk Malan was standing at the door. He must have only just arrived, because he hadn't switched off his car engine or headlamps. Through an open rear door they could see a black man slumped against the seat.

"I found him on the road, near the gas station," said Henk.

"Who on earth is he? Is he alive?" asked the duty officer, going up to the car.

"How should I know? But he's not stiff yet."

He watched as three policemen dragged the guy out of his car. Showing no sign of life, he flopped in their arms. Once they'd carried him into the police station, under the bright lights they saw that his face was badly injured and covered in blood. His teeth had been knocked out, his nose was crushed, his right eye was buried in swollen flesh, and there was blood trickling from his ear. Dark bloodstains were spreading across his pale shirt.

"I wonder who messed him up?"

"He was like this when I found him," said Henk, shrugging.

"Is he going to recover?"

"He took a pretty good beating. What was a kaffir with no car doing at the gas station in the middle of the night? And the night after the election? That's asking for trouble."

The policeman sat down at his desk to write a report. Henk flinched when he was told he had to make a statement and sign it.

"I'm not signing anything. What's it got to do with me?" he bristled. "I just brought him in. A man takes pity on another and at once he's got nothing but trouble," said Henk, getting more and more upset. "I just brought him in."

"Anyone might think you thrashed the kaffir yourself because he was pleased about the election win, and now you're feeling sorry for him," laughed the policeman.

"Or else he got cold feet because the blacks are going to be in charge around here now," added the duty officer. "Right! Wasn't it you who was driving around town this evening with those two cops from Ermelo who came to see Eugène?"

The policemen from Ermelo were members of the white brotherhood who had come to Ventersdorp before the election in answer to a call from Terre'Blanche, who was threatening to disrupt the local voting. Henk had run into them on election day when, bored and irritable, they were aimlessly driving about the streets. They had nothing to do, but they didn't feel like going home yet, to Ermelo, in eastern Transvaal.

"Bloody kaffirs," they'd said, their anger rising as they looked for a fight to offload it. For lack of anything better to do, Henk had joined them.

"They've gone. They went before nightfall," he quickly said. "So what about this black? Will he survive?"

The policeman gave him a long stare.

"He was lying in the road," Henk continued, breaking the oppressive silence. "I'd gone to get cigarettes, because I'd just run out. I was driving along, and I saw him lying there, so I stopped."

"Then what? You were suddenly filled with pity? It's not very like you. Wasn't it you and Eugène who thumped him, more like?"

"Eugène who?"

The policeman shrugged.

"If the guy snuffs it, and whites turn out to have done that to him, and on election day too, I wouldn't like to be in their shoes when the blacks take over. Eugène himself won't be able to help them. And they'll take the chance to have a go at us too. As if we haven't got enough trouble!"

That afternoon it was announced on the radio that the blacks had won the election and were taking over the government. Henk went to the police station to ask about the battered man.

But the police told him the man had disappeared. They'd left him in a cell for a doctor to examine him. They hadn't locked the door; clearly he had got up and left. Nobody had noticed him disappear, and that was that—he had just vanished into thin air.

The story soon went round the town, with people telling each other various versions of the incident. There were plenty who swore it was just the policemen, who'd brought out a body and buried it. Some claimed Henk had a hand in it, while others insisted the guy had survived, but had holed up somewhere in the township in fear of his life.

Nobody knew if he was local or just passing through, or

whether he'd lived or died. And if he had survived, whether he would remember and be able to recognize his assailants. And whether he would report his injuries to the new authorities and the new mayor of Ventersdorp.

On hearing that he was the new mayor and would be moving into the town hall in the white part of town, Meshack Mbambalala got cold feet.

He could actually have expected this. Until now, only the white citizens had elected the mayor of Ventersdorp. The town had had fifty-six mayors, every single one of whom had been an Afrikaner. But since abolishing apartheid, the authorities had decided that not just the citizens of white Ventersdorp would choose their new administrator, but also the blacks from Tshing, the township, whose population was several times bigger. Everyone knew that only a black politician from Mandela's party could win. And the ANC had chosen Mbambalala as its candidate for mayor of Ventersdorp, so he should have been prepared long ago to move into the white town hall. However, he kept putting it off, procrastinating, with the excuse that he still had so many things to do in Tshing. Although three weeks had gone by since the election, he hadn't even been to visit his mayoral office in the town hall.

He should have been packing up, but every day he came to the ANC office, a lean-to shack supported by the wall of a roadside bar selling beer. Goodness knows why. There was no furniture in here, so visitors to the party office sat on bundles of election leaflets and posters tied up with string, which had been sent from Johannesburg, too many of them, and too late, so some had never been unpacked. For his part, Mbambalala couldn't see the point of sticking up ANC posters in Ventersdorp, where no white person was going to vote for Mandela anyway.

So instead of taking up his post as the first black mayor of Ventersdorp, Mbambalala sat in the party office day after day, holding meetings with his colleagues and talking to the visitors, including people who had just dropped in accidentally, mistaking the entrance to the bar. He also received journalists there, who had come down to Tshing in droves to meet the white town's first black mayor and write about it. He sat them down on the unpacked posters and leaflets, while he squatted on the concrete floor and told them his plans for governing the town.

The days went by, until finally people in Tshing began to whisper that Mbambalala was afraid of the whites. They hadn't forgotten that in fact he had grown up on a white farm, where the blacks were instilled with blind obedience and the conviction that they were only there to serve whites and to bow down to them.

"I'm not afraid of whites, though it's true I don't feel too confident in their company," he said, when I went to see him in Tshing. "It's not about skin color, it's just that I don't know them, I've had almost no contact with them."

Mbambalala wasn't at the ANC office anymore when I arrived in the black township one afternoon. The regulars at the bar next door were happy to show me the way to his house, and the children who came running at the sight of a foreigner raced along in front of my car and escorted me to the right place. The mayor lived with his mother in a corrugated iron hut with no electricity or running water, where the only decoration was a color poster of Bob Marley, pinned to the kitchen wall.

"I'll manage, everything will be fine," said Mbambalala haltingly, so quietly that he was almost whispering. He cracked his knuckles as he said it. "It's not easy for the whites either to accept the fact that their new mayor has black skin. They're not used to a black man giving them orders. They're sure to be afraid I won't be able to cope with the administration. They don't know me, but once they do, they'll take to me and they'll give me a chance."

But since election day he hadn't been to Ventersdorp to meet with any of the white citizens. He had just talked to four white councillors who had driven down to Tshing and invited him to the local administration building. They promised they wouldn't obstruct him in his new job, but would even try to help, so the town wouldn't come to any harm.

He was twenty-six years old, and before the party proposed him as an election candidate he had led the deprived life of an unemployed teacher. He hadn't finished his studies at the black university in Soweto, because after his father's death he had had to look for a job. The wages his mother earned as a cleaner for some white people in Klerksdorp were just enough to provide something to eat at home. He had come to Tshing to help her, but had simply proved an extra burden for her—she had to maintain him, because there was no work for a teacher in the township. He didn't even ask about work in the white town, where blacks were only needed as store assistants, porters, farm laborers, and servants.

Like most of Tshing's residents, he was extremely poor, but by giving private lessons to help top up his mother's wages, he soon became known in the township as a man who was educated, well read, worldly, and worthy of respect, and also as a good neighbor and compatriot—"one of us." Nobody here had known him before—he was actually a stranger in Tshing.

Most of Tshing's residents were Tswana, whereas he was one of the Xhosa people, from the eastern and southern coasts of

Africa. His father had travelled to Transvaal in search of a living, and had found a job on a farm less than twenty kilometers
from Ventersdorp. He and his family had settled on the white
farmer's land. He had only rarely ventured to the town to buy
things, and had made even fewer trips to Tshing. He had nothing to do there, and no friends. He didn't even have to take
his sons to school there, because the white farmers told their
workers to send their children to the schools that they opened
specially for them on their properties.

As a result, the farm laborers had nothing in common with
the blacks living in Tshing, and there was even hostility between them. Envying the laborers for their permanent jobs and
guaranteed income, the township dwellers also despised them
for being at the mercy of the white farmers, carrying out all
their orders, and letting themselves be treated like livestock,
like slaves—for being good kaffirs.

When Mbambalala's father died, and the white farmer told
them to get out, the family didn't go to Tshing, where they knew
nobody, but to distant relatives living in a black township in
Johannesburg. Only when his mother was hired as a domestic
by white people in Klerksdorp had the entire family moved to
Tshing. They had rented a hut made of planks and corrugated
iron in one of the yards, with no electricity, water, or toilet.

Meshack Mbambalala was no different from the other paupers in the township. He didn't know anyone there, and nobody
knew him. Only when he started going about the neighbors'
houses, teaching their children, did he gain their respect. People
liked the fact that he didn't drink or even smoke.

The trust he inspired didn't escape the notice of the local
ANC leaders. Although they were young—Benny Tapologo
and his friends—they were eager to take power locally; the old-

er residents of Tshing hadn't forgiven them for the fuss, riots, and strikes, and regarded them as hooligans, not revolutionaries. The ANC authorities were not at all certain that when faced with a choice between the young black rebels and the experienced white administrators, the residents of Tshing might not vote for the latter.

Mbambalala hadn't taken part in the uprising. He was older than Benny, and had been to university, which appealed to the older people. Even when he said he was a communist, they burst out laughing and patted him on the back appreciatively, as if he'd told a good joke. It never occurred to them that Mbambalala could be saying it seriously, or that someone educated, intelligent, and so well mannered, could be a communist.

With his erudition, moderate views, and conciliatory style he even endeared himself to the whites in the town whose mayor he was going to be. As he hadn't worked for any of them, it seemed they would accept his candidacy more easily than if a kaffir were going to move into the town hall who only the day before had been tanking up their cars or handing them goods in the store.

That was also the view of the ANC envoys who came from Johannesburg to persuade their party comrades in Tshing that the best candidate for the first black mayor of Ventersdorp would be Meshack Mbambalala. When he learned what task the party had decided to entrust to him, he ran to the local library to flick through some books and find out what exactly a mayor did.

When his victory was announced, he delayed moving from his hut in Tshing to the town hall. He fobbed off questions about it with jokes. He said he simply felt better in Tshing—this was his home, and he had no reason to look for another one. He was afraid that the large house and garden, which belonged to the mayor, wouldn't be his palace, but his prison. If he let himself be shut in it, he would lose his freedom, lose his connection with the people in the township, and would stop understanding them.

"I don't want anyone to think it's just about having a house with a swimming pool," he kept saying.

Sometimes he let himself be carried away by fears and lack of faith in his own abilities.

"Why did I let them persuade me?" Tall, thin, and shy, with glasses on his nose, he looked more like a student facing a difficult exam than a politician. "I just wanted to be a schoolteacher."

However, he didn't complain about his fate in front of me; he seemed to forget I was there, or maybe as dusk fell I simply vanished out of sight, with the remains of the closing day. He went on talking to himself, in the darkness, which was only lit and enlivened by the flame of a candle flickering on the table.

As she clattered pots on a fire-blackened cast-iron hotplate, Mbambalala's mother listened in on our conversation.

"Why did you take it up at all? You're too gentle, you're too scared of everything."

"Don't worry, I'll manage," he replied as usual.

He was hoping his mother wouldn't hear the rumors the whites in Ventersdorp were spreading about him, that he was a drunk and a troublemaker, who had been in prison for theft and couldn't read or write. He himself had read articles in the Afrikaner press saying he'd stolen cattle from white farms, and cruised around the neighborhood in a car while drunk. He had never stolen a thing, and he didn't drink alcohol, or smoke tobacco. Nor did he have a car—he didn't even know how to drive.

He'd been getting threatening letters and phone calls since before the election. Some police officers had come to his house from Ventersdorp and advised him to be careful, because he had enemies in the town who wanted to get rid of him. They might just falsely accuse him of a crime, to have him excluded from the election at the last moment, making it impossible to find a replacement. But they might also set his house on fire at night. Or they might catch him and beat him like a mangy dog, to frighten him, force him into subservience, and turn the future mayor into a submissive puppet. Or they might even try to kill him, but so that it looked like the result of an ordinary fight of the kind that often occurred between blacks. They'd hire an assassin, and then get rid of him, to hush things up.

At first Mbambalala was grateful to the policemen for the warning, but once they had left, he started wondering if it might have been a threat. The day after the election, when it was clear he had won, his friends informed him that Eugène Terre'Blanche was questioning blacks in town about him.

That evening in the bar at the local hotel in Ventersdorp, everyone already knew I had been to the black township and had spoken to the mayor. In those days the hotel bar was still the only place in town where you could relax by listening to the jukebox, have a beer or a whisky, meet people, and swap gossip and news.

The Blue Crane tavern, which Henk Malan had opened, was still going, not far from the hotel, but after dark it was totally abandoned.

"It's a shebeen, a bar for blacks, not for you," said Jannie the barman, putting a frosted bottle of Castle beer on the counter. "Whites don't drink there. They drink at my place. You too, if the fancy takes you, should come here."

Apart from whisky and beer, Jannie served cocktails for

which he made up his own names. He especially recommended the Multiracial and the Bloody Nelson.

"People are saying you've been to see our mayor," put in a mustachioed man sitting at the bar in heavy cotton shorts and work boots.

He bunched up his hair, which was being blown around by a fan whirring above the bar.

"Kobie! Hey, Kobie!" he called toward a group of men throwing darts at a target hanging on the wall. "What's our new mayor called?"

"The kaffir?" asked Kobie, coming over to the bar. "Who'd remember those names of theirs?"

"Bambo. He's called Bambo," replied one of the darts players.

"Bamboo!"

"Black mamba!"

The gales of laughter and words bellowed not just from the dartboard, but also from the billiard table and the bar, crossed in the air, drowning out the music from the jukebox. The fun seemed to be hotting up. The delighted Jannie put another mug of beer on the counter.

"So black people don't come to your bar?" I asked.

"Oh yes they do! And how!" he replied. "The cleaning woman comes every morning. And a black guy brings the beer barrels too."

The men at the bar roared with laughter.

"So what did you talk to our kaffir mayor about?" asked the mustachioed man in shorts.

The silence that suddenly hung in the air was crackling with curiosity and now barely concealed irritation.

"You know he's been in jail?" said Jannie, wiping mugs with a cloth. "He got drunk and knifed a guy."

"He's not just a moron, he's a criminal too," added Kobie, prodding me with a finger. "Who'd have thought we'd have a kaffir as mayor here? Everything's going to the dogs."

Suddenly, as if awoken from a trance, the men in the bar forgot about the black mayor and went back to playing darts and billiards, and to chatting quietly over their beer mugs. Music from the speakers filled the smoky bar again.

"The blacks don't want to come to my bar," said Jannie. "I can't prohibit them anymore, but they prefer to drink at their places. And things are fine as they are."

The mustachioed man in shorts took a pistol from his belt.

"I carry it just in case a black ever tries to take my car off me or break into my house. He'd get a lesson for the rest of his life," he said, laying the gun on the counter. "I'm not saying we're better than them. They might be richer than I am, live better, or drive better cars. I might even do business with them. But I don't want them coming to pray at my church or buying houses in my neighborhood. I don't want to live with them. My Bible forbids it."

In the evenings before the election that deprived the whites of government locally and nationally, members of the white brotherhood had sat around in the hotel bar. Eugène Terre'Blanche himself was often to be found here too.

"Eugène?" said Jannie in surprise. "I haven't seen him for ages."

He said he didn't know anyone who belonged to the AWB, though a year ago the white brotherhood had bossed the town around.

"Who'd remember that?" he said, waving dismissively. "Ancient history."

As representative of the town's whites, Piet Terre'Blanche was meant to be deputy to the black mayor, Mbambalala.

"The surnames are just a coincidence," he explained as soon as we met. "Eugène and I are not related."

Unable to wait for his boss, Piet Terre'Blanche was working away at the town hall, in his own comfortable office with a phone and a leather armchair. He had a secretary to whom he assigned tasks, and who organized his official agenda. One of the walls of his office was decorated with a large flag representing the independent Boer republic of Transvaal, its colors a reminder of the recently lowered flags of white South Africa.

"We have met with this Mr. Mbambalala. Excuse me, but I can't remember his first name," he said when I questioned him about the mayor and his lack of hurry to move to the town hall. "He made an excellent impression on me. I think he's a very sensible fellow. I really don't know what's keeping him in Tshing, he must have his reasons. But I'm sure we'll be fine working together."

He snorted with laughter when I asked if he thought the black mayor was afraid to take over the administration in the white town.

"Where do you get that idea? He's not in any danger here."

His gaze automatically strayed to the window, and the view of the town outside. Despite the abolition of the racial segregation laws, not many blacks had moved to the white area.

"I heard lately a local teacher fellow and a couple of others bought houses in town," he said. "But nobody saw them moving in, so it may just be hearsay. If the blacks don't buy houses in Ventersdorp it's because they can't afford to, not because they're afraid."

The whites I spoke to in the town kept saying that if anyone had a reason to be afraid of the new order, it was they, and not the blacks.

"To tell the truth, we don't know much about our black

neighbors, we're not acquainted with them, we don't know what they're like. We Afrikaners aren't against them having a better life now. But not at our cost. Have you seen how they live in Tshing? Totally differently from how we live here. Here people care about cleanliness, order, and security. They're afraid that under a black administration the town will soon start to look like their ghetto."

Piet Terre'Blanche didn't know much about the white brotherhood whose leader was his compatriot and namesake, Eugène.

In his view, the AWB had ceased to function after the elections that surrendered power to the blacks.

"The white brotherhood?" he said in surprise. "It's just gossip."

As he showed me to the door, he assured me that he was convinced things would go well in town, it would all work out fine.

"Please come and see us again. Maybe not in a year or two, but in four or five," he said. "We'll welcome you to the Afrikaner republic."

"And what'll become of Mayor Mbambalala then?"

"I'm sure he'll still be mayor," said Piet Terre'Blanche. "Mayor for the blacks."

It was the first cup of coffee he'd ever received from the hands of a white person. His secretary brought it to him on a tray. One by one, she put a saucer, then a china cup the color of ivory, a sugar bowl, and a milk jug on his desk.

"Would you like a sponge finger?" she asked.

"No, thank you very much," said Benny Tapologo, shifting nervously in his chair.

Never before had any white person ever served him, carried out his orders, or asked his permission. Once it had been his dream, but now he felt awkward as the secretary knocked gently at the door of his office, and once invited in, asked if he wanted tea or coffee. He had asked for coffee.

"Black or white?"

She had surprised him with that question. And then at once it occurred to him that it might by chance be an allusion. In those days an innocent question about the color of your coffee could have a political subtext.

"White, please," he spluttered.

"Of course," she said, and once again Benny was beset with doubts in case there were hidden irony and hostility behind the white woman's courtesy.

He was the first black man to have his own office as a town councillor in the town hall in white Ventersdorp. Apart from Benny and four other councillors elected in the free election, all the other blacks at the town hall served as secretaries, messengers, cleaners, and guards, who bowed low and got out of the way with humble, ingratiating smiles stuck to their faces. They reminded him of his father begging the farmers for work and scrambling clumsily into the beds of their pickups.

Years later, Benny could still remember his first day at the town hall. He had been filled with joy, pride, and a desire for revenge.

"I looked at those white officials in the corridors and thought to myself: now it's my turn, now I'm going to be the boss around here, and you're going to listen to me. Who wouldn't want to get their own back for all those years when they treated us like thin air, nobodies, kaffirs? And now the kaffirs were going to be in charge. I'm not at all surprised they were afraid."

He liked casting his mind back to those days. Whenever we met at his office in the new town hall, he always set a date and a time slot he could devote to me. But our conversations always went over the set limits, and my audience with him was never interrupted by any clients or official business.

"Many of the whites couldn't bear the sight of us and turned away to avoid encounters. But there were some who tried to help us, explaining what to do and how. Probably out of fear that we wouldn't know how to do anything and would ruin it all."

If the votes cast in the election were all that counted, there would be nobody but blacks from Tshing at Ventersdorp town hall. However, in striking a bargain over the division of power, Mandela and de Klerk had established that to mitigate the shock to the whites after losing power, for some time they would have guaranteed influence in parliaments, and district and town councils.

In Ventersdorp, apart from Mbambalala and Tapologo, three other blacks had joined the town council, including Kabelo Mashi, Benny's friend who had been joint leader of the street revolt in Tshing. The other four councillors were white. It had also been decided that the new mayor would take a white as his deputy. The white officials responsible for the functioning of the town were to keep their jobs at the town hall. They were to train the blacks for the job, and until the new staff had gained proficiency, they were to make sure the trash was collected, the water system was running, and that in general everything was working properly.

The victory had been won, and after it there was to be a period of dividing the spoils and overturning the old order—or so at least the young people from the township, such as Benny and Kabelo Mashi, were hoping. With envy and fire in their eyes, they watched the television news as black members of parliament in

Cape Town took down portraits of the former white rulers and heroes, had their busts put away and their statues removed.

Apart from some modest memorials on tombs in the old cemetery, there were two others in Ventersdorp—the triumphal arch in honor of the first white settlers, and the black marble obelisk erected in memory of the seven members of the AWB killed during local riots and in the unsuccessful raid on Bophuthatswana. Both stood in the square outside the town hall, the headquarters and symbol of the local authorities. The young people from the ghetto wanted to blow up the white brotherhood's monument, just that one at least. They couldn't imagine having to go on staring at the evidence of their own humiliation, downfall, and injury from their office windows.

Although he himself had often had to run away from Afrikaner Resistance Movement squads, Mbambalala had no thought of knocking down the monument.

"They're just as much part of the town's history as we are. They have a right to their monuments, just as we do to ours," he explained, straightening his wire spectacles with a fingertip. "And the white brotherhood is a thing of the past—it died along with the old order."

With each day farther away from the election and the great victory, Benny lost patience with Mbambalala. More and more often Benny suspected him of being a common coward rather than a cautious politician. He was even starting to wonder why the people in Johannesburg had chosen somebody like that to be the new mayor. Probably not merely to leave everything in the town as it was, just put a black mayor in the town hall but not change anything else, and do nothing that might annoy the Afrikaners.

These thoughts occurred to him each morning as he passed

the white brotherhood monument on his way to his office. Each morning there were fresh white flowers at the foot of it.

After the election the white brotherhood disappeared from Ventersdorp. There were no more torchlit rallies, no more processions or fairs, and Eugène Terre'Blanche closed the party office located in his own home.

In fact Terre'Blanche himself vanished too. He left Ventersdorp the night before the election and hid away at the family farm. He had no wish to watch his own defeat. He stopped answering the phone, and wouldn't let his wife or adopted daughter answer it either. He wasn't accepting any invitations or arranging any meetings. He didn't want to see or speak to anyone.

He even stopped talking to the journalists, whom he'd been happy to have around him before now. Suddenly they'd started to annoy him. They weren't taking him seriously anymore, not even when he warned that the end of the world was nigh; they twisted his words and his name, calling him "ET," like the alien in the American movie then on release.

After Ventersdorp's black mayor was sworn in, unable to reach Terre'Blanche on the phone, I decided to go find him at the farm, expecting him to receive me and spend an evening talking to me.

I passed the black township, and beyond a crossroads I drove straight on, down the road to Klerksdorp. The veld, flat and even, starts to undulate here, rising and falling between hills dotted with groves of eucalyptus and acacia trees. Gray and yellow like dried grass, in summer it took on vivid shades of green and a full figure.

Terre'Blanche's farm lay behind a hill, separating it from the surfaced road to Klerksdorp. The first to inherit the place from their father was the oldest son, Andries. But he didn't have the soul of a farmer or cattle breeder, and had sold it to Eugène. He didn't feel a vocation for it either, but he kept the land because he thought it suited the image of a Boer settler and patriot that he was building for himself.

As I drove to his farm, I was mentally forming the questions I wanted to put to him. He must have had a crushing sense of defeat. He was bound to feel humiliated, bitter, and angry. Everyone had abandoned and betrayed him.

All his plans had gone wrong. He had failed to disrupt negotiations with the blacks and the election that had put them in charge of the country. His plan for twenty-one Afrikaner-governed towns in western Transvaal to announce a unilateral declaration of independence and secession on the day of the election hadn't worked.

To the very end he had been hassling the Zulu king Goodwill Zwelethini to prohibit his subjects from voting. But by tempting the Zulus with a share in the government, Mandela had persuaded them to cast their votes and renounce their own kingdom. Yet why should Terre'Blanche be counting on the Zulus, when the Afrikaners themselves weren't listening to him, but to Viljoen, who was promising to protect them from war and to secure them a state of their own, separate from the blacks? He was boasting that Mandela himself had made him a promise, and that he would achieve their purpose without any fighting, unlike Terre'Blanche, who wanted to shed blood for it.

I wanted to ask what he planned to do next. "What mistakes have you made in your political calculations?" Did he still think the only salvation for the Afrikaners was to establish their own white state in Africa? As the assumption of power by the blacks hadn't triggered violent conflict, maybe the whites would be able to live with them in a shared country after all? And what had changed in the town since a black mayor had been running it? "Have you really dissolved the white brotherhood?"

The gate from the side road into the farm was standing wide open. As I drove up to the house, I caught sight of Terre'Blanche. Dressed in the sort of dirty overalls worn by black farm laborers, he was shifting some heavy sacks from the back of a pickup truck.

Hearing the engine and seeing a stranger, an uninvited guest, he stopped work and reached into the cab for a shotgun.

"Get out! You're on my land!" he shouted.

"I just want to ask you some questions," I replied. "We've spoken before now."

"Wolf! Saldhana!" he called his dogs, two German shepherds. "Get him!"

The Boardmans farmed seven hundred hectares outside Ventersdorp. Raymond's grandfather had bought Buckingham farm, which was more than three hundred hectares in size, almost a hundred years ago from one Harry Munday. Raymond's father had bought more than twice as much land again from the local Methodist church, to which the Boardmans belonged. That farm had been called Uitkyk, which in Afrikaans meant "View," in the sense of "landscape," as well as "prospect," or "view of the future." It was on this farm that some black strangers had appeared and set up camp.

Raymond's workers came to tell him about it.

"Raymie! Raymie! There are some black strangers occupying the farm!" cried Tsepe, out of breath.

Petrus, outrun because he was older and slower, silently waited to answer Raymond's questions. He knew the farmer would ask him to explain, not young Tsepe. Petrus and Raymond were contemporaries who had grown up on the farm together. Raymond, the farmer's son, was learning to run the place. Petrus, son of a rural laborer who had worked on the Boardman's farm, now had to work for Raymond, just as his father had for old Mr. Boardman.

"Did you see them, Petrus? Are there a lot of them?"

He nodded in silence.

"What sort of people are they? Did they say anything?"

"None of our guys has ever seen any of them before. Nobody saw them arrive. Only yesterday William didn't see anyone on his way back from town, but this morning they were there. About twenty, with women and children."

Raymond went alone. He knew that before Uitkyk had become the property of the Methodist church, and later the Boardmans, some blacks had lived there, but they'd been evicted in keeping with apartheid. Now they had evidently returned.

He pulled over and stopped on the dirt road. From the hill he had a clear view of Uitkyk and the black people's shacks. He'd always been amazed how quickly they could cobble together primitive huts, at the speed of light, out of nothing. And he was even more amazed at how long they were able to live in these improvised dwellings. They seemed to prefer adapting to discomfort than changing, perfecting, or modernizing anything, as if they didn't believe in anything that could last, or to show that making an effort wasn't worth the bother.

From the road on the hill Raymond saw the smoke of bonfires rising in a white screen among branches spread low to the ground. He was a few hundred meters away from the squatter camp on the opposite slope of a shallow gorge. He could hear voices, distorted and fragmented by the wind.

Leaving his car unlocked by the road, he headed downhill across the meadow. After last night's rain the ground was as red as blood, soft and springy. It yielded beneath his feet, as if about to cave in and suck him under, making him quicken his pace spontaneously.

The thought that in just a moment those people would easily be able to see him on the veld made him stop. He wasn't ready for this encounter yet. They were bound to regard his inactivity as a sign of weakness and fear, readiness to capitulate, which could only encourage them, and frustrate everything he was planning to do.

He turned round, and as he was walking back to the road, he impulsively grabbed at blades of grass, thistles, and herbs. Crushed in his fingers they emitted a warm, heady scent full of mystery and magic, stirring memories of his childhood on the farm, and bringing back that illusory sense of power over time and destiny.

Once on the road, he glanced at the sky, looking for clouds heralding another downpour that night. It flashed through his mind that the rain would soak the people occupying Uitkyk. But the afternoon sky was clear and bright; the only marks in its flawless blue were the black shadows of falcons and snake eagles, nervously hovering above the windswept veld.

When he moved to the farm from Pretoria, in neighboring Zimbabwe on the other side of the Limpopo River, the blacks had just taken the land away from the whites, who had originally deprived them of it many years before. Squads armed with clubs, machetes, and rifles had attacked and occupied the white farms, dragging the owners out of their houses and telling them to get out. If they met with resistance, they inflicted violence, beat up the farmers, their wives and children, killed the dogs guarding the farmyard, and set fire to the farmhouses and other buildings.

Summoned to help, the police came too late or didn't come at all. At the sight of the combatants, who were brought to the white farms on government trucks, the police had shut themselves away in their stations and let the phone ring, to avoid having to listen to people begging to be rescued. Beaten up and maligned, with no hope of any help, the white farmers had run away from their estates, packing into their vehicles only the most vital objects nearest to hand. They drove off to the cities, abandoning everything that they and their ancestors had achieved.

Everyone on either side of the Limpopo knew that the attackers were supported and encouraged by the Zimbabwean president, Robert Mugabe. Just like South Africa, before being handed over to the blacks, Zimbabwe had belonged to the whites; there too racial segregation had been in force, and the best land had belonged to the whites. When the blacks took power, their president had assured the whites that as long as they served him loyally, not a hair would fall from their heads. So they'd kept their farms, estates, large houses, golf courses, and private clubs, where they went on meeting up for a game of tennis or a glass of whisky as before.

Finally they came to regard the aging black president as tame and harmless. They felt so confident that they started to criticize him, ridicule him, and help his enemies to get rid of him and put a more tractable new president in his place. They had underestimated the old one. Suddenly attacked, he retaliated furiously, like a wounded beast. He summoned his former rebels to the capital and also some young combatants, who couldn't recall the days of war against the whites, and ordered them to invade the farms. He gave them free rein.

As he was making the final preparations to move back to the farm, Raymond Boardman had seen a report from Zimbabwe on the television news, showing petrified white farmers covered in blood, expelled from their own homes and farms, farmyards burning, and black aggressors singing combat songs and dancing around the flames.

Although these scenes filled him with horror, they also attracted him with a force he couldn't resist, absorbing him entirely. He was careful not to miss a single TV news bulletin, and once they were over, he switched to foreign channels in the hope of seeing more, or at least watching and experiencing it all again.

"Haven't you thought better of it yet? Do you still want to move back to the farm?" asked his neighbors and workmates in Pretoria. "It's going to be just the same here. It's just a matter of time. One day they'll take away your land and tell you to get out."

Many of them originally came from the Transvaal veld and still had relatives and burial grounds there. They had left for the big cities so long ago that by now they'd forgotten what life was like in the countryside, or even in towns such as Ventersdorp. So, at least, thought Raymond, who despite moving to Cape Town and Pretoria had never broken his ties with his old life. With the superiority of an experienced, knowledgeable man, he explained to his friends and neighbors how very different Zimbabwe was from their country, and how wrong it was to compare them.

He believed that what had happened on the northern banks of the Limpopo would be a lesson to those living south of it. Seeing Zimbabwe's collapse as clear as day, South Africa's black government wouldn't dare to displace the white farmers. They in turn, not wanting to lose everything like the whites across the Limpopo, would understand that they would have to stop being greedy and share their property, wisdom, and experience with the blacks. That was exactly what he was going back to the family farm in Transvaal to do.

Events across the border and the attacks on whites that he had seen on the TV news only confirmed the conviction that he had made the right choice. The major change of order that was occurring right before their eyes set new rules, he said, and those who kept them would survive. But those who didn't understand, or rejected them, would be condemning themselves to disaster.

One day at work, when he was talking about the move to the farm, on hearing the name Ventersdorp, one of his colleagues asked about Eugène Terre'Blanche.

"You're still going to pay for him," he said.

"Not everyone in our town is like Eugène," replied Raymond.

"Maybe not. But that's how everyone thinks about you."

"Actually in Ventersdorp people know who's really who," said Boardman. "But our blacks have never had a reason to complain. We've treated them well, and they've always had a better life with us than with other white farmers."

"And you think they're going to be grateful to you for that now? You think they'll defend you?"

Boardman had read in the papers about the murders of white farmers in Transvaal. They were happening more and more often, almost every week, and they were all committed with inconceivable, particular cruelty. These were not ordinary robberies. It looked as if theft, arson, and even killing were not enough for the attackers, but as if they only felt sated by their victims' suffering.

Experts on crime asserted in the papers that the attacks on

the farms were only to do with robbery, and were in no way different from the wave of muggings that had flooded the big cities when the old order collapsed and the new one had not yet been enforced, gaining South Africa a global reputation as a land of crime. They said the only reason for the cruelty the criminals inflicted on their victims was that the farms were so isolated.

Scattered widely across the veld, far apart and a long way out of town, their owners couldn't count on being rescued. The way their borders were designed, from one farmstead you couldn't see the smoke from the neighbor's chimney. Here, by contrast with the populous urban districts, the attackers didn't have to hurry or worry about help coming for their victims. They only had to overpower the white farmers and their families, ordinary people of advanced age, to carry out a robbery slowly and methodically, and to feast on cruelty and the power provided by violence.

In one of the papers Raymond had read that in most cases the persecutors and their victims had known each other in person. "All this is about more than just stealing money and cars," the journalists were told by a white farmer from Transvaal who lived next door to a farm that had been attacked. "If it were just about money, why would they torture people like that? Before they shattered my neighbor's skull with a bullet, they smashed his knees with a hammer. And they poured boiling water over his wife's head, although she's an old woman who couldn't even think of defending herself."

"You think your blacks will defend you?" As he drove home from the occupied Uitkyk farm, Raymond remembered his friend's question. He rolled down the window to let the balmy scent of grass, wildflowers, and herbs into the car.

At the time he had replied that life in the city was far more dangerous than in the countryside. But did he really believe that by removing his family from the big city to the farm he'd be guaranteeing them safety? And that he'd be able to count on his own black workers, who had a better life at the Boardmans than other whites in the neighborhood would have given them?

Nothing bad had happened in the Ventersdorp area, but white farms had been attacked in other parts of Transvaal, and also in Orange Free State, and more often than that fires had broken out, consuming fields of ripe maize, tobacco, and sunflowers, and sometimes cowsheds, barns, stables, granaries, and farmhouses too. Nobody knew who was setting fire to the veld. As he drove along the N14 highway from Johannesburg to the farm, Raymond passed signs along the way prohibiting the lighting of bonfires on the roadside verges.

On the television news, which he watched as avidly as cricket, he saw some young Zulus in Natal, dressed in animal skins and feather headdresses, waving spears about as they danced at an occupied farm, just like the vigilantes in Zimbabwe. "*Iswelethu!*" they sang. "The land belongs to us!"

Raymond Boardman was mentally preparing for the blacks to appear on his land too. Their leaders in the townships had been inciting the poor to demand their rights by occupying white farms without waiting for the government, court decisions, or agricultural reform. Rather than prompting anger or fear, the sight of strangers at Uitkyk had made him feel relieved—the inevitable had now happened, so he wouldn't have to keep watching out for it, and the anticipation and uncertainty were finally over.

He turned off the dirt road into the driveway leading to Buckingham. Petrus, Tsepe and the other workers had seen his car in the distance, and were waiting in the yard. As he drove up, they made way for him, but immediately came up to the car to hear what he would say.

"Move the big tractor from the barn to the gate," he told Petrus. "Nobody's driven it for ages, so you'll have to check the oil. Take William with you—he knows what to do."

Petrus nodded.

"Tomorrow we'll get on with mending the fence along the railroad tracks. The holes in it are so big the cattle can get out of the pasture and all the way to Potchefstroom. Once you've got the tractor started, take people with you and go to town to buy some wire netting."

Petrus agreed with a smile.

Seeing how the workers carried out his instructions and went back to their familiar, everyday tasks, the established status quo, Raymond felt calm and relieved.

I met her at the bank on one of my trips to Ventersdorp. Small and thin, with her hair cut short, she was standing beside me in the line for the next window. Her figure, the look on her face and in her eyes, emanated strength, confidence, and determination, the hallmarks of a person of deep faith, who firmly believes their own views are right.

I joked that I'd never stop thanking Divine Providence for inventing money transfers, which always got me out of trouble at the other end of the world.

"We should all never stop thanking the Lord for everything he gives us in his bounty," she said. "For every day we have. For every safe homecoming."

Like everyone here, she immediately recognized me as an outsider, a foreigner. Just about everything betrayed the strangers in this town: their license plates, accent, behavior, clothes, hairstyle, glasses frame, and even their brand of cigarettes.

She didn't tell me she was Eugène Terre'Blanche's sister, and as I didn't know to whom I was talking, I didn't mention that I'd come there to find her brother.

A few days later, as I was trying to find Terre'Blanche's farm, I got lost among the farm tracks, and drove up to one of the neighboring homesteads to ask the way. The gate was opened for me by a tall white man with bow legs, in riding breeches and boots.

"The name's Don van Zyl," he introduced himself. "I know about you. You met my wife at the bank."

Van Zyl was married to Dora, Terre'Blanche's favorite sister, and his farm was on the opposite side of the valley. Brought up in Ventersdorp and on the family farm, in her youth Dora had left for the identical town of Sannieshof, where she found not just a job as a teacher, but also a husband. She had stopped working at the school when the black government took over; from then on, black children would attend the same classes as the white ones. She said she wasn't going to teach blacks.

She and her husband returned to Ventersdorp, where they bought a piece of land bordering the family farm, and founded an Arab horse stud. They lived by selling saddle horses and riding lessons, which Dora gave.

The Boers had always been proud of their superb horsemanship. They were said to have been born in the saddle. They had crossed mountains, deserts, and the boundless veld on horseback on their long trek from the Cape of Good Hope to the Limpopo River and the shores of the Indian Ocean to found their own independent republics there. And when the British went to war against them, for many long years the Boer partisan cavalry had hounded the imperial regiments hunting them down on the veld. Horse-riding skills were virtually inscribed in the Boers' national identity, an integral part of their history and tradition.

Like all the Terre'Blanches, Dora had always been an excellent rider. Before he met his future wife, Don hadn't been too good at riding, but in time he had learned, and even Dora praised him for sitting well in the saddle.

"It wasn't easy to join a family like that one," said van Zyl, as he showed me about the farm.

He was as tall as a beanpole, and so thin that his riding breeches were hanging off him like a sack. The farmhouse, furniture, and fittings were modest, simple, and inexpensive.

"We've always lived modestly here, we're not used to comforts," he explained apologetically. "And now times have become so unsure that we hardly ever buy anything for the house at all."

Dora joined us in a break between riding lessons. She greeted me politely, but without letting it show if she remembered me, her chance interlocutor at the bank. She behaved as if we'd never seen each other before, but at the same time as if she'd been expecting my visit.

"Eugène isn't a racist, he's never regarded the blacks as inferior, just as another species. They're different from us, the same way white is different from black or any other color," she said, handing me a glass of chilled lemonade. "Our black servants were always treated well. None of them ever ran away."

She said the Terre'Blanches belonged to the Boer nation. "Not Afrikaners, but Boers," she stressed. Almost all the whites in Ventersdorp and in Transvaal regarded themselves as Boers too. According to Dora van Zyl, to be an Afrikaner, it was enough to use the Afrikaans language and be a good Christian, a Calvinist. Whereas only those who declared themselves in favor of freedom, racial separation, and an independent Boer state could call themselves Boers—only those who wouldn't tolerate any alien higher authority, neither black nor British.

The Boers had fought wars for their freedom, whereas wealth and comforts were enough for the Afrikaners. The Boers called themselves the white tribe of Africa, and behaved like an African tribe. The Afrikaners were ashamed of being African, and envied the Europeans, modeling themselves on them, trying at any cost to be like them, and always seeking their approval. According to Dora, de Klerk and Viljoen were among the Afrikaners whom the Boers regarded as traitors and capitulators. She called them Judases.

"They believed someone was going to give them their own state and liberty!" she said, with a smile of pity. "Only total morons would let themselves be taken in like that."

In order to exist, a nation needs land, its own place under the sun. The Creator had assigned Africa to the Boers as their place. When they first came to the African continent, the Boers hadn't taken the land from anyone, they hadn't stolen or robbed. They had bought it from the local chiefs, and had mainly occupied unclaimed or deserted territory, abandoned because of wars, epidemics, drought, or floods. It wasn't the Boers who had taken other people's land and liberty, but they themselves who had been deprived of those things by the greedy, perfidious British.

"They deliberately sent black soldiers against us in the war to put us on a par with them. Boer women and children died of disease and starvation in concentration camps, and pigs dug up the partisans' bodies from their graves because there wasn't any wood for coffins and the dead were buried in canvas," she said, cataloguing the wrongs done to the Boers. "And when the British finally beat us, they took all the best jobs and land for themselves, leaving the Boers to a life of humiliation and adversity."

The only people to resign themselves to it were the traitors who went across to the Afrikaner camp. The real Boers had never stopped dreaming of freedom and their own state.

"Eugène embodies all the most authentic and valuable features of us Boers. All of us in this town supported him, listened to him and applauded him. But when it came to the test, on election day, they all turned away from him. They betrayed him."

Henk Malan felt betrayed too. Betrayed by Eugène Terre-Blanche.

"The only real leaders are in the army," he said one morning to his stepson Frank. "They're the only ones you can trust."

He liked the boy's company and took him along whenever he had something to do. Henk was regarded locally as a loner and a hothead, quick to quarrel and fight. He had never had many friends here, and after the election and the change of power he only hung out with Frank. He'd spend days on end with the boy, talking to him alone, or rather lecturing him for hours at a time. Frank just listened without ever interrupting or asking any questions.

Henk liked to reminisce about his years in the army, especially when he went to the war in Angola. He put it about town that he'd fought in lots of battles and served in a commando unit—a team of killers assigned to particularly tough and dangerous missions. He never said it directly, but implied that he'd looked death in the eye and knew what it was to kill.

"Not everyone's suited to it," he told Frank, narrowing his clear blue eyes meaningfully. "It's not as easy as it looks."

Very few of the locals believed these stories. It seemed to them strange that such a seasoned soldier had simply been discharged from the army and had to look for work on the railroad, where in the days of apartheid jobs were set aside for white paupers, losers, and castaways who couldn't shift for themselves in life.

"We had real leaders out there, in the bush. Everything was in its place, a man knew what he had to do, and that the guys giving the orders knew what they were doing too. You only had to carry out the orders—the rest of it wasn't your problem," he told Frank. "But these civilians . . . What a waste of breath. Tub-thumping loudmouths! They told us to gear up for war against the blacks. But when it came to it, they took to their heels, and a man was left to deal with all this alone. Now they're not bothered anymore. Manage for yourself, man! And if you don't know how, tough!"

After the blacks had taken over nationally and locally, Henk made lots more visits to the police station near the town hall to ask about the guy who'd been beaten up on election night. The policemen shrugged. They had no news of the missing man, and seemed to have forgotten the whole incident.

"Is he a relative of yours or something?" they said, surprised by Henk's concern. "Don't worry, if he survived he'll find you. He'll come and repay you."

And one day Henk found out from the policemen that Eugène Terre'Blanche had applied to the black authorities for an amnesty for himself and the other AWB members for the bombs planted on election day and the earlier attacks in Johannesburg and Bophuthatswana. In a letter to Mandela, Eugène wrote that he wasn't asking for impunity for common criminal acts, murder, assault, or rape, but for armed action, resulting from the struggle for freedom, which each man conceived in his own way. There was a war going on, asserted Terre'Blanche, so the white brotherhood should be seen as equal to the black rebels who fought for the abolition of apartheid. Hadn't the black rebels planted bombs in white cities? Hadn't Mandela himself, before being locked away, incited war? "*Wat is verby—verby. The past is the past,*" he wrote to Mandela.

Henk was bursting with anger. Always excitable and quick-tempered, in those days he kept getting into rows and starting fights. Even in his own home, where in fits of rage he flew at his stepson and wife with his fists. He decided to leave Ventersdorp and join his brother, who lived in Goshen, and was always encouraging him to move there. He spoke highly of this place, which a hundred years ago had briefly been declared an independent Boer republic. His brother swore that the blacks would never take charge in Goshen.

Henk was itching to leave. He kept saying there was no point in waiting, and that he couldn't stay here any longer. He started looking for a buyer for his house. He found it impossible to stay put, and felt compelled to keep moving. He would walk into the town and wander around it restlessly, as if going out to meet something. He would accost people, or tour the bars, as if constantly checking up on something, and endlessly repeating that it was impossible to live under such stress. One day he brought home a buyer, and tried to sell him the house for almost half its value. At this point his wife Anita, who so far had endured it all quietly, put her foot down and opposed both the sale and the move. Luckily, the house was half her property.

Nor did she want to move away from Ventersdorp, where she had been born and was so firmly rooted that she couldn't imagine living anywhere else. She worked as a clerk at the town hall, and didn't want to lose her job. She said that as the blacks were going to run the whole country, sooner or later they'd take over in Goshen too. So better stick to what you know, she explained, than go racing after the unknown.

"What are you so desperate to run away from?" she asked.

She was sure that if he was so scared of the blacks, then with her job at the town hall and her contacts, she could help both of them to find their place in the new times. She said life would be easier for them in Ventersdorp than anywhere else. But Henk only agreed to stay when he got the chance to buy the Blue Crane tavern from Anton, Anita's first husband.

It was he who had opened the bar on the road into town, counting on it being an easy place to make money. He ran the bar with his daughter, but when she got married and fell pregnant, she told him she wasn't going to sit among clouds of cigarette smoke and drunks a moment longer. Anton realized that he couldn't keep the business going on his own, but he didn't want to go into partnership with a stranger. So he sold the bar to his ex-wife and her husband.

Although they had taken over the administration in Ventersdorp and moved their mayor and councillors into the town hall, the blacks didn't have a bar of their own in the town where they could meet up and have a drink without fear of being refused service, or not admitted at all. The Blue Crane tavern suited them down to the ground. It wasn't conspicuous, and it didn't aggravate those of the whites who were finding it hardest to come to terms with the end of racial segregation.

When Henk went to the town hall to extend the alcohol license for the premises, Anita persuaded him to specify in the application that he planned to run a tavern for blacks. She explained that this was sure to appeal to the new authorities. The first black bar in Ventersdorp. That was something!

The local whites were surprised that it was Henk—a man known for his hostility toward blacks and for coming from a family that wanted nothing to do with them—who was going to open the first bar for them in town. Malicious tongues were saying that maybe he couldn't stand blacks, but he didn't mind their money. After all, they were going to buy alcohol somewhere, so he realized that at least he'd have a pretty good income from it. "He'll fleece them," they said.

He really did need money. He'd quit work at the railroad, saying that he'd chosen to leave, rather than have them throw him out and give his job to a black. He was in no doubt that the new government would push blacks into jobs that didn't require any particular qualifications, and had previously been reserved for whites. Nor did he believe that his dream of serving in the police force could come true, now that the blacks were in power. He tried dealing in parrots, but only lost the last of his money; all he had to show for it were some large wire cages, cluttering up his entire yard, and now he couldn't get rid of them, not even at half price. There were no job prospects in Ventersdorp. The Blue Crane tavern, which he bought with a loan from his brother and mother, seemed the only possible source of income; alcohol was a failsafe commodity, always in demand, regardless of the weather, the system, or the government.

However, he knew that opening a business of this kind would stir up a storm. "You know what they'll call you? A white kaffir!" his mother lamented when he told her what sort of a bar he was planning to open. In a little place like Ventersdorp nothing worse could have happened to him. The very thought of it made him boil with helpless rage and the feeling that fate had cheated him.

He felt the burning pain of betrayal whenever Eugène Terre'Blanche dropped in at his bar. He came by in his pickup truck at least once a week. He'd tank up at the gas station, and then drop in at the Blue Crane to buy Bell's whisky, Smirnoff vodka in small, two-hundred-milliliter bottles, and weak white wine. "It's for my kaffirs," he'd say, without being asked. Another time he'd explain that he needed alcohol for his wife, who had caught another rotten cold.

"He couldn't drink—two whiskies and he was done." Whenever he described Terre'Blanche's weaknesses, there'd be a tone of forbearance and satisfaction in Henk's voice. "He had a weak head."

To tell the truth, apart from the new flag flying over the town hall and the black mayor, not much had changed in Ventersdorp. Life went on unhurriedly, at the usual well-established pace.

A few new houses, stores, workshops, bars, and churches had appeared, but the layout of the streets and the character of the town remained unchanged.

Sleepy and absent as before, it only woke up properly after midday. Only then did the traffic on the main street increase, as the local farmers drove in to do their shopping. A bit of animation on the main street meant that any moment there'd be some activity at the Wild West Saloon. For now, however, a drowsy atmosphere prevailed in there. Clouds of cigarette smoke hung motionless over the bar, like slumbering phantoms of the day before. On the green cloth of the billiard table there were still some colored balls sitting in the triangular frame.

When I entered, the barman was busy changing the channel on the TV set above the door, taking no notice of his one and only customer, Douglas Wright, who had been sitting over the same mug of beer for the past hour.

At almost a hundred he was the town's oldest citizen; these days he rarely came to the bar, where once he had loved to spend his time. He was famous for telling his stories, whether somebody was listening or not. As well as telling me the stories of how he'd once played rugby for his country, he'd say there were Indians selling chickens at the store he used to own on Carmichael Street, whoever heard of such a thing? They were living in his old house, which he'd had to sell to them, in the hope of saving the store. As a result he and his wife had ended up in a bungalow where they'd once had a stable and rooms for the black servants.

"Indians!" he cried, raising his voice for the whole room to hear. "In my house!"

The barman just shrugged and turned up the television—he wanted to watch the latest episode in a TV serial before the rush hour came.

The Wild West was the only bar downtown. It was in the spot where there used to be a licensed hotel, but since the blacks had taken over, the hotel had closed down, and part of the building had been turned into an office for the ruling party, the African National Congress.

"It's just people that are moving about," said Douglas Wright, "but in fact nothing's changing."

The door creaked, and for a moment bright sunlight lit up the gloomy interior of the bar-room. The barman didn't even turn his gaze from the TV screen.

In the afternoons, once they had done their shopping and seen to their official business, the white farmers dropped in at the Wild West to forget about the heat over a mug of cold beer and to hear the latest news from the town and its environs. They often arranged to meet their black workers outside the bar, and then drive them back to their farms.

The Boardmans knew the Wrights. Isolated among the Afrikaners, they tried to keep in with their compatriots, the descendants of settlers from Great Britain. They too belonged to the Methodist church and prayed at a small chapel on the main street.

"Nothing's changing here," repeated Douglas Wright emphatically. "Well, maybe except for the fact that you're not allowed to call the blacks kaffirs anymore. Apparently it's against the law."

Most of the officials at the magistrate's court and the officers at the police station next door to here were still whites. White people still owned the attorney's office on the market square, the pharmacy, and most of the car repair shops and stores where the farmers came to do their shopping in their pickups, with their black workers in the back. Just as before, the blacks mowed the lawns outside white people's houses, removed the trash, laundered, ironed, and washed the cars. They served.

Except that at the butcher shop on the main street the meat was no longer stored in three separate refrigerators, for whites, blacks, and dogs. The customers no longer stood in two lines, one for whites and one for blacks. Nor were they served by separate assistants anymore. The first black person had moved into Ventersdorp, a young teacher from the township called Japhta Duma, with his wife and daughter. At first the white neighbors took him for the gardener, and his wife for the cleaner, working in a white couple's home. But when they realized their mistake, they sold their house and moved away.

The blacks were coming from Tshing to the white town in ever larger numbers and with increasing confidence, staying there for longer periods of time; no longer accosted by white people, they weren't returning to the township until later and later at night. But they still knew there were places in town where they wouldn't be admitted.

So they never dropped in for a beer at the local hotel, or at Jacklins Pub at the edge of town, where Eugène Terre'Blanche and his white brotherhood had held their preelection rallies. Nor were blacks accepted at the local golf club. Not even Mayor Mbambalala's cousin was allowed onto the golf course. In fact, the rich Indians weren't admitted there either, so they had to drive from Ventersdorp to Potchefstroom, Carltonville, or Stilfontein to play a round of golf.

At his office in town a certain physician was still admitting his patients through two separate entrances, as in the old days, the whites through one door, and the blacks through another. When this was mentioned in the papers, the physician explained that the front entrance was for patients who had made an appointment, while the back one was for those who came without notice and had to wait their turn.

"It so happens that my white patients always call first, to make an appointment, while unfortunately, the black ones aren't in the habit," the physician told the journalists. "Everyone in town knows this and nobody's surprised. But someone from outside might think I'm separating my patients according to the color of their skin, treating one lot better, and the other worse."

The officers at the police station were reluctant to accept calls and complaints from blacks and couldn't be bothered to go and intervene in Tshing, where they immediately got lost in the labyrinth of nameless alleys and numberless houses. On hearing an African accent, they hung up the phone.

One day Mayor Mbambalala called the police station. His girlfriend had gone into labor, and he didn't have a car to take her to the hospital. In panic, he called the police station to ask for a police ambulance. He didn't know Afrikaans, the language the Afrikaners spoke, so he asked for help in English. Without a word the duty officer hung up.

Mbambalala finally found a driver in the township, and once he had taken his girlfriend to the delivery room, he went to the police station to complain.

"How could I know it was you?" said the duty officer.

That night Mbambalala's first son was born. His father named him Nhlanganiso. In the language of his tribe, the Xhosa, this word means "Reconciliation."

It was another thousand days after Mbambalala had moved into the town hall before the first black person was buried at the local cemetery in Ventersdorp.

The old cemetery was the town's communal property, and burial plots were allocated at the town hall. While apartheid was still in force, only whites had been buried in Ventersdorp. The blacks were laid to rest in their own cemetery in Tshing. After the election, when the ghetto was incorporated into the town, there were no longer any formal obstacles to stop blacks from being buried in Ventersdorp too.

Benny Tapologo had never forgotten the day when a black man from Tshing applied to the town hall for permission for a burial at the old cemetery.

"The white councillors objected. They said the blacks from the ghetto had their own cemetery, and that this man's whim would provoke war in the town," he said, recalling a stormy session of the town council. "But there was one more of us blacks, so we outvoted them and had it our way."

News of the first black funeral to be held at the white cemetery ran round the area like wildfire. On the day of the burial, half the town gathered on the main street, which the funeral cortege would be coming down on its way from Tshing to Ventersdorp. That day a large number of white men came out in AWB uniforms for the first time since the election.

"There they stood on the sidewalks, they didn't say anything, they just watched. As if wanting to commit everything and everyone to memory, not miss a single detail, as if they needed to do that for some reason."

At noon, when the mourners from Tshing were due to reach the cemetery, Benny left the town hall, as did all the councillors, black and white, and most of the clerks, messengers, secretaries, and caretakers.

"Everyone was curious to see what would happen," said Benny. "But nothing did. It was a funeral like any other. They buried the coffin and went their separate ways."

The first black person to decide to bury a relative at the white cemetery was called Chris Maherry. Benny knew him from meetings of the ANC, the party to which they both belonged. He told me I'd be most likely to find Maherry at Lewis's furniture store, where he worked as a sales assistant. The store was located opposite the party office.

I found him there in the hour after lunch. He was asleep in a leather armchair displayed for sale. Woken from deep slumber, he looked around vacantly with bloodshot eyes. Fumbling, he took a crumpled pack of cigarettes from his shirt pocket and lit one. For a while the odor of tobacco blotted out the sour smell of the beer he'd been drinking that morning.

"If you want to smoke, go outside," the white manageress snapped in his direction.

She regarded him as an idler and a drunk. She only kept

him on because of the town's black authorities. Maherry was an activist for the ruling party, and firing him could be seen as a political act, the result of white nostalgia for apartheid, a form of rebellion against the new system.

Outside Maherry sobered up and told me what had happened. When his grandfather died, he had the idea of burying the old man in the whites' cemetery.

"I thought to myself that as none of us will ever be able to afford a decent house like the whites have, or to go and live among them, Granddad could at least lie in their cemetery," he said. "And at the party meeting they said we should be getting rid of all the divisions into white and black."

He wasn't afraid that members of the white brotherhood would prevent the funeral cortege from entering the town, or that there'd be a riot at the cemetery, despite the fact that in Tshing everyone knew that although Eugène Terre'Blanche had officially dissolved it, the AWB hadn't disappeared from Ventersdorp at all.

"In the daytime there was no reason for fear," said Maherry. "And we buried Granddad at noon."

Members of the white brotherhood appeared in the town after dark, as employees of a security firm registered at the town hall, whose boss and owner was Eugène Terre'Blanche. Armed, in black uniforms, on horseback and with dogs, they patrolled the streets, guarded stores and warehouses, and maintained law and order in Ventersdorp.

"Terre'Blanche started to take on blacks too, hiring them as night watchmen. They went to him because it was so hard to find work here," Benny admitted. "It was impossible to get a foothold. The whites in Ventersdorp were delighted. Even the police officers, because they didn't have to go out on patrol or do any night duty at all. After dark the city came under Terre'Blanche's control."

The Boardmans were the only farmers in the neighborhood who allowed black people to bury their dead on their farm. The graveyard, where the nameless graves marked with wooden crosses and boulders were overgrown with weeds and grass, lay in the dip of a valley, at the very bottom of it, far from any human settlement.

With each passing year the old graves had sunk farther into the cold, damp earth, which was slowly and furtively consuming them, unsure of its prey, swallowing the final mouthful in a single, sudden snap. Yet people remembered the old burial sites and could recognize them, even when they had completely vanished under scrub and grass. No new grave was ever dug in a spot where somebody's remains were already lying.

The graveyard was separated from the dirt track by a meadow and a fence, of the kind that surrounds cow pasture. Nearby, in the middle of the wilderness, stood a single clay hut. This was where Anna lived, the *sangoma*—herbalist, healer, and witch, who could communicate with the spirits of the dead and remove evil spells, but also cast them. She lived alone, away from other people. She was summoned to the farm for births and ailments, which she knew how to cure with herbs and charms.

The blacks at Buckingham lived in small, two-room cottages, built in even rows out of gray breeze-blocks, roofed with fiber cement, and packed with clay. Each of the houses had its own piece of land for a small garden. When Raymond came back to Buckingham, there were about fifty blacks living in twelve houses on the farm. But he could remember the days when more than a hundred of them had lived and worked on the

Boardmans' farm. Raymond's father had let them live there on condition that from each house he gave to the blacks he would have at least one laborer to work in the fields. When Raymond took over the farm, there were eighteen black employees.

On returning, he knew exactly what he wanted to do, and he had a clear plan of action.

He was sure that the great change, which he hadn't fought for or even demanded, would provide a chance to redress everything that was wrong, unfair, and unpleasant about life—to wash away the guilt and shame, to exonerate and start all over again, with a clear conscience and a clean record. Providence rarely hands out opportunities like this one on a plate. In the stormy events that were changing the system, laws, and customs, Raymond saw a deeper, spiritual significance, a prophetic sign that couldn't be ignored or wasted. He realized that for the bounty of great change to rain down on everyone, each individual must discover the need for it and its meaning, and most importantly, without waiting for it to change life, to try to do it himself. "Everything around us is changing," he kept saying feverishly as he got ready to go back to the farm. "And we've got to change too."

In those days he read a lot about Reverend William, the first Boardman in Africa. Like other missionaries from Europe he came here from England, to serve the white settlers and bring the natives the true faith and salvation, but he had another aim too. He wanted to improve their earthly life, rescue them from paganism, enslavement, and savagery, and introduce them to the world of progress and modernity.

Reverend William had failed to complete his mission. Overcome by stress and exhaustion, he had worked himself to death. When Raymond decided to give up his comfortable, affluent life in Pretoria and return to the Transvaal veld, to Ventersdorp and the farm, he felt he was completing the pastor's work and vocation.

Brought up among the Afrikaners, he understood and shared their attachment to the land, family and tradition. The Afrikaans word *bur* meant a farmer, someone who cultivates the land, who comes from it and has a lifelong connection with it. They regarded it as their sacred duty to maintain their family farms, seeing it not just as a matter of honor, but of survival as a community and a nation.

But Raymond knew—more by instinct than understanding—that in the new era, to preserve what mattered most, you would also have to give something up, make a sacrifice. Thabo Mbeki, Mandela's anointed successor, had been talking about it ever more often and ever more clearly. "Not many whites actively opposed apartheid and the white government, though nowadays almost all of you are claiming that you didn't support that unfair system. All I can do is take your word for it," he had said recently on television. "But even if you weren't against us, you weren't with us either. Now too, if you shut yourselves up in your castles, if you don't join your black fellow countrymen and combine forces with them to build a better world, we'll suffer a defeat and will never succeed in destroying racial prejudices and enmity."

That was to be the principle underlying the change on a minor scale, in the mind and heart of each person, so that the major change could be a success, establishing a new, better order. For if everyone paid a price, they would no longer be divided into winners, dictating the conditions, and losers, humbly accepting capitulation, into rulers and subjects, privileged and persecuted, insiders and outsiders, friends and enemies.

As he watched what was happening in neighboring Zimbabwe, Raymond came to the conclusion that the only way to avoid defeat in a war over land was not to let it erupt in the first place. Instead of destroying everything in a fit of blind rage and desire for revenge, it was better to try to save the achievements of unjust times and share them out more honestly.

Raymond was ready to sell part of Buckingham farm to the new government, first and foremost Uitkyk's pastures and wasteland, so that it could be parceled off among black people. However, disposing of land was his last resort; his primary plan was to convince his laborers that from now on Buckingham farm, where they had been working for generations, would in a certain sense belong to them too.

"I can't deal with everything on my own, I can't carry it all alone, but you won't be able to manage without me either. I need you, and you need me," he explained to the workers, as they were coming to the end of their working day. "*Isandla sihlamba esinye*—you can't wash with a single hand," he quoted a Zulu saying, mispronouncing the foreign words. "We're riding on the same wagon. The more we earn, the more each of us will have. But if the economy goes to the dogs, there'll be no gain for you either. If you want to change your lives, it's down to you alone."

He didn't have to teach them to work on the land, to sow or harvest maize, protect the fields from pests, plough, fertilize, and use the combine or the tractor. They knew how to do all that better than he did, but he could teach them how to run the farm, how to plan crops and expenditure, how to forecast profits and the economic outlook, and above all how to take decisions and bear the consequences of them. He wanted to give them the training to develop from laborers into farmers.

Then he'd be able to lease or even give them part of the farm,

provide help in the form of advice and cash, and lend them agricultural machinery. He could give them the old tractor. Since
his father had bought a new one, they rarely used it anyway.
Once they were sharing the work and the income, the blacks
might finally regard Buckingham as their land, and start to
feel responsible for it. And if by joint effort they managed to
achieve better harvests and greater profit, ultimately that would
win the blacks over to the new partnership, lead to its profit-
ability, and make Mandela's vision come true—from being at
odds with each other and divided by skin color, South Africa's
citizens would unite in racial harmony, a multicolored nation,
like a rainbow.

Many of the whites in Johannesburg or Cape Town thought
the same way as Raymond. Ready for major change, they were
looking forward to it, and saw hope and salvation in it. There
were very few whites who shared their attitude in Ventersdorp.
In fact, apart from Raymond, there were none at all.

"Boardman! Hey, Boardman! I hear blacks have moved into
your farm!"

Arjen Strotmann was the Boardmans' neighbor. His farm
bordered Buckingham. Perhaps it was because of the shared
boundary, but among the local Afrikaners Arjen, who was Raymond's age, was the friendliest toward him.

"Is it true?" he called from a distance, waving at Raymond.

His questions about the uninvited guests who had invaded
Uitkyk were undoubtedly prompted by concern and sympa-
thy. Holding his mug overhead, he pushed his way through the
crowd of farmers gathered on the grass, probably without even
noticing their malevolent smiles as they let him through, or the
mocking, unfriendly glances they cast at Raymond.

"Is it really true about those blacks?" asked Strotmann, catching his breath. He was panting as if he'd run part of the way. "That's what I heard."

Boardman nodded and raised his whisky glass to his lips, as if to shrug off the whole matter and avoid an exchange of remarks that he found unpleasant, which additionally would be overheard by Afrikaners who were ill-disposed toward him. Their dislike, which he explained as an obsession arising from historical prejudice against the British, had increased when he'd continued to allow his black workers to bury their dead on his land. They couldn't forgive him for yielding to the blacks and for seeking their views, but also for setting a bad example to other laborers, who'd cite the system at Buckingham and start making demands. Or, God forbid, get it into their heads to rebel.

At gatherings of the local farmers the Afrikaners had been threatening Boardman, saying he was making a noose for his own neck and that he'd lose his farm. If he allowed blacks to establish cemeteries he'd never get rid of them from his land—he'd be giving them a right to it. As soon as they buried their ancestors there, they'd regard it as their own. He replied that this was exactly what he wanted—for the blacks to regard Buckingham as their place, and to care for the farm as their own. "Only then," he said, "will I be able to feel safe and secure."

This infuriated the local Afrikaners. In fact, he annoyed them with almost everything he did, said or thought. He had taken part in the election, and what's more he hadn't voted in town, with the whites, but on the farm, with the blacks, at the polling station set up for them at the village school. He had sent his sons to the public school, with the blacks, and not to the private school founded by the whites for their children.

He believed that these were the requirements of the great

change, to which they had to adapt, in order to build a new life for everyone. As from now on they had to live with the blacks, share with them, and be mutually supportive, they should get to know each other and drop their prejudices. It came most easily, almost imperceptibly, to the children. After conferring with his wife, Raymond had decided that his sons would go to the public school in town, where he too had studied years ago, and where nowadays most of the students were black.

The local whites were angry that he paid his workers decently and always on time, and made no deductions from their daily wages for breaks, as others did, not even the long ones caused by heavy rain. When word got about that in the winter he'd cooked up soup with meat in it for his blacks and fed it to them while working in the fields, the Afrikaners regarded him as a freak. He enraged them by habitually giving black people rides in his car, instead of leaving them to walk into town from the farms. Worse yet, when he drove a pickup truck, he didn't put the blacks in the back, but invited them to sit in the passenger seats.

Raymond was fully aware that his attitude would make him new enemies in Ventersdorp; he had plenty of old ones already. But he never thought of backing off and giving in. He was sure the change was inevitable and positive, and that it would bring everything and everyone into line, even the Afrikaners from Ventersdorp, who were so strongly opposed to it. Since it covered the entire country, sooner or later it would happen here too. After all, the place was not an island in the middle of the ocean, nor could it hide from the rest of the world under an invisible dome.

Raymond felt and knew that he was the one acting properly, making the correct choices, and also that one day the local whites would admit he was right. And with no alternative, they would finally change and adapt to the new life. Otherwise they wouldn't survive, there'd be no room for them, and they'd die out like an endangered species.

"They've got to change," thought Raymond, as he glanced at the farmers with their beards and mustaches, their khaki hats, shirts, and shorts, and their heavy boots. Despite the lack of common ground, they went on inviting him to their meetings, as if they couldn't accept the idea that a white man from this town could be such a misfit, and as if they still believed he'd come to his senses and start behaving like the rest of them.

"It's incredible how spoiled they've got!" said Arjen Strotmann, still talking at the top of his voice, as if striving to shout over the crowd. "Did you call the police?"

They were standing on the grass, surrounded by a circle of farmers with their ears cocked, curious about every word and gesture. Loud, jaunty music came from the open door and windows of the restaurant. Lately the farmers' gatherings had been held on the lawn at Jacklins Pub.

"And what are you going to do with them?" Strotmann persisted.

Raymond could feel the gazes of the farmers on him, and sensed that dead silence had fallen—everyone had stopped talking to hear what he would say.

"I'm going to talk to them," he replied. "I'll find out what they want."

"Well, I wonder what?" he heard a voice behind him.

"Don't forget to offer them soup," put in another from the crowd, but the farmers standing closest to them remained silent, maybe waiting for the right moment, at another point in this conversation.

"Aren't you going to the police about it?" said Strotmann in surprise. "They can get up to two years in jail for that sort of trespass."

The only sound in the silence that followed these words was of somebody's rapid breathing. Someone had switched off the music.

"Well, exactly," said van Bommel, as if this was the moment they'd been waiting for, the right start for this conversation.

Van Bommel owned a large tobacco farm and employed several dozen blacks. He took a step toward Raymond, so that their arms were almost touching. Strotmann looked around, as if only now aware of the menace in the pressing crowd.

"Hello, there! Now now, gentlemen," he said. "No falling out…"

Van Bommel leaned so close to Raymond that he could feel the farmer's breath on his face.

"You've got to do something about it, Boardman," he said quietly. "We don't like it, see?"

Strotmann forced a laugh.

"Raymond understands perfectly, he's sure to deal with it. He'll report it to the police. No, the police here are useless. He'll report it to Eugène. Eugène'll sort it out in a trice."

"The police are useless," more farmers chimed in. "Better go straight to Eugène and get him to send his men from one of the security firms."

"But seriously, what do you want to do about it? You've got to see to it somehow."

"It's not just your affair. It affects all of us. Today they're on your land, but if it's not stopped right now, tomorrow they'll spread onto mine, in a week to Strotmann's, and in a month the whole place'll be full of them."

"Better do something about it because we can't leave it like that, you get it, Boardman?"

Raymond didn't answer. He drank up his whisky, nodded to say goodbye and left. And so he headed home. He hadn't come to town to seek advice on what he should do with the blacks who'd occupied his farm, but for a meeting about repairing one of the grain silos by the railroad tracks.

After the cautious, extremely restrained Meshack Mbambalala, the next person to be elected mayor of Ventersdorp was the ardent revolutionary, Kabelo Mashi, Benny Tapologo's friend and comrade.

Ever since former president de Klerk and his ministers had stepped down from the government and split from the coalition offered by Mandela, the whites could no longer be sure of guaranteed seats on town councils; being so greatly outnumbered by the blacks, they had been defeated in every election, losing important positions and thus influence on the exercise of power. Now the Ventersdorp town council, which had elected Kabelo Mashi as mayor just three years after the end of white rule, was almost only composed of blacks from the ruling African National Congress.

"When we chose Kabelo for mayor, he joked that he'd accept the post on condition I took it after him." As he remembered his friend, Benny didn't hide his emotion, but used a fist to wipe away the tears that came his eyes. "He was like a brother to me."

Both had soon been disappointed by Mbambalala's submissive attitude to the whites. He was afraid of everything, and made no changes at all, or any attempt at change. As his replacement, Kabelo Mashi was not just going to move into his office and leave everything as it was.

"He knew exactly what he was taking on," admitted Benny.

So the town had a black mayor, black councillors, officials, and policemen, but Eugène Terre'Blanche was still in charge of it. Apart from the AWB, now he had a second army too, the civilian militia that he had registered as a private security firm. The Mapogo a Mathamaga movement had originally been founded by blacks on the banks of the Limpopo. Unable to count on the police to save them from the robber gangs that prowled along the river, the residents of the local black villages had banded together to form this volunteer force. Some of them took part as soldiers, while others simply paid for its maintenance. They gave it the name Mapogo a Mathamaga, taken from a Pedi proverb: "If you want to turn into a leopard, remember that someone else might become a tiger."

With two tiger heads as its emblem, this force soon had a reputation for merciless cruelty in its fight against the criminal gangs. Mapogo a Mathamaga's soldiers kidnapped people suspected of murder, theft, rape, or casting spells, tortured them to extract evidence, and once they had proof of guilt, they meted out severe punishments, without any courts, lawyers, or lengthy trials.

Mapogo a Mathamaga's sinister reputation had soon spread across the whole of Transvaal, with more and more white farmers joining the black vigilante force. In Ventersdorp, Eugène Terre'Blanche had founded a branch of Mapogo a Mathamaga, which recruited members of the white brotherhood, who now embellished their old black uniforms with patches featuring the tigers' heads.

The Mapogo soldiers hunted down vagrants, burglars, cattle rustlers, and horse thieves and subjected them to summary justice. In the town of Brits, when summoned by some white farmers, they caused the death of a black worker who was suspected of stealing tomatoes. They battered and bullied him into confessing and giving away his accomplices. After the interrogation they stuffed him into a sack, tied it up, and left him there for the night, but by morning he had suffocated. According to the local blacks, it wasn't because of the stolen tomatoes at all, but because the unfortunate man had joined a trade union and had quarreled with the farmer about money.

In western Transvaal, the rich farmers paying a thousand times more to support Mapogo than the residents of the black townships made use of the civilian militia to maintain discipline and obedience among their agricultural workers, and also to remove blacks who refused to wait for the government to give them land and had occupied white farms.

The blacks in Ventersdorp were sure Mapogo soldiers had killed the son of Velie Paty, who had been stirring up farm workers, encouraging them to rebel and take land from the whites. One day Velie's small son went missing. After two days of searching, his body was found by a stream. Although the police said the boy had drowned while bathing, Velie was in no doubt his son had been killed by Mapogo soldiers, summoned by a white farmer to teach the troublemaker a lesson.

Mayor Mbambalala had put up with the lawlessness of Mapogo's squads in humble silence. He had pretended to know nothing, and when Benny and Kabelo Mashi had insisted that he stop complying with this dual regime, he explained that his hands were tied, and that as long as Mapogo didn't break the law, he couldn't ban it. Because although Mapogo's soldiers were applying summary justice, and people were being killed as a result, they were never tried for homicide, but only for manslaughter or for being involved in unfortunate accidents, and were either released with a caution, or else after trials lasting for months they only had to pay a fine.

Kabelo Mashi was determined to make changes. Before he'd

even sat down in the mayor's office, he'd told his staff to fetch from the archive every file concerning Mapogo a Mathamaga, including the license authorizing it to operate as a security firm. While he was reviewing the documents, he found contracts that the town hall had concluded with Terre'Blanche and his security firm. Soon after, Kabelo was murdered.

On the Saturday when he went missing, Benny was out of town. Easter was approaching, and he'd gone to visit relatives in Mabopane outside Pretoria, but he came back when friends called to say that Kabelo had disappeared without a trace. He'd left home on Saturday afternoon, telling his family he had a meeting with a distant relative called Johannes Bota Monatle, and that he'd be back late, because he was going to drive him to a farm in Lichtenburg where he lived and worked. He was never seen again.

On Sunday his family had informed the police, who had immediately started looking for the lost mayor. But only his car had been found, abandoned on a dirt road among the maize fields near Elandskuil. The police had also issued a warrant for Johannes Monatle, the man Kabelo had been planning to meet.

They found Monatle at his home on the farm outside Lichtenburg. He wasn't even trying to hide, as if he wasn't at all scared of being caught. He admitted killing the mayor, and showed the police where he'd hidden the body in a sunflower field. Near the corpse the investigating officers also found a knife—the murder weapon.

In court, Monatle swore that he hadn't meant to kill Mashi, but had found the knife on the dirt road while waiting for the mayor, who had told him to meet him there that day. The mayor was going to pay him a sum of money from the sale of diamonds that Monatle had stolen from a mine near Lichtenburg. He claimed that Kabelo Mashi owed him two thousand rand.

Monatle admitted that during the drive he and Mashi had quarreled. The mayor had refused to give him the money. At some point he'd stopped the car and told Johannes to get out. When he resisted, the mayor had got out of the car himself, opened the door on the passenger side and dragged him out into the road. Then he'd pushed Monatle so hard that he'd lost his balance and fallen over. That was when he remembered the knife he'd found while waiting for the mayor, so he took it out of his pants pocket to defend himself against Mashi's attack. Monatle swore that Mashi had impaled himself on the knife. He couldn't explain why he had dealt him a few more blows, fatally stabbing him in the heart and lungs. He just kept repeating that he had acted in self-defense.

The police established that on the day of his death the mayor had withdrawn four thousand rand from the bank. However, Benny never believed his friend was illicitly dealing in stolen diamonds. Or that he'd been killed in an ordinary fight. Kabelo Mashi was very fit. He pumped iron and practiced eastern martial arts. In a one-to-one duel he'd never have let himself be beaten by just anyone.

He didn't believe a word of the killer's statement, and nor did the residents of Tshing who had elected Kabelo Mashi as mayor. On the first day of Johannes Monatle's trial, a thousand blacks gathered outside the courthouse, demanding that the killer be handed over to them to mete out the punishment he deserved.

The trial went on for months. It was transferred from Ventersdorp to Potchefstroom, and from there to Pretoria. In time, just about everyone in Ventersdorp had forgotten the whole affair. Their memory was not even refreshed by the twenty-five-year jail sentence that the judge imposed on Johannes Monatle, who immediately lodged an appeal.

Whenever I went to see Henk Malan, I got the impression he knew what I'd been doing the day before, whom I'd met, and what I'd been talking about.

He knew where I'd slept, and usually where I'd had breakfast and dinner too. He normally suggested local places for me to spend the night and to eat. He also knew why I'd come to Ventersdorp, whom I was seeking, and what I wanted to find out. His bar was usually my first stop on arrival, so he was the first person I questioned and asked for advice and favors.

Like everyone in Ventersdorp he always answered politely, but only to the questions I asked. He never said a word more than necessary, or added anything of his own. He knew I had been to see Douglas Wright at his house and about my visits to the van Zyls' farm, he nodded appreciatively, but never dropped me any hints. One day I asked him to put me in touch with a local farmer, and he took me to Buckingham farm to see Raymond Boardman. Julianna, the girl he employed at the bar, had just got married to Raymond's son, Mike.

Like all the townspeople Henk was secretive toward outsiders, and only revealed as much as was necessary, as much as courtesy and hospitality demanded. He was counting on the fact that if I managed to find out anything, I'd think that now I understood everything, now I had the answers to all my questions. All foreigners were treated like that here. That was the best way of making sure a visitor would stop inquiring and delving, wouldn't ask any more questions, but would go away feeling pleased with himself, without really having a clue and understanding nothing.

If I left Pretoria in the morning, I reached Ventersdorp at noon. I often found Henk opening his bar. He'd remove a large padlock fastening the chains on the security bars and raise the steel shutters. He wasn't in a rush to open the bar because he never expected his first customers until later in the afternoon. First to drop by were a small number of whites who were ashamed of their dependence on whisky and had to hide it from the neighbors. They'd appear at Henk's as if to say hello, have a smoke, and swap news over the first whisky of the day, drunk discreetly in the back room. On their way out, they'd stuff their pockets with small bottles they'd bought to get them through the day.

The black customers only came toward evening, after work or before returning to the farms. That was the time of day, before sunset, when Eugène usually came by too. He'd drop in as if to say hello, not to buy anything. He'd greet Henk like an old friend, Julianna too, if she happened to be helping at the counter. After chatting for quite a while, Terre'Blanche would glance apologetically at his watch and take his leave, excusing himself with urgent business at home or on the farm.

Julianna told me about Terre'Blanche's visits to the tavern. She talked about things that Henk would not or could not say. But Julianna wasn't like anyone else in Ventersdorp.

"Eugène only used to buy drink when he was just about to leave, as if he'd only thought of it at the last moment. He bought whisky or vodka in small, quarter-liter bottles."

He'd search his pockets for some cash, but not finding any, he'd ask Henk how much he owed him, and to add his latest purchases to his account, which he'd settle next time. Henk didn't even scowl as he packed the bottles into a brown paper bag. He cared about Terre'Blanche dropping in at his bar, even though the man took longer and longer to pay his debts.

One time he walked Eugène to his pickup truck outside the bar. Julianna carried his shopping out to the car—half a dozen small bottles, two plastic crates of beer, and a carton of cheap cigarettes.

"You've had a good idea with this bar for blacks," said Terre'Blanche to Henk as he got into his car.

"Well, I'm not going to make a fortune out of it," grumbled Henk, casting a glance at a few blacks sipping beer in front of the store. "It costs me more to replace the broken window panes than I earn on what they drink."

"But you hear what they're saying, you know what's going on and what they're up to," replied Terre'Blanche. "Keep your eyes and ears open. And if there's anything going on, let me know."

Mike acted as his father had taught him. One day Raymond sent him to a car repair shop in town to get a new fan belt for the tractor, and his mother gave him a shopping list too.

"Take Petrus with you," advised Raymond.

Petrus was the oldest and most senior of the black workers on the farm, as well as the most experienced.

Mike had already driven the tractor as a boy, and could also drive a car; even the police regarded sixteen-year-olds as adults in Ventersdorp. The young man was eager to work on the farm and loved driving vehicles. Boardman often sent him to town, but for peace of mind, always asked him to take Petrus with him. Following his father's instructions, Mike told Petrus to get in the cab, in the passenger seat.

They were just setting off for home. Mike had decided to do the last of the shopping at Overland, the biggest store in town. Recently opened, it was locally regarded as an attraction, a fun place to go. Mike was sitting behind the wheel, happily listening to music on the radio, while he waited for Petrus to put the shopping bags in the bed of the pickup truck. He didn't notice the Afrikaners coming up to the car. He only saw them when Petrus opened the door and got in next to him.

Suddenly one of the white men opened the door on the passenger side, a second grabbed Petrus by the arm, and with a single tug pulled him out of the car. Surprised, Mike tried to get out, but two other whites held onto the car door from the outside, keeping it shut. Trapped behind the steering wheel, Mike could only watch as they pushed Petrus to the back of the pickup. When he fell onto the dusty sidewalk, they grabbed him by the arms and legs and threw him into the truck bed.

"Don't forget where your place is, kaffir!" cried one of the whites.

Mike turned the key in the ignition and reversed the car abruptly. The assailants jumped aside. Pressing down on the gas pedal, and without even looking where he was going, Mike turned the car and raced at full speed toward the Caltex gas station. In the rearview mirror he could see Petrus floundering in the back, trying to keep his balance. Only once they were outside town did he stop to check that Petrus was all right, and to move him into the cab.

They drove down the highway in silence. Petrus only spoke when they turned into the dirt road to Buckingham.

"Better not say anything about it to Raymond," he said.

Mike looked at him and shook his head, as if he couldn't understand what was being said to him. At home he told his father what had happened in town.

As he listened to his son, Raymond felt his face tighten; his jaw clenched, and his mind filled with cold, boundless rage, ha-tred, and a desire to kill. He got into his car, ignoring Petrus's entreaties to leave matters to their own course, and his assurances that nothing much had really happened.

At the farm he tried not to show his agitation, but once he'd driven onto the road to town he gave vent to his fury. Beating his fist against the steering wheel, he yelled the worst abuse. As he angrily stepped on the gas, the roar of the engine going at full speed calmed him and soothed his rage. From the compartment under the dash he took out a crumpled pack of cigarettes that he'd hidden from his wife in there. The smoke made him cough, but it also helped to clear his mind.

First he went to the Overland store. He slowed down to cast a close eye at the cars and people standing outside the place, as if trying to recognize the ones who'd attacked Mike and Petrus. He didn't know them, and Mike too had admitted that he couldn't remember their faces. But Raymond assumed they knew whom they were attacking and why, and so they also knew him, Boardman. He hoped that by drawing attention to himself, he would get them to give themselves away. But nobody was staring back at him; the people outside the store were busy with their shopping as usual, and as he was blocking their way, the car drivers were sounding their horns at him. He turned around and drove to the police station by the town hall to make a complaint.

"I can't accept it," said the duty officer, shaking his head.

"My son was attacked," Boardman repeated insistently.

"Your son, or your kaffir?" asked the policeman.

"Petrus was attacked, my worker, but he was with my son."

"So why isn't this Petrus making the complaint himself?"

"I'm making it."

"But what exactly happened to him?" asked the policemen. "Did they beat him up?"

He snorted with laughter when Raymond explained that the attackers had thrown Petrus into the bed of the pickup.

"You want to report that?"

"Yes. Don't you think I should?"

"If people were sent to prison for things like that around here, the place would be deserted."

Raymond persisted, so the policeman switched on his computer to take a statement and lodge a formal complaint.

"You're just adding to my paperwork," he quipped, as he printed out the completed form.

On his way back to Buckingham, for the first time since returning to the farm, Raymond felt doubt. Had he acted too hastily, had he let himself be seduced by the vision of great change and harmony that were meant to replace the unjust order of the past? He knew, he was sure that what he intended and thought was right and good, but was he entitled to drag his sons into it? By raising them according to the values and norms that he regarded as correct, but which did not apply in this town, he was condemning them to be outcasts.

Suddenly he felt weary, and reluctant to face up to adversity. He was sorely tempted by the constancy guaranteed by this town, living in the safe illusion of permanence, with no need for further expeditions, crucial searches and choices, or to take on the challenges involved in any sort of change. Ventersdorp offered him a life without change, without having to keep adapting and battling; it was like warm rain, you could hardly feel it on your skin, it made no demands, but instantly provided every solution, all of them simple, familiar since time began, the full, complete picture.

For the first time he wondered whether he had the right to demand of his sons—of his whole family—something that only he was so very sure about. Maybe he'd do better to give them the best education in the first place, and then the freedom to choose; he should even recognize their right to reject what he regarded as sacred. It crossed his mind that he should remove his sons from the public school in town and send them to the one only white children attended. He found the obstinacy with which it continued to maintain racial divisions offensive, but by employing all the best teachers in Ventersdorp, it guaranteed a better education and a brighter future.

Not long after, he ran into Eugène Terre'Blanche at the gas station. Busy talking to the black boy attending the pump, he didn't immediately notice Terre'Blanche walking up to his car.

"What's this story about your son?" he asked.

"Nothing, just a trifle," replied Raymond.

"But you went to the police with it."

"How do you know?"

"This is my town," said Terre'Blanche, shrugging. "So I hear all the news."

The pump attendant filled the tank, took the banknotes Raymond handed him, and raced to the till.

"People say the blacks have a good life at your place," continued Terre'Blanche. "I treat mine well too, but there's no point in overpaying them. Only as much as they really need, to send their kids to school, for food and clothing. They never know what to do with extra cash. Pay them too much and they'll drink the lot at once. You still have to tell them what to do and how."

The pump attendant came back with a receipt and change. Raymond pressed a five-rand note into the boy's shirt pocket.

"If you have any trouble, let me know. If needs be, I'll find out who accosted your Mike outside the store and I'll make sure nobody round here sets a finger on your boys," said Terre'Blanche.

"Does it really suit you to send them to school with the blacks?" he added as a parting shot. "They won't learn anything useful there. Why don't you send them to our school, like everyone else in town? You and your family speak Afrikaans, don't you? They'd manage. I can talk to the right people for you to get them in. Think about it."

The Terre'Blanches—Eugène, his older brother Andries, and their sister Dora—were among the founders of the school attached to the church, which only accepted white children. Armand van Zyl, the pastor from the Afrikaans Protestant Church who was the school's spiritual patron, denied suspicions of racial prejudice. Maybe because he had only moved to Ventersdorp recently, unlike the other townspeople he didn't avoid conversation, and was even willing to answer questions that his parishioners would certainly have regarded as provocative.

The pastor and his family lived in a small, modest house hidden in the green shade of eucalyptus trees. I always thought him bashful, as if embarrassed because his boyish face was so much at odds with his mild, patient preacher's voice.

"Our criteria for accepting students have nothing to do with their skin color, but with whom we are to educate them to be," he explained. "We are an Afrikaner church, and our school is Afrikaner too. If somebody wants to raise his child to be a good Afrikaner, he'll find all the help and support he needs here. But would a Zulu, British, or Jewish father want to deny his roots and raise his son to be somebody alien to him? So there's probably nothing odd in the fact that although we don't close our doors to anyone, only Afrikaner children attend our school."

Since the blacks had taken over the country, the Reverend van Zyl's church had been advising its congregation not to take part in any more elections.

"People go to vote, wanting to run the world just as they please, and not as God would please, though he created it," he replied when I asked him about it. "The number of votes cast doesn't determine what's good and what's bad."

The church school taught all the subjects required by the authorities, but also offered extra courses in Afrikaans, and the history of the Boers, their culture, literature, and tradition. The lessons were taught in Afrikaans, which meant that children who didn't know the language were excluded from the school. It also charged high fees, which the vast majority of the blacks simply couldn't afford. The school was even expensive for many of the white residents. Some of them took out loans just to get their child through the final class along with the other whites. Others gave in, and shamefully moved their children from the Afrikaner school to the free public school for the last few years of their education.

That was what Julianna's parents had done, Raymond's future daughter-in-law, who after several years at the Afrikaner school took her graduation exams at the public one with the black students. She remembered that although nobody had ever taught her that black people are an inferior species, they had implied that each should stick to his own, and that there was nothing wrong with keeping apart. The literature teacher was particularly heated about it. "Good fences make good neighbors," he was always quoting—out of context, and thus misquoting—a line from a famous poem. "Do you know who wrote that? Robert Frost, an American! And he was a man who read his poems to John Kennedy when he took the presidential oath!"

"We were endlessly taught about the history of the Boers, the Great Trek, the wars against the Zulus, and against the British, but it was always about the past, never the present," said

Julianna. "I didn't know much about the world and nobody ever required it of me, or even expected it."

All the way back to the farm, Raymond thought about the offer Terre'Blanche had made. It wasn't that he considered the idea of transferring his sons to the white school, but rather that he drank in the plain nature of the choice Eugène's words had confirmed to him. He had a revelation, as on the day when he'd decided to return to the farm. Suddenly he saw everything clearly and simply again.

By sending his sons to the black school, he certainly wasn't sacrificing them on the altar of his own dreams. He wasn't serving a sentence on them, condemning them to be outcasts or taking away their choice, but saving them from all that. He wasn't limiting them or marking out a single road for them to follow, he wasn't blocking their opportunities, but was flinging the gates to the future open wide for them.

He would have been imposing a sentence on his sons if he had taken Terre'Blanche's advice. The school he was talking about educated the young people to be carbon copies of their grandfathers and fathers, imbuing them with the same values and principles, the same way of thinking and acting, and so it chained the town to immutability, constrained it and locked it under a dome of set habits and prejudices, well-trodden paths and ideas. That was why everything here seemed to keep repeating ad infinitum, it was always the same, from generation to generation. The present had its sights firmly set on the safe, familiar past, and ran in fear from the unknown future, even when it offered a tempting promise of change for the better.

Raymond could see it clearly now. If he took his sons out of the public school and sent them to the one Terre'Blanche was recommending, they'd become just like everyone else in

Ventersdorp. That was actually what Eugène, the town's self-appointed ruler and sentinel of its inability to change, wanted from him. That was what it was really about, not about a choice of school, or how you treated your workers.

If he had let himself be tempted by Terre'Blanche and had accepted his offer, Raymond would have been denying himself, agreeing to defeat, and sealing his own humiliating capitulation by surrendering his sons to Eugène and his town. He would merely have condemned them to everything he regarded as hateful evil and was trying to keep at bay.

Without a moment's hesitation, he decided that his sons would go on attending the public school in Ventersdorp along with the black children.

Although Benny Tapologo had jokingly assured Kabelo Mashi that he would be the next mayor of Ventersdorp after him, he didn't stand for the post when his friend died. He didn't even resent the fact that nobody had offered it to him.

For the first time it occurred to him to break out of the enchanted circle of static lack of change by leaving Ventersdorp. A new election was approaching, and Benny thought of moving all the way to Cape Town to become a member of parliament. And if not there, then at least to Mafikeng, where the provincial authorities were based. Even that seemed better than being endlessly stuck in Ventersdorp, where everything always stayed the same.

He decided to take action. With some difficulty, in Johannesburg he managed to locate one of the ANC envoys who had come to Ventersdorp years earlier to found a branch of the party there. Some of them didn't answer his calls, and others had disappeared without a trace. The one he finally managed to

reach on the phone was called Moses. They agreed to meet in
the Shell tower in downtown Johannesburg, where the ANC
rented two floors for its head office.

As Benny, intimidated by the size and wealth of the city,
awkwardly stated his case, Moses just shook his head.

"It's no use," said Moses. "The candidate lists are approved
at the very top. Anyway, they've already been prepared. Serfontein's going to parliament from your area."

"Serfontein?" Benny goggled in amazement. "Jan Serfontein?"

Jan Serfontein was an Afrikaner who owned a chicken farm
near Potchefstroom, one of the biggest in the country, and everyone in the entire vicinity knew he belonged to the white
brotherhood.

"Mandela gave orders for him to be put on the list," said Moses. "Are you so surprised?"

Even among the other Afrikaner farmers in western Transvaal, who didn't exactly pamper their black workers, Serfontein
stood out for his cruelty and contempt toward blacks. He punished the mildest offense with the greatest severity. He beat
his workers with his fists and with a stick. He even hit their
children if they forgot to bow to him and call him sir.

He also had a reputation for firing a shotgun at any black
stranger on his farm, regarding them all as thieves. He even
shot at people who took shortcuts across his land without asking. He was known to have had the water and electricity cut off
from a black village whose inhabitants had refused to sell him
their allotments to increase the size of his farm.

When the blacks took power nationally, and Terre'Blanche
and his Afrikaner Resistance Movement not only failed to prevent it, but didn't even manage to carve out a small piece of

land to be a separate republic for the Afrikaners, Serfontein left the AWB and announced that he was joining Mandela's party. The Afrikaners of western Transvaal and their black workers thought it was a joke. But Mandela gave orders for Serfontein to be accepted in the ANC, and even made him an offer to be one of its members of parliament.

Benny went back to Ventersdorp with a heavy heart and his mind in chaos. Years later, when he told me about his trip to Johannesburg, he said he had felt strangely split in half. One half of him understood what had happened, and could see the party's rationale for such a decision, while the other simply couldn't deal with the unreality of the situation.

For some reasons the ANC and government leaders were depending on a man like Jan Serfontein becoming a member of parliament for their party. The grateful Afrikaner organized receptions at his farm for ANC dignitaries, wasn't sparing with money for party expenses, and also encouraged his neighbors, the brothers Pieter and Robert Haagner—also former members of the white brotherhood—to join the party, which they had once regarded as a band of heathens and criminals.

The honors and favors showered on Serfontein were meant to prove to the mistrustful Afrikaners of western Transvaal that Mandela and his people had no ill feeling toward them, and that under the black government no harm would come to anyone. There would be no mention of past sins, acts of vengeance, or witch hunts. Instead of picking at their wounds, it was better to leave them alone to heal up, until they were forgotten and stopped causing pain. Once and for all. And then the enemies would unite into one harmonious nation, as multicolored and beautiful as a rainbow.

Many of the whites, who not long ago had been ardent supporters of apartheid, now joined Mandela's party. Some were prompted by a sense of guilt, a wish to compensate for past injustice and to start all over again. Others acted out of fear of punishment, or sometimes plain calculation, tallying up the profits and losses. As members of the ruling party they still had power and influence on the course of affairs, and kept their privileges and importance.

One after another, former white ministers, officials, army and police officers signed up for Mandela's party, and finally, to universal amazement, the entire National Party joined the ANC, although it had been Mandela's bitter enemy and persecutor, and had introduced and defended the apartheid system for half a century, ruthlessly and violently stifling any sign of rebellion by the blacks.

"People change," said Moses, as he bid Benny farewell in Johannesburg.

"People change," thought Benny on the way home. "But do they really change that much?"

He was traveling alone, driving slowly and cautiously to avoid damaging the car, which he'd borrowed from a neighbor. In those days he didn't have his own car yet, and was still living at his mother's house. The road was empty, so he could allow himself to sink into thought and memory.

Everything was blurred, starting to fade and go gray, what had once been a cause for celebration was now becoming daily fare. People were no longer divided into innocent and guilty, victors and losers. Declaring yourself to be on the right side and openly supporting a just cause, which used to demand courage and strength, were no longer enough of a counterweight to believing in a bad cause and sticking by it. Or even plain cowardice. So there was no real way of parading your martyrdom, the memory of your sacrifices, your fortitude, and the hurt you had suffered.

The oppressors had gone over to the victims' camp; they had merged with them, and now both sides were patting each other on the backs. Jan Serfontein, who told his black workers to call him sir, called the black activists at party meetings his "comrades." They too addressed him as "comrade," as if talking to a communist.

Memory had been wiped clean, and thus the memory of who had stood on which side of the barricade had been erased too. It was as if nobody in the entire country had ever supported apartheid or gained advantage from it. Those who had once enjoyed privileges because of their skin color now asserted that they had hated doing it. Even those who had defended apartheid now insisted that they had actually been its secret enemies, the most dangerous kind, destroying it from the inside.

Near Krugersdorp, where the highway runs past some rocky hills, turns onto a flat plain covered in maize and tobacco fields, and then leads straight to Ventersdorp, Benny's doubts evaporated.

He firmly believed that the top party leaders were greater experts at running things, as proved by all the elections they'd won. So he hadn't taken offense or objected when it wasn't Kabelo Mashi who was selected as candidate for the first black mayor of Ventersdorp, or even himself, but Mbambalala. Only later was he somewhat surprised by the new mayor's submissive attitude to the whites, but he ascribed it to Mbambalala's naturally cautious and fearful character.

Benny was also surprised by how many whites were joining the ranks of the ruling ANC since losing power, and that they were being so readily received, welcomed with open arms, with nobody asking them any questions.

Mandela was courting their favor to show the sincerity of his intentions and a conciliatory spirit, but also because he feared the Afrikaners. He realized that it would be hard to replace them in the civil service, courts, police, and army, and that without their cooperation his kingdom wouldn't last, but would collapse soon after he ascended the throne. After all, the Afrikaners, so influential in the army, the forces of law and order and the administration, could not only refuse to serve Mandela, but could turn against him, attempt to sabotage his government and his state, and possibly even resort to extreme measures by declaring open war.

Benny had often heard blacks from Ventersdorp and the local farms grumbling that Mandela was afraid of Terre'Blanche, and that as a result—even though they'd been given the same rights as the whites—their lives hadn't actually changed at all. Of course, now they had a new black president whom they had elected, but they still had the same white master as before, and continued to be his subjects and servants. Town councillor Benny Tapologo usually reacted to complaints of this kind with a shrug; he'd assure them it wasn't possible to change everything at once, in an instant. And that the party leaders knew better what to do, and how. Now he was beginning to wonder if there wasn't a grain of truth in those people's words.

That would explain the lack of response from the head office in Johannesburg to the letters and calls from the party organization in Tshing complaining about white farmers who humiliated their black workers and refused to pay them. It would also explain the passivity of the town hall officials, and even of the police at the local station, who silently ignored any request to intervene on the farms.

As Benny caught sight of the silvery grain silos at the town line ahead of him, it crossed his mind that perhaps Ventersdorp had been sacrificed on the altar of another, greater cause. Confined under the dome of the old system and unchanging habits, it had been handed over to the white leader Terre'Blanche to live in as he had before; satisfied with a domain of his own in his hometown, he wouldn't cast his gaze any farther or make any more demands.

Every Friday evening, after finishing work in the fields, Raymond gathered the workers in the yard outside the barn. On that one day everybody came—there was no need to hustle or remind them. They never made any excuses, dragged their heels, or turned up their noses. He didn't even have to wait for them to assemble.

Once they'd seen to the tractor and other agricultural machinery, they'd be shifting from foot to foot impatiently, waiting for Raymond to wash up after work, change from his work clothes into a clean shirt, and come out to them, carrying a cardboard box. Inside there were some pink envelopes containing banknotes, their weekly wages. Eager to be paid, they'd be glancing skyward to see how high the sun was standing, calculating whether they'd still have time to get to town with the money and back to the farm before dark.

If Raymond had simply paid them their wages, they'd have gone there and back easily. But on Friday afternoons he gathered his workers not just to reward their efforts, but also to confer with them, to appraise the past week, to know what had gone well and what hadn't come out right, and to plan the work for the following week, month, or even year.

He came outside clutching bottles of cold beer and handed round cigarettes.

"Not a bad week, was it?" he opened the conversation.

"*Yebo*," mumbled Petrus, Willem, Jomo, Harry, Tsepe, and Modise in chorus. "That's the truth and no mistake."

They repeated these words mechanically, like a lesson learned by heart, a weekly, necessary ritual, which had to be performed to do their duty, and then be able to get on with other, everyday matters. As usual, they praised the week, but Raymond knew they weren't happy at all. At any rate, not about everything. Not about the fact that he'd told them to dig a well in the meadow occupied by the strangers at Uitkyk. They'd been amazed when he took them there to work.

"That well . . . Now we'll never be rid of them," muttered Petrus.

As the oldest of the workers he always spoke first. The rest waited to hear what he would say, and only joined in the conversation later.

"They've got a right to be here," replied Raymond. "This was once their land. They've got documents to prove it."

"But now it's yours," insisted Petrus. "And you've got documents too. You have got some, haven't you?"

Raymond had the purchase deeds for both farms, both certified by a notary. But the people occupying the meadow at Uitkyk had also shown him an extract from the state register confirming that they used to live here, but the white government had forcefully relocated them to a homeland outside Mafikeng, and had given their land to the Methodist church. A long list drawn up by a court official scrupulously recorded the first name and surname of every black evicted from Uitkyk.

They had come back on the suggestion of an ANC activist, to whom they had gone to complain and to ask for help. They had nowhere to go, because the white farmer on whose land they used to live and work had told them to get out so he could change his fields and pastures into a wildlife park, and charge rich tourists for hunting trips and safaris. Raymond had read that many white farmers were doing the same thing to get the blacks off their land.

The ANC activist had informed them that he couldn't help, but had advised them to reclaim the land from which the white government had evicted them years ago. "Go back there, and see what happens," he'd said. "Somebody has to take care of you."

They hadn't occupied the farm at Uitkyk just for the government to share it out between them as a way of compensating for past injustice. It would be of no use to them. They knew how to work the land, but they had no money, tools, or seeds to start farming. Nor did they have the time to wait months on end to harvest crops that would allow them to survive. Instead they were counting on striking a bargain with the authorities: they'd stop occupying the farm, and in exchange they'd be assigned free houses of the kind the government was building for penniless blacks. But although several weeks had gone by, apart from Raymond, who owned the meadow, nobody had taken any interest in them.

"When winter comes and there's frost on the ground, they'll feel the cold and they'll get the hell out," said Petrus.

"You're so rattled it's as if they'd moved into your cottage," muttered Raymond. "They won't be staying here, so don't get upset about it."

"So why did we dig that well for them?" said Petrus, not backing down.

"Just to help them out. Why not?"

Petrus shrugged.

"I'd help you too if necessary," added Raymond.

The sun was slowly starting to set, gradually acquiring a reddish tinge.

"Jomo!" said Raymond, breaking the silence. "Have you had a look at the carburetor on the tractor? The choke's always cutting out."

"I checked the needle valve and the nozzle, but I couldn't find anything wrong. It'll have to go to the mechanic."

"Have another try tomorrow. Better get to the bottom of it yourself than hand it over to a repair shop and not know what you're paying for. That's the easiest way."

Jomo was the brightest of the workers, but also the one with the least initiative. He only ever did what he was told to do. On his father's side he was Zulu. His father worked at a gold mine in Johannesburg, where he lived in a laborers' hostel, for men only. At first he'd visited his family once every six months, but later he had just sent them money, less of it by the month, until finally he had vanished into thin air.

At home, Jomo's mother had brought him up as Xhosa, as that was her ethnicity. When his father disappeared, she had to get a job as a domestic servant for a white couple in Potchefstroom, and only came home on Saturdays and Sundays. She looked after some Afrikaner children, but her own kids grew up without maternal care, in the street, watched over by the neighbors, who were Tswana. That was how Jomo had become a Tswana.

As Petrus put it, Jomo had no roots. He knew all the black languages, and Afrikaans and English too, but he hadn't acquired any sense of belonging to a community. He never applied himself, and did everything with the minimum effort, as if he regarded any exertion as pointless, because nothing it produced would last. He hadn't started a family, but lived at Buckingham farm with a series of different girlfriends.

"We need to decide what to sow in the fields for the year

ahead. They're paying a low price for maize, so maybe we should plant tobacco?" said Raymond.

"Are they paying more for tobacco?" asked Tsepe.

"No comparison," nodded Petrus.

"If we sowed it all with tobacco, how much would we earn?" wondered Tsepe.

"It depends on the harvest, and the quality of the leaves. But more than for maize," explained the farmer.

"But you have to work so much harder than to grow maize," said Jomo.

"Pests can get into tobacco more easily and destroy it all," added Petrus. "And who'd harvest it? There are too few of us, we'd have to hire people."

"What about taking on those fellows from the meadow?" suggested Raymond.

Petrus shook his head.

"So maybe we should sow half of it with maize and half with tobacco?" asked Raymond.

"Maize may be cheaper, but it grows by itself. And sunflowers. You don't have to harvest them by hand, you can do it all with the combine," added Jomo.

"Why don't we raise stock?" said Willem. "Other people do. It's no work at all, the cows just graze by themselves. You just have to keep an eye out to make sure no one steals them. You don't have to worry about drought or pests."

"We haven't got enough land," said Raymond. "If we turned Buckingham and Uitkyk over to pasture, we could only keep about a hundred, at most a hundred and fifty cows. Or about three hundred sheep. The norm round here is that each cow needs five hectares of pasture, and each sheep or goat needs three. No, livestock won't bring us any profit."

"In that case, buy some more land," muttered Petrus.

The evening was setting in, and the cooling sun was gradually sinking over the still, silent veld. The shadows of the trees in the yard were losing their definition, their shapes were blurring and melting into the cracked, darkening red-brown earth.

Then Tsepe hesitantly suggested growing vegetables—peppers, cucumbers, and tomatoes could be supplied to the superstores that were springing up in the suburbs of most of the cities. Many of the local farmers had moved over to farming vegetables, which they were selling to the supermarket chains, Pick n Pay, SPAR, Woolworths, and Checkers. Those who'd managed to secure contracts for their crops were jealously protecting the market from competitors, and the supermarket owners were reluctant to give up on their tried-and-tested suppliers.

The big stores had started appearing in almost all the larger towns in the area too, including Potchefstroom, Krugersdorp, Klerksdorp, and Carltonville, but not in Ventersdorp. Here nothing had been built, though every year it was said that any day now one of the large superstore chains would open a branch in this town too. The delay was explained by the far smaller number of citizens and their lack of money, but also by their dislike of outsiders, whose arrival would be bound to change habits around here, and destroy the old way of life. To prevent strangers from coming in and to make sure they kept away, the citizens of Ventersdorp and the neighboring farmers refused to sell them the land to build stores, factories, or houses.

Nor were the rich entrepreneurs from Johannesburg eager to spend their money in a town with a bad reputation nationwide as the realm of the white brotherhood. It didn't offer a promising business prospect, and could easily lead to trouble, by bringing down on the incautious investor the suspicion that he ranked among the supporters of Eugène Terre'Blanche and was opposed to the new system. As a result, despite the major changes taking place all over the country, Ventersdorp remained on the sidelines of everything, shut away in its own world, breathing its own air and living in its own time.

"Vegetables aren't an option. First you've got to have a definite purchaser who'll buy everything you grow," Raymond explained to the worker. "Otherwise you won't sell it. You can't just take it to the market and sell it by the item."

They nodded sadly. There was a silence. The conversation about the farm had long since ceased to hold water, and now it had fallen apart entirely. Without saying another word, they drank the bottles of beer. The blacks kept glancing at the darkening sky, then at Raymond, trying to guess whether their weekly conference had come to an end. They saw their attendance as a duty, just like all the others they were paid to perform.

Raymond watched as with their heads lowered they waited for him to hand each man his week's wages, and then they'd race off to town to buy beer, the cheapest whisky, and a kind of sweet hooch called *mampoer*, distilled from peaches and marula fruits. At night they'd hold a drinkfest round a bonfire. To begin with, they'd have a good time together, but after a while the first argument would erupt, followed by noisy squabbling. They'd start yelling, waking up the Boardmans.

The first fight usually came well after midnight. The workers' wives, who joined in the drinking with them and got just as drunk as the men, would try to seize the rest of the money from their husbands' pockets. The pint-sized Tsepe would go for his wife Angelina with his fists flying, while she, as big as a closet, would give him a thrashing and throw him out of the house.

The others would mock him, so Tsepe would fetch his knife out of his pocket. Then they'd come running to the Boardmans' house and rap on the window, calling on Raymond to come and save the knifeman's victim.

Raymond would take the wounded man to the emergency unit in town, telling the others to find Tsepe and stop him from causing any more trouble. Still drunk, staggering as they lit up the darkness with flashlights, they'd wander the fields of ripe maize, where the terrified Tsepe would be hiding, as they called to him to come out, with no fear of punishment or vengeance. Only in the gray light of dawn, once the beer and whisky were wearing off, would they come home exhausted; the next day they'd apologize to Raymond, beg him not to call the police, and promise nothing like that would ever happen again—it was the last time they'd cause him trouble.

It was always like that.

Lost in thought, he was staring at the flower bed in front of the veranda. He liked gazing at the purple asters. He liked purple—it put him in a good mood, made him feel calm and safe. He associated it with the jacaranda trees in Pretoria, which blossomed in the spring, painting the city purple. He missed Pretoria's lavender-colored springs.

He had never liked the fall, which he associated with things ending, never to return, a painful reminder of the limits of what's possible. He had once read in a newspaper that these feelings were typical of people who were unfulfilled, insecure, and fearful, and that the end of something didn't actually have to involve fear, but should bring a sense of satisfaction and achievement. Still, he preferred the lavender-colored spring, when unclouded faith blossomed in him, when he gained strength and certainty that everything could be fixed and started anew.

Petrus woke him from his reverie.

"Raymond! Can we head off to town now? We might still catch a ride along the way. Otherwise we won't have time to get back by nightfall."

They'd had enough by now. They refused to go on puzzling away or conferring any longer. They couldn't understand why he kept asking them all these questions. He'd make all the decisions himself anyway—he'd be the one who determined what to do and how.

He nodded.

"Mike's driving in to the video store this afternoon. You won't all fit in the car but he can take some of you there and back."

"*Ayoba!* Great!" said Jomo happily. "You're a really nice guy, Raymie."

Mike Boardman was going into Ventersdorp to meet up with Julianna, the Afrikaner girl he'd met at the video store recently opened behind the Engen gas station on the way into town.

The petite blonde with laughing blue eyes and a slender, shapely figure had attracted him at first sight. He kept glancing at her as he browsed the shelves of videos, pretending he couldn't decide, or couldn't find the movie he wanted. He did his best to extend his visits, putting off the moment when Julianna would write down his name and the return date, and take his payment.

At first he went there once a month, then every three weeks, then every two. She must have found him attractive too, because one day, as she was handing him the videos, she gave him a flirtatious look, straight in the eyes, and said she could put aside his favorite movies if he told her what he liked best. From then on he stopped at the video store even more often, every couple of days.

"I wanted to give him a sign, to encourage him." Julianna talked about her relationship with Mike openly, frankly, as if by saying things aloud, by recreating it all from the start, and calling things by their proper names, she could discover and understand the reasons for the disappointment and misunderstandings that would mark their life. "I remembered him from school, I knew he was English, though I had no idea what that was supposed to mean, I'd never known anyone English before."

A year older, Mike didn't remember Julianna from school. Like almost all the other Afrikaner kids in Ventersdorp Julianna had started her education at the white church school. She had moved to the public school in the penultimate year, after her parents' divorce, when they hadn't had enough money for the high tuition fees. By then, Mike was preparing for his high-school graduation exams. He said goodbye to the school, and to the town as well for a while, never seeking or expecting to find any new acquaintances there.

Of his three sons, Raymond was proudest of Mike, though he was also the one who caused him the most trouble and concern. In an exaggerated way he embodied everything that Raymond wanted his sons to learn, and everything he wanted to protect them from. Sometimes, as he watched him anxiously, Raymond felt as if he were looking at himself, his own unfulfilled dreams, his old longings and fears, moments of triumph and humiliation. But he couldn't see any of the doubts that he himself had always had, and that he'd so badly wanted to overcome.

Mike was never hesitant about anything. He was a determined person, with sophisticated views on all sorts of matters, self-confident and sure of his opinions. He had no wish to impose them on anyone or to persuade others that they were right. Once he believed in something, there was no way he would ever gainsay it out of fear, or for the sake of peace and quiet.

For him there were no authorities, nothing was sacrosanct or indisputable. He even questioned the faith, saying openly that he had left it, because it had been appropriated and falsified by the clergy. They made him feel hostility and disgust. They had been entrusted with the task of serving their congregation, but they wanted people to believe that they had been called upon to guide them. They had usurped the right to interpret the word of God and his intentions, and even thought they could give absolution and penance in his name.

Raymond recognized himself in Mike, his better, improved incarnation. But just as often he perceived a stranger, whom he didn't know, but who knew everything about him and could see right through him. As if all his thoughts, desires, fears, and obsessions were embodied in Mike. And in an uncompromising, unadulterated form that seemed exaggerated, extreme, downright reckless, heading for self-destruction. Mike had in him everything that Raymond held dearest, and had once wanted for himself, and then for his son, but there was also something in him that filled Raymond with fear and anxiety.

What worried him most was the tenacity with which Mike stood his ground and aimed at his chosen target. He was a quiet boy, but if accosted by the Afrikaners in town he counterattacked, and was always getting into fights with them. Sometimes he won, and sometimes he took a beating. But he never hesitated to get up for the next fistfight if he thought it the only way to avoid having something imposed on him that he refused to accept.

At school he hadn't been a top student, but on the rugby pitch he'd been one of the best. Although not heavily built, he had exceptional grit and endurance. He fought until he dropped, and was never afraid to tackle opponents who exceeded him in height, weight, experience, and strength. Several times he was carried off the pitch on a stretcher with concussion or a back injury. He went out to play with as much determination as if he were going to fight a battle of life and death.

Raymond sometimes came to watch when Mike was playing for the school rugby team; seeing the reckless dedication with which his son went for his rivals, he remembered the burning humiliation he himself had suffered some years earlier on the very same pitch.

After military service, which was compulsory for all white males, he had been transferred to the reserve units. From time to time they were called up for exercises, usually near the town where they lived, which meant that the civic militia was similar to the Boer volunteer force from the time of the wars against the British.

The Afrikaner farmers in the area were rarely called up for exercises, but for ten years Raymond had received a summons from the army on an annual basis. Regardless of whether he was living in Cape Town or Pretoria, he was ordered to come to Ventersdorp for exercises.

One time the exercises ended on a Sunday, when the Afrikaners were holding a festival in Ventersdorp to mark a special holiday. There were celebrations, entertainments, and a fair on the sports pitch where the reservists were practicing their drill in field uniforms.

That particular Sunday, some old friends of Raymond's from Johannesburg had decided to visit him at the farm. When they found out he was doing exercises, they sought him out at the pitch. He was sure it was the sight of Charlene hugging him that had roused the anger of the Afrikaner sergeant.

The man had accused him of being late for the roll call, and had made him put on a gas mask and run around the pitch, holding his rifle overhead. Dripping with sweat and purple with embarrassment, he had performed his penalty rounds to the delight of the Afrikaners gathered for the festival, who had found out somehow that the sergeant was disciplining the upstart Englishman. Only when Raymond fainted from the effort and fell to the ground did the Afrikaner NCO regard it as adequate punishment. As he watched Mike on the rugby pitch, Raymond had no doubt that his son would sooner have gone for the sergeant with his fists—he'd have preferred arrest to public humiliation.

Raymond, his brothers, and even his father had never been fond of Ventersdorp and had avoided visiting the town. They had no friends or acquaintances there. Raymond's two other sons, James, the oldest, and Matthew, the youngest, regarded the town as alien too. Their world was at Buckingham farm and in Potchefstroom, where they studied and had friends.

Mike was the only member of the family to regard Ventersdorp as his town. By contrast with his father and brothers, he cared about the place. He used to go into Ventersdorp, and although he had no friends locally, at least he was known there. Like all the Boardmans, he wasn't popular, was marked out as British, and was laughed at for his black person's accent in Afrikaans, but he was regarded as a fellow citizen, a local.

The town annoyed him, and was sometimes hostile to him, but he believed he could change it—he had enough strength and resilience. After graduating from high school he didn't apply for university, but enrolled on a course for wildlife trackers and national park rangers, thinking he could get a job at one of the private hunting parks established on the white farms in

Transvaal. It looked as if he had found his vocation; he did extremely well on the course, and was the tutors' favorite, star student. But he was caught smoking *dagga*, the local version of marijuana, and thrown out of the course.

After that, for a short time he worked as a barman at the Irish Pub in Potchefstroom, until finally he came back to Buckingham farm to help his father and learn about agriculture.

At the same time Julianna came back to Ventersdorp too. After school, very few of the local Afrikaner girls ever decided to go to college in Johannesburg, Cape Town, or Potchefstroom. They more often learned a profession, looked for jobs and husbands, and started families.

For three years Julianna trained as a hairdresser at one of the beauty salons in Potchefstroom. In Ventersdorp, where she was regarded as one of the prettiest girls, she had a boyfriend whom she had been dating for several years. When the blacks took power and it became hard to get work in the area, he'd decided to leave for America. He'd promised to come back in a year, and asked her to wait for him. But Julianna had told him she wasn't going to waste her life waiting.

To earn the money for her own hairdressing salon, she got a job at the video store, where she met Mike Boardman. Julianna liked talking about those years. There was nothing to do in town, and nowhere to go. The local hotel had closed down for lack of guests, and Buffalo, Ventersdorp's first restaurant, hadn't opened yet. There was a billiard hall, but the young Afrikaners in there were always accosting Mike, trying to provoke him into a fight.

"They didn't like the fact that one of their girls had chosen an Englishman," said Julianna.

Usually Mike drove out from the farm in a pickup truck after work, and took her to the river or the Rietspruit dam, where the local youth liked to go. Nobody pestered or accosted them there, the sight of them didn't annoy anyone, and they could enjoy themselves far from everyone and everything.

They also used to go to the cinema and to cafés in Potchefstroom, and sometimes Mike took her all the way to Pretoria, to the vast Loftus stadium, where the biggest rugby games were played. One Saturday he invited her to Buckingham farm and introduced her to his parents. Julianna stayed overnight. Although she'd lived her whole life in this farming town, she'd never been on a farm before.

Raymond said that as no evidence had ever been found to prove who had set light to the field in front of the house, nobody should be accused of it. But Mike said straight out that somebody from the town had done it, and that they should take a sober look at things and weigh the facts. That was this town's only form of response to any attempt to change things, or any way of thinking that differed from the accepted norm. His father must have known that long ago.

If somebody really had set fire to it, they'd done it at sunrise. It's hardest to notice flames when the whole sky looks as if it's on fire. If Raymond hadn't got up before five that day to drive to Johannesburg before the rush hour traffic, more of it would have burned, and the fire would have come right up to the house.

The field had been set alight from the road that ran across Buckingham farm to the grain silos and the railroad station. If maize had been growing here as it used to, the dry straw would have provided fuel for the fire. However, that year Raymond hadn't sown this field, but had let Mike grow pumpkins there.

The rest of the ground was covered in weeds and grass, which gave no strength to the flames.

He hadn't noticed the fire when he'd gone out onto the lawn with a mug of coffee. The tall, spreading trees surrounding the house like a palisade shielded his view of the dirt road. But when he raised his head to look at the sky, the wind began to wreathe them in a thick cloud of fresh black smoke.

Crackling vigorously, the fire was spreading across the field, greedily consuming dry stalks and leaves. Raymond summoned the workers, and they put out the flames. He also phoned the police and called them out to the farm. They wandered about by the road, looking for evidence, anything that might explain the cause of the fire, or betray the culprit, but they failed to establish anything certain.

In his office at the town hall, town councillor Benny Tapologo started the day's work by sorting out and recording the complaints lodged the day before by voters from the black township, Tshing.

Choosing their words with difficulty, farm workers, gardeners, store assistants, and cleaners told him about the wrongs done to them by the local whites, whom they were still serving as before. They came to complain, but also to ask for advice or help, and sometimes for money.

Benny would listen carefully and make notes, filling blank sheets of paper with neat rows of letters; sometimes he asked for details. When he was done, he'd place the complaint on top of a towering pyramid of similar sheets of paper, detailing the residents' grievances and the injustices they had suffered.

On Friday, at the end of the working week, Benny would review the complaints, sort them by subject, put aside the local ones that could be settled without help from outside, and then write a report, which on Monday morning he'd put into an envelope and send to the party authorities in Johannesburg. The complaints divided into two main kinds. Most frequently, black agricultural workers came to complain that the white farmers hadn't paid them their promised wages on time, or at the rate fixed when they'd hired them for the job. Most of them made verbal agreements, and very rarely signed contracts or discussed the details. When arguments broke out, it was hard to establish who was telling the truth, and who was trying to cheat or exploit the other.

There was an equal number of complaints of beatings, often severe, by white employers, who resorted to violence to punish any disobedience, any mistake or lack of enthusiasm, just as they always had.

Modise Molete had been hired to work on a white farm as a cowherd. He agreed the rate of his weekly wage with the farmer, and that it would be paid to him each Friday. So that he wouldn't have to travel to work from Tshing each day, with the farmer's consent Modise stayed overnight in the barn, but in exchange for his accommodation, as well as tending the cows, he was to do other jobs at the farm. But soon these extra duties, for which he wasn't being paid, became his only occupation at the farm.

He no longer kept an eye on the cattle, but spent all his time cleaning out ditches, mending fences and the roofs of farm buildings, digging the garden, and tidying up. But when he demanded payment for his work, the white farmer replied that he only had to pay Modise for looking after the cattle—for everything else all he owed him was a free bed in the barn. And if he didn't like it, he could get out at any time—there'd be ten others to fill his place.

Molete hadn't given way, but had gone on demanding his money, and on payday he had threatened to take legal action. At this point the farmer had come up and punched him in the face.

"Are you trying to frighten me?" he said. "Just you try, and you'll soon find out who should be scared of whom around here!"

Molete hadn't taken his complaint either to court or the police, but to Benny Tapologo, whom he had known since the old days, before he was a town councillor.

I was sitting in Benny's office when he knocked and asked shyly if he could have a chat about an urgent matter.

"When was this? I mean, when did he hit you?" asked Benny, reaching into a drawer for a fresh sheet of paper.

"On Friday, payday," replied Molete, and turning to me he added: "He has made me into his slave."

I got up to leave, but Benny stopped me.

"Wait, we haven't finished our conversation."

We'd been talking all morning about Saturday's soccer match between the Pirates, from Soweto, and the Zulu team AmaZulu, from Durban. The Pirates had unexpectedly lost, and Benny was ecstatic, because he supported their greatest rivals, the Kaizer Chiefs. I'd watched the match at the stadium in Johannesburg, and at a hotel afterward I'd talked to the Zulus' trainer, Neill Tovey, who had once been Benny's favorite soccer player.

"How much does the farmer owe you?" he asked, turning to Molete, who muttered the sum.

"Have you reported this to the police?"

Molete said no.

"And to the court?"

He said no again.

"Have you been to see Benny Malebatsi at the ANC office?"
Molete nodded to say yes.

"And?"

"He told me to write to the head office in Johannesburg."

"Yes, write to head office," sighed Benny. "You can always write to the head office."

Every week he sent his reports full of complaints to Johannesburg, but none of them were ever answered. "Your case is being dealt with at head office," he replied to those who lodged a complaint and then came back to ask what progress was being made. At first he had believed it himself, but in time he stopped. He couldn't recall a single instance of a case being settled as a result of intervention by the head office. Nor could he remember anyone in Johannesburg ever having taken any interest in his reports, neither the ones about white farmers beating their black workers and failing to pay their wages, nor the ones about them continuing to insult their employees by calling them kaffirs, niggers, and baboons.

Nor was there any answer to his letters requesting aid for the black workers and their families whom the white farmers were ordering off their land from one day to the next, even though they had lived and worked there for generations. Many of the whites were getting the blacks off their farms, in case it occurred to them to demand a piece of land for themselves. Others were evicting the blacks to make it easier to sell their land to other farmers, or to set it aside for a hunting ground or wildlife park.

The black workers' families expelled from the white farms didn't even try to object or to occupy the land, but went and squatted on the outskirts of Tshing in shacks made of boards, plywood, and sheets of metal, with no running water or electricity. They came to Benny to complain and ask for help, but apart from writing out a new report and sending it to Johannesburg there wasn't much he could do. Several times he had tried intervening with the mayor, but he always replied that his hands were tied, and that it was a matter for head office, because the farmers had the law behind them. And that in Potchefstroom the local authorities had even sent the police to supervise the expulsion of a hundred black families from farms owned by Pieter and Robert Haagner, members of the white brotherhood who on Jan Serfontein's advice had joined the ANC.

Benny could only listen to the complaints, add them to his reports, and send them to head office in Johannesburg. He used to think it was important, something that would change the fortunes of this town and its people. "A small power can't do much," he used to say. "But a great power can do anything."

Never receiving any reply from head office, finally he stopped promising the petitioners that their cases would be settled promptly, and that they'd receive compensation for the wrongs done to them. But he did go on listening to their complaints and sending reports to Johannesburg. As a town councillor he didn't have much more to do anyway.

He put Molete's complaint on the pile of documents destined for the mail. The workman got up from his chair.

"Well? Do you think something'll come of it?" he asked, shaking Benny's hand. "Should I come and ask?"

"I'll let you know if something comes back from Johannesburg," replied Benny. "It could take a while."

Molete nodded and closed the door behind him. Benny turned to me and said: "So what's Tovey like, then? You said you talked to him."

That evening I ran into Modise Molete again, at a bar in Tshing called Thobile, sitting on plastic crates with his pals, drinking beer from the bottle.

Whenever I had an appointment in Tshing I always arranged to meet at the Thobile shebeen. In the labyrinth of the black township, this was the only place I knew how to find without losing my bearings or having to ask the way—every passing stranger would confidently point me in the opposite direction. The Thobile was situated on the outskirts of Tshing, and could be reached without having to dive into the anthill of unfamiliar alleyways, and identical shacks and yards. It was also the only place in the township that I had no trouble getting away from.

It was a plain shed made of planks. After the fall of apartheid, stores had been set up in shacks like this one in the townships, selling food, clothes, and electrical goods. But the Thobile tavern sold alcohol. Lit by a naked bulb hanging from the ceiling, the colorful bottles of whisky, gin, wine, and beer stood on shelves against the wall, separated from the customers by solid steel bars, reinforced with wire netting. The alcohol was bought by the bottle, which the owner handed through a little window.

The Thobile was a shebeen only in name. There were no tables, no bar, not even a patch of floor to dance on, and no room for a stage where musicians could play. On Saturdays and Sundays, when there were league soccer matches, the owner of the place set up an old TV on a table on the grass outside, and charged people to watch football. As it was impossible to figure out who was watching TV and who wasn't, the prices of whisky and beer were several rand higher during the matches. But the customers avoided this trap by buying alcohol before the match began.

The man I had arranged to meet at the Thobile was Velaphi Qankase, a friend of Benny Tapologo's, one of his comrades from the days of the uprising in Tshing. Unlike Benny, after the great victory, Velaphi had not become a party activist, councillor, or member of parliament, but had completed an extramural degree in law, and now helped the local black workers in their disputes with the white farmers. That evening Velaphi was late, and with each passing moment I felt more anxiety, as if in the increasing darkness the fact that I was the only white man in a bar full of blacks might take on another, dangerous significance. Just then I caught sight of Modise Molete, sipping beer by the fence with several others. Recognizing me, he nodded invitingly, and pulled up a beer crate for me to sit on. He asked what I was doing in Tshing at that time of day.

"I'm waiting for Velaphi," I said.

The blacks nodded with understanding. Everyone in Tshing knew Velaphi. Molete said he'd been to see him after his visit to Benny Tapologo at the town hall.

"So it looks as if he has a lot to do here, right?" I asked.

"He can't complain of a lack of work," said Leonard, one of Molete's friends. "Whose case has he been working on lately?"

"Those two guys who were beaten up by white farmers in Ottosdal," added another. "They tried taking a shortcut home across a white farm. When the owner found out, he summoned the neighbors, and they battered the kaffirs so badly that one of them couldn't walk at all, and the other lost his hearing."

"And do you remember the guy who was tied to a truck by a white farmer and dragged about the farm for half a day? Just because he hadn't got to work on time!"

"They beat Shabalala to death for taking a tractor without permission and going to visit his family."

"And the guy who worked at the wildlife park—first the white farmer beat him up, then threw him out of the car to the lions. He sat in the cab and watched them kill the kaffir."

"And do you remember Jason Dube? The guy from Zimbabwe? He was walking across a field with some other workers when a white farmer shot him. His defense in court was that the sun had dazzled him and he thought it was a troop of baboons. 'I shot at some monkeys,' he said, and the judge let him off. He just paid a fine, but Dube will be crippled for the rest of his life."

"Can't anything be done about it?" I wondered. "You've got your own people in power here now—the mayor, members of parliament, government ministers, the president."

"They've plainly got other things to do," said Molete. "More pressing matters."

"What about the police? Can't you go to the police about it?"

The men snorted with laughter, and Molete looked at me closely, as if trying to make sure I wasn't poking fun at him.

"Old Percy went to the police one time to complain about Eugène Terre'Blanche," Leonard recalled. "To say he'd beaten him up, knocked out his front teeth, and not paid him the money he'd promised. Percy swore that right there in front of him the policemen argued over which one of them was to go to the farm and question Terre'Blanche. They all backed out of it, so eventually none of them went, and the case was dropped, because they're so scared of him."

"If you go to the police, the next day your farmer will know about it."

"If it got about town that you'd set the law on a white farmer, you'd never find work on any farm again. And there's no other source of income."

"Eugène Terre'Blanche is still in control here—he can stop me in the street any time he likes and smack me in the face."

"Clearly that's how it has to be. It was always like that, it still is, and will continue to be. If you want something to put in your mouth, you've obviously got to be ready for the fact that from time to time you're gonna get a smack in it too."

"And that's all I got out of Mandela being the president. Maybe he really is in charge over in Pretoria. I don't know, I've never even seen him," Molete Modise spat through his teeth.

John Thembine Ndzima was born and grew up on a white farm in Ratzegaai, not far from the Terre'Blanches' family property. He had gone to live in Tshing when the white farmer told him to get out because he didn't need him anymore. Ndzima moved from Ratzegaai to the town, leaving behind his parents' and grandparents' graves. He had never been back to them again. He felt bad about it, and was afraid of being punished as a result.

But fortune seemed to favor him. At first, he lived in a hut made of plywood and corrugated iron, knocked together illegally in the yard of one of the houses in the township. As a hard-working, diligent, and agreeable man, John Ndzima had no trouble finding work in the white town and on other farms. Thanks to the frugality and restraint his parents had taught him, he had soon saved enough money to buy his landlord's house from him. Though modest, consisting of just two rooms, it was neat and tidy, with a patch of garden.

He raised three children, made sure they did well at school, and borrowed money to send them all to college at black universities. His oldest daughter became a teacher, and his oldest son was an orderly at the local hospital. The whites regarded John Ndzima as a good kaffir, the kind who knows his place, knows how to behave, and doesn't take offense at just anything or put on airs.

When the blacks took power, and their mayor moved into the town hall in Ventersdorp, John Ndzima was working at the Shell gas station on the way into town. Like all the blacks, he had voted for Mandela and the African National Congress, but he didn't pin much hope on their victory.

He knew that it was impossible to change anything for the better overnight, that nothing lasting could be built in a hurry, by taking shortcuts—and that change, the genuine kind that really counts, starts inside the individual, in his heart and mind; he has to want it and be ready for it, not wait for it to happen because of other people and events over which he has no influence.

Satisfied with his lot, John Ndzima's life was measured out by shifts at the gas station, journeys on foot between the white town and the black township, suppers prepared by his wife, and testing his children on their lessons. The rhythm of his existence, which seemed to have been set once and for all, was disturbed one spring night, two years after the election they said would bring great change.

That Tuesday he was on shift at the Shell station. The sky was clear and starry, and the warmth of the approaching summer could already be felt in the wind. John was dozing off, leaning against a gas pump, when he was abruptly woken by a shrill crash of breaking glass. He leaped to his feet. The noise seemed to have come from the pharmacy next door to the gas station. Without giving it much thought, he headed in that direction.

He heard muffled voices in the darkness, the patter of feet, and the crunch of glass from a broken window crushed underfoot. When the burglars ran outside, in the light of the streetlamps John saw that there were two of them. And that they were white boys, aged about fifteen or sixteen years old.

He ran after them, but when they disappeared among the outbuildings, he gave up the chase. He went back to the gas station and called the police. He told the officers that there had been two burglars, and they were white. They took down his statement, and drove back to the police station without a word.

Two days later, John was working on the night shift again, when Eugène Terre'Blanche drove his pickup into the Engen station on the other side of the road. He always got his gas there. In town it was said that the owner of the Engen station belonged to the white brotherhood.

John knew Terre'Blanche, and like all the local blacks, he was afraid of him. He was quite capable of arriving at the gas station and ordering one of the blacks to wash his car as if he were his servant. He was always telling his workers he'd pay them if they behaved like good kaffirs. Only then could they be sure of the money, and if he was in a good mood, he got them drunk on cheap whisky. In fact the white citizens of Ventersdorp were scared of Terre'Blanche too, and feared doing anything that would rouse his anger, so they sucked up to him or kept out of his way.

Terre'Blanche came out of the kiosk, where the owner of the Engen station spent his time, went up to his car, and called over one of the black employees. John saw the boy glance toward the Shell station and point a finger at him. Terre'Blanche slowly drove over to the other side of the road and stopped his car by the pump that Ndzima was attending.

"So you're John?" he asked through the open window.

"Yes, *baas*," said Ndzima.

"And do you know who I am?"

"Yes, *baas*, I do."

"You did well to call the police after that break-in. But in future, if anything happens, you're to come to me with it first, not the police. You get it?"

"Yes, *baas*. But how do I do that? How am I to tell you, when I don't know where to go?"

"Just go to the Engen station and ask them to call the boss. Tell him everything and don't worry about the rest of it. Got that?"

Yes, baas, I've got it."

"Keep an eye on it all, John. And stop calling me *baas*. I'm called *morena*. In your language that means 'the chief,' right? Got it?"

"Yes, *baas*. Yes, *morena*."

A few days later, when John was working the night shift again, Terre'Blanche came to the Shell station on horseback. It was late by now, and the town was deserted. Terre'Blanche was in a black uniform of the kind worn by employees of his security firm for their evening patrols about town and for guard duty. A German shepherd dog was running along by the horse, on a long lead strapped to the saddle. Behind Terre'Blanche came a second horse and rider in a black uniform.

Terre'Blanche rode up to the pump where John was standing.

"Everything OK?" he asked from the saddle.

"Yes, *baas*, I mean *morena*."

"You're a decent kaffir, not like the others."

As he held out his hand to John, the dog growled. The blacks were afraid of dogs, and they all knew that Terre'Blanche trained his German shepherds to fly at the throat of any black who stretched out a hand to him. Terrified, John recoiled, but Terre'Blanche wouldn't give up.

"Come on, John, won't you shake hands with me? Don't be afraid. That dog will only do as I tell him."

As John held out his hand, Terre'Blanche seized hold of it, and with a sharp tug pulled him toward the horse.

"John, I thought you weren't so dumb, but you've been talking nonsense, saying it was whites who robbed the pharmacy. But everyone knows the burglars were black."

"No, *morena*, I saw them with my own eyes."

The dog was going mad, barking and trying to attack John.

"You're talking crap, and in statements to the police too. Tomorrow you'll go to the police station and withdraw the garbage you told them earlier. Better yet, tell them you saw blacks breaking into the store."

"No, *morena*, I can't do that. It wasn't like that, I saw them."

John was trying to free his hand, but Terre'Blanche was holding it in an iron grip. As he struggled with the white horseman, he did his best to keep away from the barking dog. Finally he tugged so hard that he reeled, lost his balance, and fell to the ground. He jumped to his feet and ran for the bathroom to hide from his attackers, but he couldn't slide the bolt fast enough. Terre'Blanche rode his horse up to the door and pushed it so hard that it sprang to the inside, knocking Ndzima to the floor.

He was scrambling to his feet when Terre'Blanche came in with the dog on its lead. He grabbed him by the throat, pressed him to the wall, and started to choke him.

"Look at me," he hissed in rage. "You see my blue eyes? It's the last time you'll see them."

He punched him in the face, stepped back, let the dog off the lead, and left the bathroom, closing the door behind him. The dog attacked Ndzima, ripping his clothes and biting his legs and arms, which he used to shield his head. Frightened to death, fighting for his life, he broke free of the beast, climbed onto the washbasin, and squeezed through a tiny window over-looking the rear of the gas station.

In the darkness he rushed among the nearest buildings, run-ning blindly ahead, jumping the fences of neighboring proper-ties, but he could still hear the barking dog, shouts, and curses behind him. When he thought he was far enough away, he headed for the lights on the main street. But when he emerged onto the empty, surfaced road, wreathed in the yellow glow of the streetlamps, he realized he hadn't run far.

Terre'Blanche, with the dog and the other man in black, were only a few hundred meters away.

"Stop! I'm telling you to stop!" cried Terre'Blanche at the sight of him. "Stop or I'll shoot!"

John Ndzima raced off toward the police station. He ran into the building, yelling that Eugène Terre'Blanche was trying to kill him. The police officers stared at him in disbelief.

"Why would he want to kill you?" asked the black officer on duty, casting an eye at his blood-stained clothes and terrified face.

It crossed John's mind that they wouldn't believe him, but would take him for a drunk and lock him in a cell for the night. As he was wondering whether asylum in a police lockup might not be the best solution, the police station door opened, and there stood Eugène Terre'Blanche.

"John!" he cried. "Aren't you being rather unwise?"

"Do you know him?" asked the duty officer, pointing at Ndzima.

John didn't wait for an answer. He rushed for the door, pushed Terre'Blanche aside, and disappeared into the darkness. He ran through the night, as fast as he could, without stopping, until he got to Tshing.

Next morning, covered in bruises and bite wounds, with his front teeth knocked out, he went back to the police station to press charges against Terre'Blanche for assault and battery. He wasn't motivated by a desire for revenge for the pain and humiliation, or a sense of injury, or by reason, but by an overpowering need for plain justice, which demands that crime should be punished.

The duty officer took out a form, wrote down his statement, and told him to go home. Through a friend, John Ndzima asked the owner of the Shell station for a few days' leave. He wanted a little time to lick his wounds and recover. He also preferred not to show his face in the white town for now. He decided to wait in Tshing until the mailman brought him a court summons for a hearing against Terre'Blanche.

The days went by, but the mailman didn't come. Nor was he summoned to the police. Finally, Ndzima decided to go to town to find out what was going on. At the police station he was told that the case had been handed over to the appropriate people, and to wait quietly. When another week went by without any news, he went back to the police station, and once again came away with nothing.

A few days later he tried again, but this time he took his shift manager from the Shell station with him, an Indian. They had only just entered the police station when Eugène Terre'Blanche appeared. Ndzima thought the Afrikaner seemed quite at home there, but then that was how he behaved everywhere in town—as if it belonged to him.

On seeing John Ndzima, he hurled abuse at him and ordered him out of town. He pushed aside the protesting Indian, telling him to get back to his own country, to India—he could demand his rights there, but here, in South Africa, he was just a vagabond with no entitlement at all.

John had just about come to terms with the idea that he would never get justice, when some police officers came to see him in Tshing—not local ones from Ventersdorp, but from Potchefstroom. He never did find out how they heard about his case. They asked him to tell them once again what had happened that night at the gas station, and then they drove him to the local police station. They asked for a copy of the complaint that Ndzima has lodged. The police chief replied that there was no charge against Terre'Blanche among his documents, so nobody could have made one. John swore on oath that he had accused Terre'Blanche of assault, and that he had signed a statement.

A quarrel broke out among the policemen. The visitors insisted that they weren't leaving town without John's statement, and threatened to send inspectors from the ministry. The local police, pinned to the wall, finally found John's statement. It turned out to have been mislaid and never sent to the court.

"It's the black woman who comes in the evenings to clean—she must have thrown it in the closet among the old documents," said the chief. "That old witch is a real curse. She can't even read."

Terre'Blanche's trial was heard before a court in Potchefstroom, not in Ventersdorp. On those days John Ndzima was afraid to go to work in town. The local Afrikaners weren't stopping at the gas station for petrol anymore, but just to shout abuse or threaten him.

"Kaffir! You won't have a life here if Eugène Terre'Blanche ends up behind bars because of you!" they cried through the open windows of their cars as they drove past. "Get out of here before we come for you!"

Seriously intimidated, Ndzima's Indian boss stopped putting him on the night shift.

During the hearing, in his usual swaggering way, Terre'Blanche claimed that Ndzima was lying, that he'd committed perjury in an attempt to frame him and have him sent to jail, and that it was he, Terre'Blanche, who was the victim of a plot.

"To be precise, Your Honor," he jeered, "it wasn't me who attacked him, but my dog Saldhana."

He was sentenced to a year in jail. This time the judge did not suspend the sentence, and rejected an appeal by Terre'Blanche's lawyers.

Whenever I met John Ndzima in Tshing or at the Caltex station, where he moved to from the Shell, he proudly told me about the days when everyone in town had been talking about him. He believed it was thanks to him, his suffering and courage, that Ventersdorp had stopped being Terre'Blanche's sovereign kingdom.

"If I hadn't gone to the police, but had accepted the injury and not demanded justice, nothing would have changed," he said. "He'd have gone on battering blacks who didn't do things the way he wanted, if not me, then someone else. And the whites would have been afraid to cross him. He always got off scot-free, and the government in Pretoria preferred to pretend it couldn't see a thing."

"If not for me, Terre'Blanche would still be the morena here, the chief," Ndzima told me the last time we saw each other at his house in Tshing.

I asked if he believed Terre'Blanche's incarceration was going to change life in Ventersdorp.

"I know one thing for sure: nothing would ever change without it."

He said that as a religious man the idea of revenge was alien to him, and that he certainly didn't intend to cause his oppressor suffering. He didn't feel hatred. He had read in the papers that Bea, Terre'Blanche's adopted daughter and only child, was taking her high school graduation exams, and he felt sorry for her. He imagined his own daughter.

He was ready to forgive Terre'Blanche, and when the Afrikaner's lawyer came to ask him to, without hesitation Ndzima wrote a letter to the authorities asking them to pardon and release him. The Afrikaans-language newspaper Beeld put it on the front page. His neighbors in Tshing tapped their foreheads in amazement and asked if he'd lost his mind.

"Jesus teaches us not to hate," he replied. "First we must learn to forgive our oppressors, and then our own crimes will be absolved too."

Ndzima's request for Terre'Blanche to be pardoned meant that after six months in prison he was conditionally discharged. When he heard about it, John battled with the thought of how to behave when they met. Terre'Blanche still filled him with fear as before. He even considered taking a few days' leave.

When Terre'Blanche finally drove up to the Shell station, he stopped alongside Ndzima and stared at him for a long while, without getting out of his car. According to John, the look in his eyes was not conciliatory or benevolent.

Soon after, Terre'Blanche was brought before the court in Potchefstroom again, this time charged with the attempted murder of Paul Motshabi, a black laborer employed on his farm, who also worked for his security firm as a night watchman.

One night, not long after the assault on John Ndzima, while

guarding a store for Terre'Blanche's firm, Paul Motshabi took a nap on the job. He had the bad luck to be caught by Eugène himself, who liked to patrol his town at night and check on the sentries. He was drunk, and that was when the devil got into him, or at least so said the local blacks.

Terre'Blanche pistol-whipped Mothabi over the head until he lost consciousness. He gave him such a thrashing that he suffered a brain injury, causing him to lose the power of speech and control of his limbs for months on end. He was only thirty, and would be crippled for life, unable to work or live independently. Realizing that he couldn't maintain the family, his wife left him, taking their children with her. He was saved from total misery and isolation by his sister Maria, who agreed to live with him in his shack made of planks, cardboard, and tin.

For beating Motshabi, Terre'Blanche was sentenced to another six years in prison. Including the punishment for attacking John Ndzima, the white brotherhood leader was sentenced to a total of seven long, hard years behind bars.

On a small patch of ground behind the tavern, Henk Malan watched as six blacks tried to shift a large wire cage from a tractor trailer. At one time he had tried to deal in parrots, but the business had failed; the empty cages had been cluttering up his yard at home, but now he had to get them out of there.

After their mother's death, his brother had paid Henk his part of the inheritance, and kept the house for himself. Then he had moved to Goshen, and Henk had lived in the house, just paying the electricity and water bills. But now his brother had written to say he'd run into trouble, and would probably have to put the house in Ventersdorp up for sale. And if so, he'd rather potential buyers didn't see the yard cluttered with parrot cages.

"Perhaps we'll finally be rid of all that ironmongery," sighed Anita. She didn't think they were going to lose the roof over their heads, but at last he'd get the cages out of the yard. "It's like living on a scrap heap! Why do you keep the things? You'd be better off selling them, even at half price. Better a few pennies than nothing."

"I can just see them flocking to buy," muttered Henk, as he watched the blacks wondering how to get the cage off the trailer.

As he was gazing at the wire box, it crossed his mind that the parrot cages were the only thing he possessed—that was all he had achieved in life.

Meanwhile the blacks were trying to work out how to spread the weight of the cage between them. Six of them had picked it up and pushed it onto the trailer in Henk's yard at home, but now they couldn't think how to get it off.

"I wonder what they'll come up with. Puzzle it out, kaffirs!" he thought.

"Mind you don't bend it!" he cried, leaning against the door frame.

They stared at him in silence.

"Bloody kaffirs!" thought Henk. "They'll just stand there staring all day! If you don't show them what to do, they never think of anything for themselves; if you don't tell them to, they won't lift a finger. What brutes!"

The tavern he ran had stopped making any profit. It was deserted. The whites didn't stop here, regarding the Blue Crane as a black shebeen, and the blacks had never entirely taken to it. If I drove over to Henk's, I usually found him in the back room, where he'd be lighting one cigarette off the last as he watched television. In the bar, which was even devoid of tables, silence reigned.

"*Foken kaffirs*! A kaffir will always be a kaffir, end of story! I've had it up to here with them!" he erupted, when I asked him how things were going. "They can't even drink like human beings. They immediately start yelling at the top of their voices, singing those heathen songs of theirs and dancing about like monkeys at the circus. You can't turn your back or they'll steal something. And when they're caught short, do you think those guys go to the toilet? No way! They just go out front and piss against a wall. I caught one of them once, and I said: 'What the fuck are you doing? Think you're in your own pigsty at home, do you?' And the guy pulls a knife on me! He didn't even stop to button his fly. He was pretty trashed and could hardly stay upright, so he went reeling when I hit him. Otherwise we probably wouldn't be having this conversation now. The old ones, who remember the past, are still bearable. They know how to behave, they know what's allowed, and what isn't. There's one guy who comes here every night. He hasn't got any money, so he buys a single beer, then comes begging after me. 'Baas, I'm a good kaffir, give me a drink on credit.' I give it to him, on the house! Because he really is a good kaffir. The worst are the young ones. You call one of those guys 'kaffir,' and he up and threatens you with the law, or pulls a knife on you. One time there were three of them having a beer here, and I called them over to bring out the trash from the back. Do you know what they said to me? They hadn't come here to be servants! I chased them out so fast you couldn't see their heels for dust!"

"What are you doing with that cage? Bloody hell!" Henk shouted at the blacks by the tractor.

As they were sliding the cage off the trailer it had tipped over, and now it was hanging in midair; Petrus and Tsepe had saved it from falling and being damaged, and were supporting it with increasing difficulty.

Jomo, who was driving the tractor, had remained sitting at the wheel. Roused from his torpor, he scrambled to the ground.

Henk leaped up to him with his hands raised, as if to fight. He grabbed Jomo by the top of his overalls and gave him a hard push. Jomo staggered, but didn't fall.

"Well? What are you waiting for?"

The blacks froze, glancing hesitantly now at the enraged white man, and now at Petrus and Tsepe, buckling under the weight of the cage. Jomo stepped back, turned around, and went to help them grapple with it. Finally, they shifted it off the trailer and onto the ground, and carried it over to the fence. Petrus went up to Malan.

"*Baas*, it's midday, and we haven't eaten yet. We could do with a break and some breakfast."

"I suppose you want me to bring you some beer as well, eh?" Henk saw them casting glances at him, curiously and hungrily, as if counting on a free meal. "It's not my fault you guys move as slow as molasses. There are four cages to be transported and you've only just managed to move one of them. Bring the second, and then you can have a break. And if you want food, go buy it at the gas station. Or the Wimpy."

As the tavern for blacks wasn't making any profit, Henk was trying to earn more on the side by mowing lawns. It seemed like a fail-safe business, because in the white town the lawns were well tended even at the poorest homes. Well-kept, neatly trimmed, and watered grass seemed to be irrefutable proof of the fact that the good times weren't over at all, and even if they were, then not irrevocably—they'd be back, fortunes would change.

He bought two lawn mowers, garden hoses, grass clippers, and rakes. Only blacks were hired for this sort of work, but none of them wanted to work for Henk. They all refused, despite the local lack of work and honest sources of income.

In his conversations with me he listed the wrongs suffered by the white citizens, in his view, under the black government. He started with the public school. The whites had built it for their children, using their own tax money. They'd built a second one, for the blacks, in Tshing.

"But the blacks wrecked their own school, so when they took power, they moved into ours," he said. "We had to fork out again and build a new school, so our children would have somewhere to study. But they'll probably try to take that one away from us too. Just as they took the swimming pool. The blacks at the town hall announced that anyone could bathe in it. Would you let your child go to a pool with blacks? We did so much for them, but they're still not satisfied. They only need us so they can take everything away from us. The day we've got nothing left maybe they'll finally be satisfied."

Leaning against the doorframe, Henk watched as the blacks drove away to fetch more cages. He walked through the tavern and stood on the sidewalk at the front, seeing the tractor off as it moved slowly down the street, silent and deserted in the midday sun. There wasn't a living soul in sight, hardly anything to prove life went on here at all. The sun-scorched air shuddered above the surface of the road, as the burning wind chased tangled balls of grass along it.

Outside the Engen gas station and the Wimpy bar located next to it there were some blacks hiding in the shade, selling oranges and apples, cigarettes, phone cards, sunglasses, and belts. "What the hell makes them think anyone could be tempted by that junk of theirs?" Henk often thought as he watched them from his tavern.

Among the black stallholders by the Wimpy bar and the furniture store Henk noticed a white girl. He saw her there every day. He knew her, or rather he knew her parents. Her name was Annike, and she was the Barnards' daughter. Old Conrad had been fond of the hard stuff, and his wife Ruth liked a drop too. They used to live on Conrad's pension, but when he finally drank himself to death and turned up his toes, the mother and daughter had been left without a penny to their names. At first the neighbors had helped, but seeing that Ruth used their money to seek consolation in the bottle, they gave up. With no other source of aid, she finally had to seek a living for herself.

She baked buns at home, which she and her daughter then sold in the street, like the blacks. Ruth traded outside the Overland store, where the local farmers came to do their shopping. Annike came to the gas station each morning, lugging along checkered bags full of the buns she sold. Henk had often seen her failing to find any takers for her wares, and offering instead to wash cars for a few rand, or keep an eye on them at the parking lot. Just like the blacks!

Henk had seen poor whites on television, homeless and jobless, squatting in shacks made of planks, plywood, cardboard, and plastic sheeting. He had seen the slums on the Magalies River outside Krugersdorp. And their inhabitants, bearded, barefoot Afrikaners in rags, with an apprehensive, acquiescent look in their eyes. He had heard about similar slums outside Johannesburg, and even about whites moving into the black townships. In Pretoria he had seen white beggars at the crossroads. The television news had reported that one in ten of the country's whites was living on benefits.

Henk had noticed that even in Ventersdorp the white citizens no longer looked the same as before. Once masterful, now they had lost their old confidence, their carefree manner and sense of being special, the hallmark of people convinced they've been chosen by fate. Deprived of this faith, they had gone gray and stale, they seemed ordinary, weaker, no different from anyone else, feeling joy and desire, pain and fear in just the same way. This new, common, human side of them was even more visible by contrast with the blacks, who were also undergoing a transformation, shaking off their old humility and timidity. They were moving about the white town more and more freely, though not long ago making a trip there had been a privilege, like a special holiday for them.

"They'll come and take away your land and houses! Then they'll take your women, and finally your God too!" Henk remembered Eugène Terre'Blanche's sinister predictions and threats. He had warned that Africa's white race would be wiped out, but he had also sworn to save it, calling for war and promising to lead the Afrikaners to victory. He had pledged that he would sooner send everything up in smoke than allow blacks to become the masters of whites. Where was he now that his prophecies had started to come true?

Henk had believed and listened to him. Like almost all the whites in Ventersdorp. Of his own choice, and out of fear of Terre'Blanche, he had become one of his followers and subjects, one of the soldiers gearing up for the great war, in which the "General" promised them a wonderful, ultimate victory. There wasn't a week when he hadn't announced that it was about to break out shortly, it was on its way, just around the corner.

"Damn and blast it!" At the memory of Terre'Blanche, Henk felt rising anger. "And now he's let himself get locked in jail! He was supposed to start a great war, but it's all ended with him beating up a kaffir! Bloody world! A man gets himself ready, like a rugby player preparing for the most important game in the season, he's done as he was told, believing he was doing what was necessary. And then it turns out the competition's off and the trainer has dissolved the team. Just like that, without giving a damn what would happen to us. They're all the same!"

De Klerk, the last white president, had let himself be tempted by Mandela and had accepted the post of his deputy. At least he had some influence on the course of things. But once removed from power, he'd let his sense of honor take him over completely, and had left the government, along with the ministers from his party. He had deprived himself of any significance; realizing his mistake, he had announced his retirement. His successor as leader of the National Party had submitted to Mandela in exchange for the post of minister of tourism and sport, and then announced that he and his entire party were joining the ANC. And so the party responsible for racial segregation had merged into one with the movement that had fought a war against it.

General Viljoen had retired too; he had called de Klerk a traitor, but had persuaded the Afrikaners to drop the idea of war, promising to force Mandela into agreeing to create an Afrikaner republic out of part of the country. Mandela had never agreed to it. The embittered Viljoen had declared that politics was a profession for rogues and liars, and that blame for his failure lay with apartheid, a mistake that had set the blacks against the whites.

"What nonsense!" Henk fumed. "Everyone was against apartheid! Both blacks and whites! Nobody was in favor of it. What a joke!"

He looked up. The sun was still high, but was starting to sink westward. Henk glanced at his watch. "If they don't hurry up, they'll never shift those bloody cages before dark," he thought. "I'll have to ask that bloody English bighead to lend me his kaffirs again."

When Terre'Blanche ended up in prison, Henk had started wondering how to move away from Ventersdorp again. He was getting cold feet. Instead of profit, the tavern was making a loss. He felt all alone in this town. The blacks scowled at him, and were frequenting the Blue Crane less and less. They complained that he treated them like slaves. Even the reverend Armand van Zyl had once stopped him after the Sunday service to say that if he was living off his black customers, he should be treating them like his guests, not shooing them away like vagrants or stray dogs.

The local Afrikaners gave him a wide berth, resenting him for opening a tavern for blacks. They started to avoid him even more when it got about that the girl who worked for him, Julianna, had married an Englishman, Mike Boardman, the son of the farmer from Buckingham. As if he, Henk Malan, had matched her up with him! He liked the girl, and he had no children of his own, so he treated her a bit like a daughter, making sure no harm came to her. She called him "*Oom*," meaning "Uncle," but the Afrikaners address all their elders that way.

People couldn't get over their amazement at her marrying an Englishman! The Afrikaner citizens of Ventersdorp weren't fond of the British, especially the Boardmans. Henk was no exception. But when Julianna married the young Boardman, he sometimes went to visit them at their farm.

He was consoled by the thought that once he fell into debt, which often happened to him, at least he'd have someone to turn to for help. But although he had no scruples about borrowing money from the farmer with Julianna as a go-between, he didn't regard Boardman as "one of us," and spoke about him disdainfully, saying, "He's such a wise guy, but he can't even maintain the farm he got from his father." Ignoring Raymond, the blacks were talking to each other in their own dialect, which the farmer knew was proof of extreme outrage on their part.

"We're never going back to him," declared Petrus firmly. "Don't tell us to do that again."

"Henk Malan is a bad man," added Jomo. "We worked for him from dawn to dusk, and he didn't even feed us. He didn't even give us a glass of water. He just ordered us about, shouting abuse and calling us names."

"And he didn't pay us," added Tsepe. "Not a penny."

When he'd sent his workers to Malan with the tractor, Boardman had promised to pay them the usual rate himself, as if they'd worked on the farm all day.

"We're not your slaves, Raymond, but you handed us over to that Afrikaner as if we were your property," said Petrus. "You've got to pay us extra."

"This is the sum we agreed."

"Oh no, no," they said, shaking their heads. "It should be extra for that. You've got to pay extra."

Increasingly often they were demanding more money from him. They refused to learn anything, train to be farmers, make an effort, or consider themselves jointly responsible for the farm. He couldn't understand it. Not only did he have to urge them to work, but he had to supervise them the whole time, watching their hands to make sure they did it properly.

They didn't want him to teach them, or explain that in order to start producing and bringing profit the land needed time. They refused to wait. They just wanted him to give them more money. And right now, this instant. "That's just how we wanted them to be," he admitted to himself. "We wanted them to obey orders mindlessly. So now we have our wish."

He explained that he wasn't a rich man and couldn't just hand out money—they had to earn it. The greater profit the farm brought, the more they'd have. They as well as he, Raymond. There was no other way, money doesn't come out of thin air, you can't just conjure it up by magic, try as you might. They shook their heads in disbelief, and complained that they'd earned more when Raymond's father was running the farm—there'd been more money then.

"Maybe you'd like to find out for yourselves how easy it is to earn money?" he replied whenever they came to insist that he pay them more. "I'll give you some land, I'll lend you the machinery and fertilizer, and you can pay me the same as for leasing pasturage, half price. Whatever you harvest will be yours. Otherwise you'll never learn to farm. You know how to work on the farm, but you have no idea how to manage it. And the more black farmers there are, the better for everyone. For the whites too, because then perhaps that government of yours will understand that they have to help farmers and care for the land. In fact it shouldn't have to be my problem at all—it should be up to your ministers."

They just shrugged. They asked why he didn't call the police to drive out the black strangers who had occupied Uitkyk. Just as Jan Serfontein, the former white brotherhood member who had joined Mandela's party and become a member of parliament, had done. When blacks occupied part of his chicken farm near Potchefstroom he hadn't hesitated for a moment. He had called the police, and they'd sent the intruders packing with their batons.

"Throw them out, Raymie, before one of them dies here,"

they warned. "If they bury someone here, nothing will ever shift them."

When they insisted he pay them double for working for Henk Malan, Raymond refused. He solemnly promised himself never to lend the man his workers again, but on Friday he paid them the usual weekly wage, without any bonus. He took his family to Pretoria for the weekend.

At dawn on Monday, when he told Jomo to fill up the tractor, he discovered that the huge fuel tank, buried in the ground, where he kept the diesel oil, was almost empty.

"It was only just filled," he said, annoyed.

"Buy some fuel and it'll be full again," muttered Jomo, casting the farmer a glance.

The farm was collapsing. Since coming back to take it over from his aging, decrepit parents, he had already spent most of his savings. When he lived in Pretoria, he had thought he was secure for the rest of his life. After just a few years on the farm, for the first time ever he was starting to worry about money. The debts were growing from year to year.

Since the blacks had taken over the country, the farms, which the previous, white government had been so proud of, had lost significance. It was hardly surprising; the Afrikaner farmers from the veld towns in Transvaal, devoutly religious, strongly attached to their traditions and reluctant to accept any change or innovation, had been the political clientele of every government in the apartheid era. It was their votes that the white ministers and presidents had courted for half a century, and in exchange for their unwavering support they had made sure that working the land brought profits on a par with those made by factories or mines in the big cities. But after the change of power the farms and their owners had ceased to count, and became a troublesome, unwanted legacy of the old system.

The ruling blacks weren't entirely sure what to do with them. Mandela had announced that he would compensate the blacks for past wrongs, and give them back the land taken from them by whites. In less than twenty-five years, he said, one-third of the country's land would belong to blacks. However, rather than dispossess the Afrikaner farmers, he wanted to persuade them to share the land of their own accord, to sell part of it to the government voluntarily, to be divided among the landless blacks.

Mandela wanted to avoid dispossessing the Afrikaners for fear of making enemies of them or bringing the country to economic collapse. He didn't want agricultural reform to be construed as revenge against the whites, which would be highly at odds with the need he was promoting for universal harmony and reconciliation. He pledged not to take the land away from anyone against their will, only to buy it from those who agreed to sell, and to pay a fair price, as much as they would get on the market.

But not many were willing to sell, and the government proved an unreliable buyer, paying late and in installments, which often meant waiting for several years. The minister of agriculture accused the farmers of deliberately inflating land prices, so the government couldn't afford to pay for it. The civil servants estimated that at such a sluggish pace agricultural reform would take a hundred years. If so, warned the minister, the authorities would have to resort to the extreme measures that they had so badly wanted to avoid. Soon a list was published of the first farms in western Transvaal that the government had decided to expropriate. After lengthy bargaining and threats of legal action, the white farmers finally agreed to the price offered by the authorities, although they were angered at falling victim to blackmail.

Taken over and shared out among blacks, the farms had soon collapsed and gone bankrupt; put on sale by the new owners, they had ended up in white hands again. Apart from land, the government hadn't given the black farmers any help. It hadn't taught them anything about farming, management, or book-keeping, nor had it explained what a business forecast or a mortgage was. It hadn't offered any cheap loans, or cash for development. Quite often the white farms taken over by the government ended up in the hands of party bigwigs and profiteers, who had no intention of working the land, but were only interested in the quickest way to sell it at a profit.

The government decided that the best way out of the fiasco of agricultural reform would be to do nothing. The unresolved issue of land ownership was also a handy argument as the next election approached. As they fought for the votes of the poorest blacks, the politicians running for office could promise to carry out agricultural reform and achieve historical justice.

But the authorities' passivity antagonized the impoverished blacks who, encouraged by the most radical political leaders, began to invade white farms and occupy them, as in Zimbabwe. There were more and more incidents involving the murder of white farmers.

"These killings are political," read Raymond in a statement by a black politician from a small, radical party, published in one of the newspapers. "They're to do with the fact that along with liberty, the blacks also expected to get land. They got nothing, so they're taking matters into their own hands and killing farmers to take the land away from them and occupy their place."

Not so eager to win the support of farmers anymore, the new black government dropped its previous habit of setting state-subsidized purchase prices, thanks to which they had been able to work out their annual plans and budgets, regardless of the state of the economy or the weather. Breaking away from everything that was connected with the old system, while also doing their best to win the world's favor and be in with current fashions, the new authorities abolished customs duty and opened the country to foreign goods.

As the prices of fuel, electricity, and water rose by the year, and so did the costs of supporting agricultural laborers, the Transvaal farms couldn't withstand the competition from cheaper maize, wheat, tobacco, and beef imported from abroad. It was more profitable to import these items from Uganda, Kenya, or even America than to farm them at home.

The uncertainty of the situation meant that neither the government, nor the banks, nor the enterprising businessmen from the big cities, were prepared to risk investments that might not bring them any return. The farms started to suffer from a shortage of cash. Mike Boardman, who helped his father on the farm, kept telling him he was employing too many black workers, and that he should lay off most of them.

"We don't need quite so many of them," he said. "All the farms are letting people go."

"The two of us can't get everything done on our own," said Raymond, irritated.

"Not everything. But what do we need all this land for? Let's sell part of the farm and buy some machines. It's a big outlay, but it'll pay off. We just need to modernize the farm a bit and we won't need the blacks to work here anymore."

"So what do you expect me to do? Am I supposed to put them in the truck and dump them in the road? They're people too—they've been living here for years."

"But where does it say in writing that we're responsible for them? Why should we have to support them?"

"You're talking like a bloody racist."

"You'd have thrown out whites without a second thought," said Mike. "But you're going to keep the blacks, even though you don't need them. Just because they're blacks? So who's talking like a racist?"

Since returning to the farm, Mike interfered in everything; he always knew better and was a greater expert. He didn't like the way anything was done, but had to change it all.

"Maize doesn't pay, it's outmoded now," he'd announced just after coming back. "Let's grow vegetables."

"But this is a maize farm, it always has been," replied Raymond.

"Is that supposed to mean it has to stay that way?"

Raymond let his son take over a large patch of land behind the barn and sow pumpkins there. Mike took them to the stores in Klerksdorp and had even bought himself a pickup truck for this purpose. He had no savings of his own, so he'd bought it on credit, though his father had warned him not to take out a loan against such an uncertain future crop. The first one was successful, but the next one was destroyed by pests. Discouraged, Mike had switched to poultry.

He had built a shed for his hens next to the house and got them special, expensive feed. He didn't want to feed them on ordinary grain or maize, though there were sacks full of them heaped up in the granary. But the profits from chicken farming never offset the costs, so finally he wound up the business, sold the hens, and distributed the ones he hadn't managed to sell to the blacks on the farm.

Whenever he told me about his son, I could sense both pride and anxiety in Raymond's voice. He liked to stand to one side and watch as Mike instructed the workers harvesting maize in the fall.

"He's a born farmer," he said, pointing at Mike. "He doesn't have anything to learn."

Raymond was worried by the state of the farm, which he wanted to pass on to his son, and also by the boy's waywardness, his lack of humility and unwillingness to be flexible. He was starting to wonder whether in his attempts to make his dream of great change come true, he hadn't actually ruined the things that mattered most to him. In endeavoring to remain true to his convictions, he had ended up at war with the town, even as he tried to change it, its citizens, their views and customs.

He himself had given Mike firsthand proof that there was no room for people like him in Ventersdorp, and it would be some time before it was possible to live there according to an outsider's principles. Raymond was gradually facing up to the idea that Mike wouldn't take over the farm from him, and everything would go to waste.

Unless Julianna kept him here, the local Afrikaner girl whom he had chosen as a wife. Raymond was fond of Julianna; he'd liked her as soon as he met her, on her first visit to Buckingham farm. But it hadn't occurred to him that his son would marry her. Although he had never said so to Mike, he was opposed to the marriage.

By marrying an Afrikaner girl, Mike was challenging the status quo, and declaring war on the town, where the British were regarded as the enemy. Knowing his son, Raymond was under no illusion that he would want to fight this war. He also knew that he'd have no chance of winning this particular battle.

"No chance," he sighed, as he watched the workers under his

son's charge burning the stubble and the grass along the roads and by the houses.

The grass was burned to clear the soil of weeds and get it ready to be fertile again. By removing the maize straw, dry grass, and leaves this way, the farmers protected their farms from fires, which on charred ground lost their destructive might and slowly went out without causing harm. The blacks also burned the grass around their houses to get rid of scrub where snakes might be hiding. They were so afraid of them that as they set the fire, they stood in their doorways, holding machetes and keeping watch to make sure none of the escaping reptiles crawled inside their homes.

"The autumn evenings on the veld can be chilly," said Raymond, as if to himself, still looking at his son. "Sometimes the blacks set fire to bundles of dry grass at that time of year to warm their hands."

They also liked to light bonfires out of boredom, and stare into the flames. Then you had to keep an eye on them, because they were capable of becoming so mesmerized that they forgot about the real world. Then the fire, escaping out of control and driven by the wind, would go racing into the dry, colorless veld, and in among the fields and buildings, where it would break into brightly burning flames.

That was how Xavier Wessels, one of Raymond's neighbors, lost his farm. The fire had consumed his house, cowsheds, barns, and tool sheds. He had lost almost everything, and only had about a dozen cows left. To rebuild his farm and his herd, Wessels had to go and earn a living in London for several years. Even so, he was lucky he had taken his family to Potchefstroom that day. Nobody was killed in the fire.

Jaco Nortje from the town of Bethlehem was burned alive in

his own pasture when it was unexpectedly engulfed by fire. Nobody could explain why the farmer had ventured so far into the veld on foot. The flames had appeared suddenly, and from all directions, so he had failed to get back to his car, parked on a dirt road. He had nowhere to run to, and no way to summon help.

"Burning the grass is a bit like saying goodbye to the past, and to everything that happened in it. Let's close the door, leave it behind us, and get ready for the new things life brings us," said Raymond, gazing at the flames, which were hardly visible in the thick, milky smoke. "It's like a purification ritual, designed to bring hope. But sometimes it turns into a smokescreen, hiding a lethal danger."

The fire from the brightly burning grass was making the surrounding earth exude heat, which could even be felt through thick boot soles. Raymond watched as the pale flames crept up to the trunks of some eucalyptus trees. They greedily lapped at the bark, and even some low-hanging boughs, but as if meeting resistance, they went around the trees and raced onward, deep into the grass, which was easier prey.

"The fire from dry grass can't hurt the old trees. They've put their roots down deep and they can easily resist it. At most it scorches them," the farmer commented quietly, as if talking to himself. "It's weak fire, although it burns brightly. At most it's a threat to the young trees—it can actually bring them down."

The smoke rising from the earth enveloped the maize field and veiled the silhouettes of the workers bustling about the fire.

"Mike and Julianna are expecting a child," said Boardman. "They're going to have a son. And I'm getting a grandson."

Julianna's pregnancy had settled the question of the wedding. It had broken the resistance of Raymond and his wife, who weren't thrilled by the match, and also of the girl's parents, who were categorically opposed to her relationship with the Englishman.

Mike was twenty-two, and Julianna was twenty-one. She had moved out of the family home to come and live with Mike in a small rented cottage near the gigantic grain silos. One night Mike had asked Julianna to climb the ladder with him onto the roof of the tallest silo. He took some champagne and glasses with him, and at sunset he proposed to her. Earlier on, he had gone all the way to Johannesburg to get her an engagement ring. They decided to have the wedding on the first anniversary of the day they met.

Once the wedding date had been set, over supper at the farm Julianna asked if she could invite Eugène Terre'Blanche to the ceremony; she had lived next door to him for many years, and called him "Uncle." Terre'Blanche had just come out of prison, conditionally released for good conduct.

"Why not?" replied Boardman, surprised. "Let him come."

Raymond was planning to invite some of his old friends from Johannesburg and Pretoria to his son's wedding. The thought of the faces they'd make at the sight of the white brotherhood leader put him into a good mood.

Although I went to Ventersdorp several times more, I never met Eugène Terre'Blanche again.

Though sentenced to seven years in jail, Eugene did not spend as much as half that time behind bars. When the judge announced the sentence, Terre'Blanche realized they would lock him in the same cell as blacks. He was horrified. He pawned his farm and land, and ran up enormous debts to cover the court costs and pay the lawyers handling his appeal.

He began to show remorse. He asked for a milder sentence, begging to be allowed to serve his term of detention on the farm. He swore that he was prepared to stay inside the house and work hard from dawn to dusk—he would even sweep the streets of Ventersdorp, anything rather than be shut away with blacks. All in vain. The judge did not accede to his requests and complaints, and had him locked up in Rooigrond jail near Mafikeng. Of the thousand criminals imprisoned there, only a few were whites. The prison guards were black too.

"I was the only white man in my cell, and it was a tough time for me," said Terre'Blanche the day he was released. "Prison was my Golgotha—it brought me even closer to God. I have always regarded myself as a religious man, but just as for many others who think of themselves as good Christians, in my life God had been the spare wheel, rather than the steering wheel. In prison, that changed."

According to one of the Johannesburg newspapers, on his first night locked in a communal cell with blacks, the white brotherhood leader hadn't slept a wink, and kept liberally treating everyone to cigarettes. Terre'Blanche himself insisted that he had quickly and easily come to terms with his black fellow prisoners. "I convinced them that I was not their enemy, and did not want war with them at all," he said. "The Afrikaners have no intention of persecuting and enslaving others. They just want to be Afrikaners, and to be allowed to live in their own way."

"I don't know how I managed to survive it all, but cowboys don't cry," he said at a press conference that he called on the occasion of his release at the Elgro hotel in Potchefstroom. "On my way to prison I put my life in the hands of the Creator, and he saved me. I rediscovered the Lord. Evidently that was the very reason why I had to undergo this test."

He came out on conditional release for exemplary conduct. He had worked at the prison farm, from dawn to dusk. He tended the cattle, took care of the horses, and even rode them.

304 ❖ Wojciech Jagielski

He galloped into the veld, far from the prison walls. "I was entirely alone, for days on end, with nobody keeping an eye on me," he said. "I quite often thought of running away. And yet I did not. In prison I matured."

He also wrote poetry, read the Bible, and led the prayers. "Terre'Blanche's world outlook didn't change," said his lawyer. "He became more patient and understanding." And Bojosi Issac Medupe, the black prison chaplain, even claimed that he and Eugène had become friends. "Prison changed him out of recognition," Medupe insisted. "I won't say he became an angel, but he came out of prison a better person, no longer judging people according to the color of their skin."

At the press conference at the hotel, the journalists asked Terre'Blanche if he regretted the crimes that had put him behind bars. "I have no regrets," he replied. "I have asked for forgiveness, and I have been forgiven. So what is there for me to regret?"

When he was released, his supporters brought his favorite horse, the black Attila, to the prison gate; he had also ridden the same horse to the prison at the start of his sentence. Dressed in a black uniform, he cantered through the streets, saluting and greeting the passersby, who were surprised to see him. He seemed oblivious to the cluster of black kids who ran after him shouting: "Hey! When are you gonna fall off your horse?"

When he entered the hotel where the press conference was being held, it was plain to see how thin he had grown in prison and how much he had aged. He looked older than his sixty years. He also upset his supporters by no longer inciting them to war, or threatening revenge. "I am an old man, and not a politician, I'm not off to parliament. We lost our war long ago," he announced at the press conference. "Now my only concern, with God's help, is to get my farm back. I know I'll have to work harder than ever before. But all I need is a piece of land I can cultivate."

Benny Tapologo learned from the radio news that Terre'Blanche was back in town.

"Well-known white politician Eugène Terre-Blanche, founder and leader of the Afrikaner Resistance Movement, was conditionally released from jail today, where he served time for assaulting two black men," said the newsreader. "The condition for his release is that he should pledge not to comment in public on his sentence and his time in prison. Nor will he be permitted to leave his home town of Ventersdorp."

"So it's all for nothing," thought Benny.

He mechanically tidied the official documents, sorting and piling them on his desk in neat stacks. He looked around the empty office, which he was to vacate by the end of the month. The first forebodings that something was going wrong had entered his mind when a report he had sent to Johannesburg complaining about the lady mayor of Ventersdorp had gone unanswered.

All he had written was what the citizens of Ventersdorp were saying about her: that she had no idea how to run the town, where the electricity and water supply had stopped working because the town hall wasn't paying the bills for them, and the public services weren't collecting the trash from the streets. In the black township, Tshing, antigovernment disturbances kept breaking out, as in the past, with rioters erecting barricades in the streets, and looting and torching stores and houses belonging to civic officials. In the old days, the rebellion had been aimed at the white government and the apartheid system. Now

306 ❖ Wojciech Jagielski

the rebels were demanding the resignation of the black lady mayor, who was good for nothing, but was issuing government contracts to her friends, and giving official posts to her relatives. Under her administration the town was on the verge of bankruptcy, while she was recklessly spending state money on her own requirements. Like the time when her car broke down, and at town hall expense she had them bring her a Mercedes luxury sports limousine from a rental place in Potchefstroom.

"The comrade mayor is harming our party and our cause, and in the citizens' view she should be dismissed from her post immediately," he closed the report. "She might provide our opponents with proof that black people aren't really capable of governing."

The lady mayor had never taken to him; she saw him as a wise guy and bighead who thought that as he'd been a town councillor for more than ten years, he knew it all and could interfere in everything. She didn't want him as her adviser at all. Benny had been offered this post the day he learned that the party wasn't going to enter him for the next town council election.

"That's the decision from on high—there's nothing to be done about it," explained his comrades from the ANC in Tshing. "Anyway, it's more of a promotion than a demotion. Everyone's happy with you. In Mafikeng and Johannesburg they can't praise you enough. Adviser to the mayor is a far more important post than just one of the town councillors."

That day it was also announced that in the provincial capital, Mafikeng, the post of minister of agriculture was going to the former white brotherhood member Jan Serfontein. "That man has a head on his shoulders," said the comrades from the ANC, shaking their heads in admiration, at the former local hotel in Ventersdorp where they had relocated their office. They appreciatively remembered how Serfontein had chosen black politicians as his business partners in order to gain the respect of the authorities, and easier access to preferential credits and contracts. "He knew who to keep in with. That sort of person always lands on his feet."

Benny had heard about the factional, fratricidal wars being waged within the party leadership in Mafikeng. Power, influence, access to good positions, privileges, and money were all stakes in the game, the spoils of war, for which life-and-death battles were fought, as if with weapons. In rich Cape Town or Johannesburg there were so many trophies to be won that even those who were defeated in the power struggle were not left empty-handed. In impoverished western Transvaal there were barely enough of them for the victors, and so whoever came out on top took everything. The loser sank to the very bottom, and his vanquisher made sure he never rose from it again. In the provinces, the rivalry for influence and a share of the power turned into such a brutal and destructive fight for survival that the participants forgot about the local administration.

Now and then inspectors had to be sent from ANC headquarters in Johannesburg to investigate and hush up corruption scandals, and also supervisors tasked with imposing discipline and order. To no avail. In Mafikeng even the most honest, most austere individuals yielded to temptation and gave in to corruption more avariciously, with even greater abandon than the people whom they were supposed to be monitoring. All the officials, mayors, governors, or ministers whom the party put up for promotion immediately changed into possessive, greedy, bloodthirsty beasts.

In this war for power and survival every foot soldier counted, every post, even that of local councillor in a town as inconspicuous as Ventersdorp. Even it could serve as sufficient plunder to repay loyalty as well as wartime defenses.

Benny didn't belong to any party faction, and so he had to give up the post of councillor. One of the ANC activists whom I spoke to in Ventersdorp told me that Benny may well have been honest, but he was a poor councillor, cowardly, lacking imagination and initiative, and wasn't suited to politics. Otherwise he would never have got stuck at the town hall for so long—he'd have been noticed at headquarters, or at least would have gained the interest of one of the congress factions in Mafikeng. But he hadn't been needed by anyone.

Not long after he was informed that he would cease to be a councillor, the lady mayor fired him from the job as her adviser. She didn't drop the slightest hint about the complaint he had written against her. She merely informed him that according to guidelines from headquarters recommending equal rights for the sexes, she had to employ a woman in his place.

He was transferred to the civic administration, located right next door in the old town hall building. He was to supervise and coordinate the work of the individual departments, which, as in the past, were run by white officials, though they no longer held management posts. But to tell the truth, he never found out exactly what his job was supposed to involve, what was required of him, or what was expected. He just had to be the white employees' superior.

"So is that all it was about?" Benny found himself wondering ever more often. "Just to take the best jobs for ourselves, and leave everything else unchanged? Not even swapping roles with the whites, but more like taking all the power and privileges from them. And then ruling over the kaffirs just as they used to, controlling the good kaffirs, patient and humble, who know their place."

Preserving the old, familiar system, habits, and customs required no effort; it was simpler and easier than creating new ones. It was enough to call the old things by new names and pretend everything had changed. It all depended on the good kaffirs. As long as they believed what they were told, as long as they agreed to it, there was no actual need to change anything.

One time I asked Benny what had really changed in Ventersdorp since the black government came to power.

"Mainly that nowadays it's virtually only blacks who hold positions of authority here," he admitted. "It's impossible to change something overnight that took shape over whole centuries. Sometimes you can destroy things, but not change them."

A presenter on the radio was encouraging the listeners to call in and say what they thought about the release of Eugène Terre'Blanche from prison. Between the conversations he read out news bulletins including comments by politicians: "The leaders of the African National Congress do not think that Mr. Eugène Terre'Blanche's release from prison represents any threat to democracy or liberty. Government spokesman Smuts Ngonyama declared that Eugène Terre'Blanche, known to his supporters as the Lion of Transvaal, no longer threatens democracy and never really did pose a threat to anything."

Benny heard a knock at the door. It was Thabang, from the mayor's office.

"Have you heard? They've let Eugène out!"

Benny smiled and nodded.

"He's sure to get here early this evening! Are you coming to watch?" asked Thabang.

He was excited, almost joyful, as if Terre'Blanche's release from prison was a reason to rejoice.

"I've got work to do," replied Benny.

"OK, I'm out of here! I wonder if he's changed!"

Thabang let the door slam behind him, and Benny went up to the window. The black officials were gathering in the square outside the town hall, talking animatedly. "I bet it's about Terre'Blanche," he thought. Apart from a policeman who, surprised by the crowd, stopped for a moment before disappearing into the police station, Benny couldn't see any whites. They weren't coming onto the streets, they weren't lining up on the sidewalks to welcome their leader back to town. There was nobody in front of the AWB monument in the park outside the town hall. If anyone was waiting for Terre'Blanche to come back, it was blacks rather than whites. So maybe they needed him more than the whites did?

The whites needed him because he took their prejudices upon himself, including the most deeply hidden ones, and justified them, removed the brand of shame and evil from them, freeing them of a sense of guilt and fear of isolation. But the blacks evidently needed him too, or at least those who exercised power in Ventersdorp in the name of the blacks and by their choice. In every deed, in every word, even by his very existence, he did them the service of absolving their mistakes, their indolence and negligence. And provided a convenient excuse for their reluctance to introduce the major changes they had promised.

As Benny stood at the window, watching the crowd growing outside the town hall, it occurred to him that Terre'Blanche's release from prison was even more gratifying for the authorities in Pretoria and Mafikeng than for the white townspeople, whom Terre'Blanche wanted to lead and guide.

Mike and Julianna's wedding was held at Buckingham farm. They had an altar set up in the garden outside the farmhouse, and a tent under the trees for the wedding guests.

Although he was invited to the ceremony, Eugène Terre'Blanche didn't come, to the disappointment of Raymond's guests from Pretoria and Johannesburg. He had called to say thank you for the honor, and to excuse himself with urgent business and previous engagements.

After coming out of jail, for some time he really did retreat to the farm, as his conditional release demanded, in an effort to recover his health, which had been impaired by incarceration and age. He also underwent heart surgery.

Thanks to help from his neighbors, and also from AWB members nationwide, he had recovered his farm and his land. When his farm was auctioned by court order to cover the costs of his trials, his neighbors and friends had agreed to buy his grazing land, fields, buildings, and agricultural equipment, merely in order to sell it all back to him at cost, without any interest, once he regained his liberty. To recover his inheritance, he had to borrow from the banks and from private individuals again. In any case, he was permanently in debt, constantly hounded by unpaid bills; times were changing, but he still couldn't get on top of the bookkeeping or tidy up his paperwork.

Times were changing, but not Eugène Terre'Blanche. He never changed, just like Ventersdorp. Once his period of conditional release was over, he went back to his old impersonation of a Boer general, to the processions and rallies, where he made fiery speeches, predicted total annihilation, and called for an uprising. He gave just the same performance as before, beneath monuments to Boer victories and martyrdom, and on their old battlefields. He travelled to Pretoria, Vryburg, and Vegkop, making pilgrimages to sites in the former Boer republics of Transvaal and Natal, now divided among the new South African provinces.

Meanwhile, Jacob Zuma was elected as independent South

Africa's third president. "The good Lord punished us with governments of traitors and losers. Our fatherland has become a land of crime, ravaged by thieves, murderers, rapists, swindlers, and liars. More people get killed here in peacetime than anywhere else in times of war. We are governed by a president who is burdened with charges of theft, who has six wives, and who takes new lovers for himself from among his own nieces," he cried at the rallies.

It was no longer thousands but barely a few hundred people who came to them now, yet Terre'Blanche had not stopped believing the entire nation stood behind him. He was confirmed in this conviction by a television poll, in which the public voted for the greatest citizens in the country's history. Nelson Mandela won the popular poll, but Terre'Blanche came twenty-fifth on the list of a hundred names.

"Do you want to live in a country like this? I don't! I want to live separately, in my own country, as built by my ancestors. That is my only salvation! This was the land of milk and honey, but since they took over, there's nothing left but smoldering ruins. I call on you, Afrikaners! Humble yourselves before the Lord and beg him for forgiveness!"

He announced that he was resurrecting the white brotherhood, but not as a volunteer force, mustered for war, but as a political party, which would demand rights for the Afrikaners in parliament and the courts, including the foreign ones. He sent a delegation to Geneva with a demand for the United Nations to recognize the Afrikaners as the same sort of native race in Africa as the Bushmen, the Aborigines in Australia, and the Apache and Sioux in North America. When he was refused, he accused the UN of racism. He announced that he would go and complain to the international tribunal in The Hague, and would demand that it recognize the rights of the Afrikaners to liberty and their own state. He claimed to have the land purchase agreements that the Boer leaders had concluded with the black kings locked in a safe, and that any court would award the Afrikaners not just Transvaal, but also part of Natal.

He started meeting with journalists again, and even invited the black Charles Mogale from the Johannesburg paper *Sowetan* to interview him. "I haven't changed my opinion of the blacks," he told him. "We are different, anyone can see that. And so it will remain. But I do not hate blacks. Why on earth should I? Being attached to my own race doesn't mean I immediately have to hate others."

He charged others with hatred—including the black government, which was closing its eyes to the killings of white farmers, to frighten other ones and prompt them to run away, then take over their farms, fields, and pastures. Shortly before his death he accused Julius Malema, one of the ANC youth leaders, of disseminating hatred, because he enjoyed singing an old rebel song about killing Boers at his public events. "That is a summons to war," he warned. "Let nobody be surprised if someone gets killed."

A month later he was dead, murdered in his own bed.

Sergeant Dhumela stood in the open doorway of Isaiah Ngobeni's house and asked about Chris Mahlangu; he wanted to know if Ngobeni really was acquainted with him.

Of course he was—Chris was his nephew, and six months ago he had actually been living in his hut. He had moved out, saying he wanted to get married and needed money for planks and plastic tarpaulin to build a house. So Ngobeni had given him the hut that had served him as a shelter when he first moved to Mabopane. And he'd thrown in almost five hundred rand for plywood to make the inside walls.

"Well then?" asked the policeman. "Do you know this Mahlangu guy, or not?"

"How could I not know him? He's my brother's son. Has something happened to him?"

"Haven't you heard? They say he killed Eugène Terre'Blanche."

Isaiah Ngobeni knew about the Afrikaner's death, but it took him a long time to give credence to the idea that it was his nephew who had taken the man's life. He only believed it when he went to see Chris in custody.

"He asked me for cigarettes. I don't approve of smoking, but I felt sorry for him in that prison cell, so I went to the store and bought him a pack."

In a navy-blue suit and woolen sweater over a clean shirt, washed and shaven, Ngobeni was completely unsuited to the place where I found him, and that was his home. I'd spent half the day wandering about until I finally found the address I'd copied from the court files.

Mabopane was a large, black town situated about two hours' drive from Pretoria. However, none of the streets was called "Phase 8," and nobody had ever heard of such a name, not even the black policemen patrolling the streets that Sunday afternoon. I was just about to give up, when the next policeman I asked said that Phase 8 was an area outside town, set aside for vagrants.

There were several thousand outsiders from poorer neighboring countries living in Phase 8, mainly from Zimbabwe, Mozambique, and Malawi, who for the past decade had been drawn to South Africa in search of work at the gold and diamond mines, in factories or on farms. The residents of Mabopane called them vagrants and strays, and didn't like them, because by agreeing to work for a pittance, they took jobs from the natives. Apart from foreigners, there were locals living in Phase 8 too, immigrants from indigent villages on the Limpopo, and even Zulus from the green hills on the far side of the Drakensberg range.

The settlement was scattered on the hillsides above a wide, surfaced road running along the valley. Huts and shacks, cobbled together from boards, poles, plywood, corrugated iron, and plastic, rose from the cracked, stony ground amid stunted acacia trees, thorny bushes, and cacti. Narrow paths amid tall, withered grass and prickly thistles led to widely scattered yards. No water supply or plumbing had ever been brought here. People drew their water from a well, relieved themselves in the bushes, and threw their trash over the nearest fence, made of rocks and branches. Only a very few of the huts had electricity, produced by fuel-powered generators. But each of them had its own identification number, assigned by the Mabopane town council. Nailed to the gate into Isaiah Ngobeni's yard there was a board marked with the number 1244.

I was guided there by a girl I passed as I drove along the road down the valley. She had suddenly appeared on the verge, as if she'd shot out of the soil. She was covered in it—on the dirty gray skin of her arms and legs, on her ragged clothes, and in her tangled hair. She stared blankly when I asked her for Isaiah Ngobeni's house.

"Ngobeni, Isaiah Ngobeni, Phase 8," I went on.

She nodded.

"You know him? Do you know where he lives?"

She nodded again.

"Can't you talk?"

"*No English.*"

She got in the back seat, and showed me which way to go by pointing. She stank of alcohol and sweat. She told me to drive off the road down a barely visible track that climbed amid large rocks to the top of a hill.

"Ngobeni," she said, indicating an acacia copse.

I nodded to say I understood. With an effort, as if feeling its way, the car slid across the grass, scraping its undercarriage on the stones.

"Chris Mahlangu," she said.

She was staring at me in the rearview mirror.

Before meeting her, as I wandered along the valley, I had stopped several people to ask for Isaiah Ngobeni. They had looked at me hesitantly, with suspicion, then either said nothing, or answered that they didn't know anyone called Ngobeni, and had never heard the name before—he wasn't from round here at all. At a crossroads I'd been stopped by a police patrol.

"You're going round in circles. What are you looking for?" asked the officer, inspecting my passport. "You're not one of those guys from Terre'Blanche, are you?"

The girl whom I met in the valley was the only one who admitted she knew Ngobeni and promised to take me to him. She also mentioned the name of Chris Mahlangu without my asking.

"Chris Mahlangu," she repeated, pointing at her belly.

Isaiah Ngobeni said her name was Ntombifuthi, and she was Mahlangu's girlfriend. They'd been living together for ages, and she'd even borne him two children. Their daughter, the older child, was eight now, and the son was three. Mahlangu was going to marry her and build a house for them to live in together as a family. He wanted a place to settle and put down roots. To get money for that, he had left Mabopane several weeks earlier and gone to western Transvaal.

Nobody in Mabopane knew how he got there or when. In fact, nobody was ever asked that sort of question round here. Isaiah Ngobeni couldn't even say when Chris had come to him for the first time, or how he had found him in Mabopane. At a court hearing in Ventersdorp Mahlangu had said he came from the town of Bela-Bela in Limpopo Province, but Ngobeni remembered that the first time he had seen him was while visiting the family in Zimbabwe, in a place called Chiredzi on the other side of the Limpopo. Chris was very small then, not yet at school. His father, Ngobeni's brother, worked as a sugarcane cutter on plantations owned by white farmers.

He had a wife and children in Chiredzi, but he also had half a dozen others in various towns on either side of the river, wherever he could find work. There were thousands of nomads like him who travelled the country, roaming about the farms and gold mines, stopping for longer where they were needed, and moving on once there was no more use for them.

They didn't take the old families with them, but left them to their fate, before starting new ones in new places. As if they were constantly beginning their lives over again. For them, endless wandering was the only familiar way to live, to survive, to struggle for existence. Doomed to vagrancy, they never settled down. They were never tied to anything or anyone forever, and regarded no place as their own. The only permanent thing they left behind them were the tracks along which their sons and grandsons followed them.

They were like balls of grass torn from the ground and tangled, then driven across the veld by the breeze. Continually chased by gusts of wind, they passively roll onward, into the unknown, never stopping anywhere for long. I once saw the wind seize a ball of dry grass and hurl it into a burning meadow. The flames engulfed it, changing it into a ball of fire, which was blown across the undulating veld, taking the fire with it, until some laborers caught up and extinguished it.

Nothing certain was known about Chris Mahlangu, neither where he was from, nor his age. Nobody even knew if that was his real name. He gave various dates and places of birth, claiming that all the documents capable of certifying who he was had burned to ashes in a fire at the hut where he'd lived with his mother and her next cohabitant. He hadn't got on well with his stepfather, and it was he, after a row and a fight, who had set fire to the shack. Since then he had wandered from town to town, looking for employment on the farms or mowing and burning the grass.

In the whole of Phase 8, only Isaiah Ngobeni had managed to break the cycle of eternal wandering. His yard was swept and clean, and in his shack he had even furnished a tidy living room, where in place of honor stood a large couch, bought at the market in Mabopane. Facing the couch, there was a television set on a small table, which he switched on in the evenings when he started up the power generator.

He had four children and a permanent job as a night watchman at one of the big stores in Pretoria, to which he commuted twice a week.

"I wanted to help him to settle down too, because endless wandering is no life," he said, when I asked him to tell me about Chris Mahlangu. "He's a good boy, gentle and quiet, the kind who respects his elders and knows how to behave, although he never finished school. He drank a bit too often for my liking, but he never did anyone harm because of it, he never got into a fight or ever had a reason to take revenge on anyone."

Isaiah Ngobeni had no idea how and why his nephew had ended up in Ventersdorp. When he was still living in Mabopane, he had mown the grass for a white man named Frans. It was clearly Frans who had got him a job at Eugène Terre'Blanche's farm. He may not even have known whom he was going to work for.

Terre'Blanche had also hired Patrick, the teenager from Tshing who had dropped out of school; in the absence of his parents who were working away from home, he had got into bad company and was caught breaking into a cookie factory. As a penalty, he cleaned the police station, washing the floors and scrubbing the restrooms.

Terre'Blanche's friends had warned him that by hiring a vagrant and a hooligan he was asking for trouble. But it didn't bother him—he was looking for cheap laborers, and he knew he wouldn't have to pay these ones much. Indeed, he was soon behind with the payments, but when Mahlangu demanded his money, Terre'Blanche just hurled abuse and hit him.

Mahlangu had gone to the police station to make a charge against him. At first the policemen had refused to accept the complaint at all, and then they spent a long time arguing over which of them was to go to Terre'Blanche's farm to caution him. Finally none of them had gone.

"You've only yourself to blame," one of them had told Chris. "Don't say you didn't know who Eugène was when you hired yourself out to him."

Mahlangu had thought of giving up the job and leaving, but in that case Terre'Blanche certainly wouldn't have given him his back pay.

Apart from tending cattle on the farm, Mahlangu mowed the lawn outside Terre'Blanche's house in Ventersdorp. In the evenings, as the sun died down, and the stone walls of the houses, the asphalt, and even the leaves on the trees emanated heat, the bittersweet, warm smell of freshly mown grass wafted about the town.

Few of the townspeople cut their own grass with motorized mowers, but most preferred to employ blacks to do it, using machetes with curved, shining blades, which serve in Africa for farmwork, but also for killing. Eugène Terre'Blanche kept a machete at home. On the farm he never took a single step without one.

4

On the day of Eugène Terre'Blanche's burial, the authorities in Ventersdorp called upon its black citizens to stay at home in Tshing, and not to drift about the white part of town unnecessarily. It reminded the blacks of the times when they were driven out of town by squads of AWB members taking it over as a rallying platform for their leader.

Although the funeral was on a Friday, willing to comply with the requests of the trade union bosses, the local office managers and store and workshop owners gave their employees the day off. To provide some sort of occupation and keep people away from the town, the union bosses and the local ANC leaders convened some neighborly gatherings in Tshing at which, among other things, they urged the blacks to refrain from singing the old rebel songs, especially the one about killing Boers.

Segregating the blacks and whites for the time of the funeral was aimed at preventing riots and street fighting. Since Terre'Blanche's death hundreds of his supporters and AWB members had come down to Ventersdorp from all over the country. As in the past, they were parading about town in uniforms, wearing swastika armbands, and waving the flags of the old Boer republics.

Journalists had been arriving too, including foreign ones. The murder on the farm was a major incident. It was being covered by the newspapers, and discussed on the radio and television. Several thousand people were expected to attend the funeral, and twice as many policemen. A helicopter had even been sent from Pretoria to keep an eye on the town from the air.

It wouldn't have taken much for a riot to erupt outside the courthouse when Terre'Blanche's killers were brought there from jail for the first hearing. When they got out of the prison vans with a police escort, the blacks outside the courthouse cheered at the sight of them. "Heroes! They killed Beelzebub! Serve him right! We should have done it ourselves long ago, but we were too scared to look him in the eye. He thrived on our suffering, he did us harm and he enjoyed it. At last we're going to be free! The world will be a better place without him! Now the whites will respect us. Chris Mahlangu for mayor of Ventersdorp!"

The whites outside the court would willingly have hanged Terre'Blanche's murderers from the nearest lamppost. The AWB members thundered that by killing their leader the blacks had declared war on the white race. "This is a land of crime! They've crucified Eugène Terre'Blanche, just as the Jews crucified Christ, because he wasn't afraid to speak the truth. Eugène was a good man, but he had everyone against him. We must be on our guard, and stay alert with our guns in our hands, to kill the bastards who are out to kill us. We want our land and our own place under the sun. We want our own country, we want to be free."

Helen Zille, leader of the opposition in parliament, declared that the death of Eugène Terre'Blanche had symbolic significance. "A symbolic murder can often be the match on the dry grass." National president Jacob Zuma appeared on television in person to make an appeal for calm and consideration. "It is our duty to condemn this crime and to refrain from acts liable to disturb unity," said Zuma in a speech delivered on the very night after Terre'Blanche's murder. "I resolutely condemn this cowardly act. The murder of Mr. Terre'Blanche is unacceptable, and we must all unite against this crime." Zuma told his minister of police to go to Ventersdorp, meet with the family of the white brotherhood leader, and convey his condolences.

The danger in the town was so great that on the day before the burial Jean and Elsa Meyer, owners of the Eli-Shammah funeral parlor, who were taking care of Terre'Blanche's interment, decided to fit extra locks to the room where his body was being kept—because there were rumors circulating that someone would try to steal it.

Terre'Blanche's widow, Martha, chose a rosewood coffin with gold fittings for her husband. She also brought a large framed photograph of Eugène on his horse to the church with her. She believed that was the way he would want to be remembered. The photo was to stand beside the coffin during the funeral service. His widow also decided that Eugène's favorite horse, the raven-black Attila, was to be given away to an unfamiliar farm near Klerksdorp. Dora didn't want him for her stud farm. She raised Arab horses, but Attila was a Friesian, and she couldn't let them crossbreed.

From the church, the funeral cortege was to make its way to the Terre'Blanches' farm at Ratzegaai, where Eugène was to be buried in the family graveyard, beside his father and grandfather. The day before the burial a digger had carved out a hole for a new grave under the old trees.

On the day of the funeral not many blacks were seen in

town. As the funeral cortege moved through the town with Terre'Blanche's coffin, they came onto the streets. They watched the procession in silence, solemnly, pensively; it was hard for them to believe this particular ceremony was really happening. Years ago the white brotherhood members had reacted in a similar way when the first black person was buried at the old cemetery in public view.

Terre'Blanche's funeral began at midday. So many people came that there wasn't enough room for them all in the Afrikaans Protestant Church on the edge of town. The pastor had speakers placed outside the church doors, for those who couldn't come inside to take part in the service too.

The funeral oration was delivered by Steve Hofmeyr, a famous Afrikaner poet and singer, who came to the town from Pretoria. "None of the white peoples of Africa has borne as much suffering as the Afrikaners, none of them has lost quite so many of the best among them. If you can't understand that, you can't understand the Afrikaners either. It's very hard to come to terms with this death. But we are calm, we shall not give in to despair or the desire for revenge. Not yet."

The reverend Ferdie Devenir, Terre'Blanche's favorite pastor, led the service and read from the Bible. He ended by calling on the Afrikaners to return to God, for otherwise doom lay ahead of them. As the funeral cortege set off on its journey to the farm, from a sky that had hung heavy with clouds all morning, a sudden downpour fell on the town.

Not long after Eugène Terre'Blanche's death, Mike Boardman finally decided to leave for Australia.

He had made the decision long ago, and was angry at himself for being beset by doubts, and giving in to the temptation to keep putting off all the important resolutions, choices, and challenges. He believed, or maybe he just wanted to believe, that something was going to make the decision for him—that without his involvement something was going to happen that would change everything, or at least resolve it.

By now he was tired of arguing with Julianna and his father, both of whom seemed determined not to notice the threat or to understand its inevitability. He didn't feel strong enough to go on fighting with them. The result of Terre'Blanche's death was that he let himself be seduced by the hope—the conviction in fact—that it wouldn't be just another murder on the veld, but would mark a turning point, the dividing line between the past and the future, a big enough shock to make it impossible simply to return to daily business and the usual status quo. By giving in to this belief, he was succumbing to weakness—like just about everyone in Ventersdorp. The whole town seemed to be waiting for what would happen next.

And then, two weeks after Eugène's murder, there was an attack on Arjen Strotmann's farm. Mike and Julianna were living on the adjacent property, in a rented house at an abandoned farm. The owner didn't even expect them to pay rent. He just wanted them to carry out any necessary repairs and prevent the house from falling into total ruin or being robbed by laborers from the neighboring farms.

Strotmann was lucky that his daughters had stayed at his house for the night instead of going home to their bungalow at the other end of the farm, where his ex-wife had been living since their divorce. The older girl called her mother at dawn on Sunday, when she was woken by the sound of a gunshot. Strotmann was on his way out to the veranda to throw the dogs some bones. He turned the key in the lock, but before he could depress the handle, the door opened and three blacks pushed their way into the kitchen. One was holding a pistol. He fired, hitting the farmer in the leg. The three men pounced on Strotmann, and tried to tie his hands. He didn't even feel the knife jabbing him several times during the struggle. The attackers ran off when they heard cars driving up to the house.

When they heard about the attack, Mike and Raymond Boardman went straight to Strotmann's farm. An ambulance had taken him off to the hospital, and several of the neighbors were gathered outside the house. Henk Malan was standing on the porch.

"So who will it be now? Who's going to be next?"

"They're going to do us all in, one by one, it's just a matter of time."

"It's all going according to their plan. The government lot stir up the blacks, by deliberately singing songs about killing Boers at their rallies," said Henk. "They want to get rid of us, but on the quiet. What do they need an international scandal for? As it is, they're sure to make us start selling the unprofitable farms and moving away from here."

That was just what Mike thought; he had said it a thousand times, as he quarreled with Julianna and his father. He was sure there was no future for him in Ventersdorp. First he'd considered California, then he'd had the idea of going to Australia.

"I'm not going to get stuck here waiting for death," he said. "You have to do something, not just hope it'll be all right."

"You want to leave? That's like giving in," replied his father. "This is your place—do you want to run away from it for the sake of peace and quiet?"

"They're not going to leave us in peace here, they're not going to let us live," he told Julianna, urging her to leave. "We're going to kill each other."

On the day Strotmann was attacked, Mike and Julianna moved out of the house on the farm. He'd come home and found her crying. She said she couldn't stand it any longer, she couldn't go on living in the middle of nowhere, left on her own all day. Mike had no objections. For the past few days he'd been bothered by the colored plastic bags tied to poles and fences along the dirt roads between the farms. They looked like signs. They hadn't been there before. Or maybe he just hadn't noticed them.

"Let's move to my grandparents' house in town. Everything's going to be fine," he reassured his wife.

Yet Julianna had had enough, not just of living in the wilderness, but of everything. Mike had opened her eyes to so many matters, shown her things whose existence she'd never even suspected. She loved them, she'd torn free of the narrow world where she'd been living. She couldn't believe that if it weren't for Mike, she'd have stayed in it forever.

"I'd been nowhere, I'd seen nothing, I knew nothing, and I had no curiosity," Julianna counted off on her fingers. "That's how I was educated. My entire world was this town. I'd lived like someone shut away in a tower."

"You only ate what was put on your plate," said Mike.

It was about so many things, big and small; customs, likes, prejudices, behavior, and trivialities, such as how they ate their meals. In Julianna's family nobody ever ate away from home, and the food was instantly put on your plate and set on the table for you. At the Boardmans' everyone helped themselves to as much of each dish as they wanted. Julianna's relatives would visit their friends without warning. The Boardmans regarded that as bad manners, and always called first to say they were coming.

It often seemed to her that although she and Mike lived in the same place at the same time, although they'd sometimes seen each other in the street, their meeting was extremely improbable. The worlds they lived in were so totally different, as if parallel, with almost no point of contact, that sometimes their love and marriage seemed quite unreal to her.

She and Mike had been discovering these differences, learning about each other, confident that they'd be able to adapt, and that all they had to do was establish in what ways they were dissimilar. It worked, as long as nobody tried to encroach on their life. But the peaceful moments were getting rarer and shorter. As a couple, they had disturbed the town's harmony, so it refused to leave them in peace. It was trying to separate them, reminding them of the old habits and order, safe and familiar. And of all the unbearable differences.

Then Mike had lost patience and understanding for Julianna's mistrust of the changes. Her attachment to the old life had started to annoy him, her inability and reluctance to break the final ties and truly set herself free. She had always seen the world differently from him, in a narrower, more solid frame that enclosed her within a small, familiar space. As he showed her a different reality, he had soon felt the resistance in her, as if she refused to see any more, as if he'd come too close to the boundaries marking her customary world.

At these times, he seemed like a stranger to Julianna. Terrified, she sought salvation and comfort. She found them with her mother, in her old home, in the old world where she'd grown up, where something still kept her, still tempted and called to her. Mike didn't fit in here. So her mother and father kept telling her; so did Henk Malan, whenever he dropped in at their house on the remote farm and, if Mike was out, stayed for tea.

Inflamed by them, she took her grievances to Mike.

"This isn't what you promised me, it wasn't meant to be like this, I'm not going to put up with the difficult life you've condemned me to."

Divided, they couldn't cope with the clash of worlds. Both stubborn and quick-tempered, they were quarreling more and more often, about everything and anything. They argued and made up, parted and got back together, feeling more and more hurt by the misunderstandings and causing each other pain.

Every time she came back to him, Mike tried to convince Julianna that they should get as far away from this town as possible, the farther the better—they must escape, that was the only hope for them.

"We're too different to succeed here," he said.

Julianna agreed, saying he was right, and shouting that she hated this town, which wouldn't accept the slightest diversity, or any kind of independence.

After Terre'Blanche's death and the attack on Strotmann's farm, Mike and Julianna moved into Ventersdorp, to a gated community of identical bungalows on the river, protected by security guards. Whenever I went to visit them, Mike came out to meet me at the main gate.

"You won't find the way," he explained. "Everything here looks so similar that I sometimes go past my own house without recognizing it."

It was a pleasant, warm evening, and the residents of the neighboring houses were out on their porches and lawns. Immobilized by the heat and wearied by the same endless pace, without hiding their curiosity, they stared after me all the way to Mike and Julianna's house. Mike opened the front door for me.

"I'm off to Australia. Julianna has finally agreed," he said, smiling at his wife.

"I'm longing to get away from here," she said. "I don't want my sons to be like the people in this town."

Henk Malan spent his time in the kitchen, sitting for hours in front of a small television that sat high up, on top of the refrigerator, almost touching the ceiling. These days he rarely went farther than his own yard, hardly ever into the street outside, and almost never into town.

Not long after Terre'Blanche's death he had closed the Blue Crane tavern. It wasn't making any profit, his alcohol license had run out, and they'd refused to issue him a new one at the town hall. This time Anita couldn't pull strings for him; she'd been fired from her job at the civic administration, and a black girl had been employed in her place.

"What on earth has happened?" said Henk in disbelief and the distress of a man who doesn't recognize his own world. "It's apartheid in reverse. Now, if you're not black, you have a tough life. Especially in a dump like Ventersdorp. There's no future here."

Lost in thought for a while, he gazed at an old corkboard, to which he used to pin press cuttings about Terre'Blanche.

"Unless you take on a black as a partner."

At the town hall they had made it very clear to him that he would only get a new license to sell alcohol if he went into business with the cousin of one of the town councillors. He had refused. He sold the tavern to the young de Beer, who changed its name to a black one, Sedibeng, meaning "Pure Water Spring," and boasted that he would finally show how to get the business going and make money out of the blacks.

"Good luck to him!" said Henk dismissively. "I don't want any part of it. I'm glad I'm finally rid of it."

Leaving the task of selling the tavern to his wife, straight after Terre'Blanche's funeral he went out of town, and disappeared without a trace. Finally, Anita was starting to wonder whether to go to the police and report him missing. As if she'd conjured him up by thinking about it, that evening he called—all the way from Mozambique, where he'd found a job as a security guard at a gold mine.

Six months later he came home, since when he had hardly been out of the house, but sat waiting for the phone to ring with news of a new contract, which an acquaintance had promised him in Zambia or Malawi, on Lake Nyasa.

"There's no future for me here now," he kept saying, when I went to see him. "And there's nothing to keep me here," he added, casting a glance at his black-haired, dusky wife, bustling about in the dining room.

On his return he'd started to drink. He'd brought back a bottle of the local whisky from Mozambique in a thick flask designed to look like the shape of Africa. The blacks sold bottles of this kind to foreign tourists. He hadn't thrown it away, but kept refilling it with the whisky he bought at the store.

"I've got to get out of here. Only a fool sits and waits for death," he said, pouring the drinks.

That day happened to be the anniversary of his mother's death, so he had been to the cemetery. He'd spent half the day walking about before he found her grave.

"It's completely overgrown, there's grass up to your waist, like out on the veld!"

There was a grave I hadn't been able to find at the cemetery too, that of an Irish soldier who had deserted during one of the Boer wars and gone over to the enemy's side. He couldn't abide the brutality of the British army, as it wiped out Boer towns and farms, and locked the Boers in concentration camps. The Irishman had run away from his platoon and hidden on the Engelbrechts' farm near Ventersdorp. When his hosts ran out of food, he'd offered to go to the market in town. He'd had the bad luck to run into a British patrol that included soldiers who recognized him. He was arrested, condemned to death for desertion, and shot.

The clerk at the town hall told me I'd find the Irishman's grave by the cemetery wall, to the left of the gate, under a large tree.

"It's a pity it's almost winter, because until late autumn that tree is covered in flowers," she said.

I was also supposed to recognize the Irish deserter's grave by the fact that it was far away from the graves of the British soldiers and Boer partisans.

Until midday I wandered along the paths between the family tombs of the town's first citizens, the Deventers, de Kocks, Mollmans, Cronkamps, van Zyls, Potgieters, and van der Bergs.

Research conducted some years ago by a scholar from Cape Town showed that almost all the modern-day Afrikaners are descendants of the first thousand Boer settlers, and half of them have the same Christian names as the pioneers. To this day almost all the citizens of Cederberg valley near Cape Town have the surname Nieuwoudt, which was what the first settler family was called. The Afrikaners in Transvaal often address each other as "Father," "Uncle," "Auntie," or "Brother," although not connected by any formal kinship.

I found the graves of Raymond's grandfather, George Boardman, and of the Jewish tradesmen, the Robinsons and the

Newmans. The graves of thirty-seven British soldiers, killed in skirmishes with the Boers in January and May 1901, were lined up in two rows, as straight as on parade.

I couldn't find the Irish deserter's grave.

"I've never heard of him before," said Henk Malan, shrugging.

Sprawled at a white plastic garden table set up in the kitchen, he was checking his correspondence. He tossed the colorful advertising leaflets into a wastebasket, and put the bills to one side. He hadn't received any letters.

Next to the television on the refrigerator there was another, smaller screen. Henk didn't hide his satisfaction when I asked him about it. On his return from Mozambique he had fixed two cameras to the high fence surrounding the house and wired them up to the monitor standing on the refrigerator. There was a remote control on the kitchen table, which let him change channels, showing images from the camera on the gate, or the one at the rear of the house. Even while watching television, by glancing at the other screen, he could see what was going on in his yard.

"Good, eh? Like this I won't be surprised," he said. "The blacks aren't fit to run this place. We tried to teach them something, but they're simply not fit, they've got a smaller cerebral cortex than us. This country was paradise on earth, but what have they done to it? They want to take it all away from us, and then cut our throats. There's a great big war ahead of us. The blacks won't give way to us, but it's impossible to live with them."

He belonged to the semilegal Suidlanders (Southerners) association, founded by a former intelligence officer called Gustav Müller and open to Afrikaners who believed that one day the blacks would murder all the whites, and take away their land and houses. The start of the "night of the long knives" was to be the death of Nelson Mandela.

This had been predicted a hundred years earlier by the Boer "prophet" Nicolaas van Rensburg, who at his farm on the Transvaal veld had almost a thousand visions. This clairvoyant predicted the outbreak of both Boer wars, as well as the First World War, the collapse of the British Empire, Irish independence, the Spanish flu epidemic, and AIDS.

In the days of the Boer wars, he predicted the advent of a black president, during whose government Muslims originally from India would take power. The black president would be murdered, a seven-day mourning period would be announced, and all the world's leaders would come to his funeral. But the next day a great war would erupt. In Johannesburg the blacks would murder thirty thousand whites in a single night. However, the Boers would emerge from the war triumphant, they would rout all their enemies, and regain power over the country.

The Southerners weren't going to be beaten easily or wait passively for their apocalypse. At the farms on the veld, under the tutelage of retired army and police officers, they became skilled in the craft of soldiering, and at some chosen sites they stockpiled food, medicine, fuel, weapons, and ammunition, stolen from army stores.

And when the hour struck, at an agreed signal from their supreme leader, Gustav Müller, the Southerners would all head for the impoverished white town of Bethlehem, located on the Jordan River in a valley in the Rooiberg Mountains. There would be a fortified camp ready and waiting for them, where they would survive the war, and then they would start to build a Boer republic.

"Eugène Terre'Blanche would have liked that," I said.

"Eugène? You must be joking! He was just a loudmouth. What sort of great leader lets himself get killed by a stableboy?"

He fell silent, then reached for a cigarette and the Africa-shaped bottle.

"Did you know that Mike Boardman's back from Australia?"

From the window of his office at the civic administration Benny Tapologo saw two whites and their black laborers dismantling the AWB monument in the park between the town hall and the courthouse.

They must have arrived at dawn, when the town was still deserted. They probably didn't want to attract attention or prompt a scandal. Benny watched as the black workmen in navy-blue overalls efficiently unscrewed the plaques from the plinth and carefully loaded them into the beds of some pickup trucks. They made short work of it, in half an hour. The whites slammed the cab doors shut, the blacks hopped in the back, and they drove away, never to be seen again.

Although long since removed from town hall affairs, Benny did know that neither the mayor nor the town council had given orders for the AWB monument to be taken down. But nobody tried to find out what had happened to it, or who the people were who had taken it away at dawn.

Nor did it occupy Benny's thoughts. Nor did the town council election, due to take place in a couple of weeks. He wasn't running in it, he wasn't included on the ANC candidate list for Ventersdorp, but was in first place on the reserve list. He would only have a seat on the council if one of the candidates died or withdrew. But Benny wasn't worrying about that either.

On his fortieth birthday he had paid *lobola*—a dowry—to the father of the girlfriend with whom he had been living for several years. He had given his future father-in-law a sum equivalent in value to several cows. The *lobola* had been accepted, so according to African custom they were already a married couple. Now they wanted to get married at the registry office.

"It's time to think of myself," said Benny, smiling broadly.

Although he didn't admit it, I got the impression that he was feeling resentful. I could definitely sense bitterness as he assured me that he'd quit politics and the power game, and that everything would have to be the same as in the past before he'd ever go back to it.

"It's time to think about myself," he repeated like a refrain.

The first time he thought about himself was when he found out that as a town councillor, at very low cost he could lease a Nissan SUV, bought by the town hall at public expense. The second time was when he stopped being a councillor and lost his job as adviser to the mayor. His party comrades had prompted him to register himself as officially unemployed and homeless, and apply to the state for the free housing that the authorities were distributing to the poor. He got a small, three-room house in the newest, fifth district of Tshing.

Now he was starting to look round for a business.

"Maybe I'll set up a transport firm, or maybe a diamond polishing company," he wondered aloud. "I just have to find a partner, a white partner with experience, the sort of person who knows a thing or two."

To reward the blacks for all the years of discrimination, the new authorities had started showing them favor, giving them the most important posts in business and public office, and points for racial origin also facilitated entry to universities. Firms that had blacks on their board of directors could count on preferential loans and concessions. They had even set a legal upper limit on income, above which business owners simply had to take on a black partner.

In the distant past, when they took over the country from the British, the Boer leaders had supported their own compatriots in a similar way. Now it was the blacks' turn to be granted property rights. From one day to the next former revolutionaries, rebels, political prisoners, and trade union activists were made the chairmen of the boards of major concerns, becoming rich men, among the wealthiest in all Africa.

"And what do you think about it all?" asked Benny.

From the start of our conversation I had felt as if he were dodging, circling, wanting to ask me a question, but at the last moment something kept putting him off, so he changed the subject. He told me about the dismantling of the AWB monument, and then about his disenchantment with politics. He even showed me a newspaper issued in Johannesburg, *City Press*, and read out an article by Andile Mngxitama, a journalist famous throughout the country, who had grown up on a white farm near Potchefstroom and knew better than just about anyone how matters stood on the Transvaal veld, and was aware of all its residents' darkest secrets, dreams, hopes, obsessions, and fears.

"Just listen to this," said Benny, seeking out the right passage. "If we want to understand South ¬Africa, then we need to look more closely at Ventersdorp, a town that springs up at you in the heart of the North West maize belt . . . When I go to Ventersdorp, I see a microcosm of South Africa—racist, untransformed, supremacist."

But even as he read it, I could tell that his mind was on something else.

"Or maybe I should buy a farm in the neighborhood?" he said at last. "I've heard about that Buckingham farm, apparently they're not doing too well. You're staying there, with that Boardman guy, aren't you? What's he like? Do you think I could make a deal with him?"

That year, Boardman hadn't sowed the fields. The purchase price of maize had fallen so low that in the spring he'd realized it would make better financial sense to lease the land to cattle breeders as pasture than to cultivate it.

"The government is buying cheap maize in America and isn't protecting the farmers," he informed his workers; in that case, they asked, clearly alarmed, what was he going to harvest, and what were they going to live on?

He can't have reassured them, because several times after that they wanted to know if he was thinking of selling the land. Apparently someone in town had been asking questions about his farm.

He no longer had any work for them, but kept them on at Buckingham, and still paid them a weekly wage every Friday. As there wasn't much happening on the farm, there wasn't much to do, apart from routine jobs in the farmyards. So they no longer started the day at dawn, but later, sometimes not until eight or even nine.

Time passed more slowly, dissolving in the sunshine that grew hotter by the hour, and stopping in the dark shade on the grass in front of the veranda, under the spreading black acacias and eucalyptus trees. After midday, life on the farm came to a standstill. After finishing the routine tasks, with nothing better to do, the blacks would go home, not knowing how to occupy themselves.

Raymond was happy with the sudden excess of time. He said it might actually be a good thing, as he'd finally get on with sorting out all the family papers he kept in a safe in his study. He'd been meaning to do it ever since returning to the farm, but the farming and the blacks had taken up all his strength, time, and attention.

"I put it off for a quieter moment," he said. "Who knows, maybe that quieter time is now."

He no longer went out to confer with the blacks as he used to. I hadn't seen Petrus or Jomo for a few days, though I'd been spending almost all my time at the farm. The blacks didn't even come in range of the house, as if they'd suddenly ceased to have anything in common with Raymond. There was no connection between them anymore, not even the usual relationship between worker and employer.

"They just come every Friday for their money, but I don't think they associate it with any community of interests. I don't think they care where I get it from or what I'm paying them for. They just believe it's their due. I don't really know what I'm to do with them," said Raymond one day, when unusually he was sitting out on the veranda with me.

Once we used to sit out there until late at night, over cigarettes and whisky, listening to the crickets and cicadas, watching as the glimmers of light went out in the windows of the houses where the blacks lived. Raymond told me about the farm, about his plans, about Mike and Julianna, and Gareth, his grandson, the fifth generation of Boardmans to grow up in this town.

The previous year, when Mike had gone to Australia, Gareth had lived at Buckingham. His toys still lay scattered around the house, including teddy bears, a hippopotamus, a rabbit and a dog, and a little orange car with no front wheels. Raymond often said he missed the boy. On his return from Australia Mike had taken him and Julianna to Pretoria, where they had settled on a chicken farm.

He hadn't wanted to come back from Australia at all. He'd ended up near Brisbane, on a pig farm. The work was tough, but he was in seventh heaven. He wrote home to say he'd found his promised land. But eventually Julianna had refused to go to the other end of the world. She couldn't tell Mike straight out that she wouldn't go to Australia, but she did everything to prolong the formalities involved in making the journey.

Pretoria proved a mistake. For Mike it was too close to Ventersdorp, and for Julianna it was too far away. All the more since the chicken farm where they lived was in an isolated place almost an hour's drive from the city center, right next to a black township called Shoshanguve which bordered Mabopane, from where Eugène Terre'Blanche's killer had come to Ventersdorp.

Julianna wanted to go back there.

"Mike suspects me of stirring Julianna up, as a way of bringing him back to the farm—he thinks I want to run his life," Raymond had told me the night before after supper, which Charlene had served in the living room.

We weren't eating outside in the garden in the evenings anymore. Now Raymond was chasing me inside, the shadows were only just gathering in the yard, and the first chill was drawing in from the veld. We only ate supper outside when guests came. When we were alone, Raymond closed the shutters from the inside and brought the dogs in. They were trained not to bark in the daytime, but after dusk fell, once they were in the house, they announced everything that was happening outside. Raymond said it was enough to keep an eye on them to be relatively safe.

He spent all day long going through the family archive, and each evening he told me about his grandfather George. George was regarded in the family as a hero, on a par with the pastor William, the first Boardman to have settled in the south of Africa, who had founded one of the first schools.

Grandfather George, great-grandson of Reverend William, was the first Boardman to be born in Ventersdorp. He was sixteen when the war between the British and the Boers broke out on the Highveld. Although he was English, the British army had imprisoned him and his entire family along with the Boers in a concentration camp.

He had fought in the First World War, and had volunteered for the second one too, even though he was approaching fifty by then. He served in the Second World War with his son, Raymond's father, who had fought in Egypt, Libya, and Tunisia. Grandfather George had repaired military aircraft in Italy.

After supper, Raymond spread out proof of his grandfather's merits on the dining room table.

A yellowing photograph of his grandfather and father, in army uniform, standing outside the farmhouse. A large framed portrait of Grandfather George, and also his uniform, hanging on the wall in Raymond's study.

His army medals and insignia.

Ration cards issued by the British to Boer concentration camp prisoners, dating from 1901 and 1902, for ten adults and two children. There was exactly that number of people in his grandfather's family at the time.

A certificate of inoculation against smallpox issued by the military authorities in Potchefstroom.

A copy of a land purchase document dated November 30, 1918, 250 acres at Buckingham.

A certificate of baptism dated 1884.

A farmer's notebook recording the harvests of 1912.

The birth and death certificates of Raymond's grandmother, Rotha May Coventry Fell, whose family came to Africa all the way from New Zealand. An envelope containing locks of her hair.

A license to hunt wild birds on the territory of Ventersdorp dated 1907. Raymond remembered his grandfather as a keen hunter. He was never parted from his shotgun, and fired at everything that moved on the farm.

A petition signed by his grandfather, from the citizens of Ventersdorp to the government, requesting the construction of a railroad station.

Raymond couldn't come to terms with the fact that although the Boardmans had been living in Ventersdorp for more than a hundred years, they had no friends or acquaintances here. Apart from the Boardmans, there were only about three of four families of British origin in the entire municipality. The Afrikaners did not regard them as their kin, and they related to the Boardmans worst of all. It had always been like that—nobody in the town had ever wondered why.

One evening Raymond came into my room.

"I think I may have found out why they don't want me here," he said.

One after another, he placed some slips of paper on the table.

A permit to ride a bicycle and travel to Potchefstroom, dated 1901.

A permit to go about Potchefstroom after ten at night, dated 1902.

Some notes and instructions handwritten by British officers on pages torn from a notebook. "Supply a mattress, pillow, sheet and three blankets. Immediately. August 1, 1902."

A firearms license issued in 1905.

A letter from George Boardman to Her Majesty's government, complaining that although he had fought for Great Britain as a loyal soldier in three wars, he had been discharged from army service without a word, thrown away like a broken rifle.

"Bloody hell! In three wars! You see? The British shut him up in a concentration camp, but then he must have gone over to their side. He was a collaborator." Raymond looked at me inquiringly, as if the truth of his own words hadn't sunk in yet. "Maybe they just took him on as an interpreter? But if they issued him with a firearms license immediately after the war, he must have been someone they trusted. That's why the local Afrikaners are convinced he got the farm as a reward from the British for his treachery!"

Outside, some chaotic singing rang out from the direction of the road, somebody was bellowing in a fitful, guttural way, and bursting into laughter. It was Friday, and the blacks were celebrating payday. They had lit a bonfire under a tree and were drinking moonshine. Someone began chanting a song, then others joined in, their voices full and steady. We listened in silence.

"They've joined the party, and they say they're going to take away the land," said Raymond. "They go to rallies and sing 'Dubul'ibhunu.' Have you heard it? 'Kill the Boer, kill the farmer.' Do you want to wait a bit? They're sure to sing it later on."

EPILOGUE

Dear friend,

Hope you and your family are well. We are all doing fine.

Not sure if I mentioned before that we have another addition to the farm—Stacy Jean was born on May 17, 2012.

Most of the farm burned down yesterday. Fortunately the crops were off the lands but 8 percent prime grazing was destroyed. No arson suspected—just negligence two farms farther west from us.

I have fought worse fires but this was the worst fire we have had at Buckingham and Uitkyk in my memory. It came from the west and continued easterly, branching off north and south—so unpredictable. At one stage I thought Mike had been overcome by the flames—being trapped between fence and flames—I watched as he raced through the flames. He is fine but there were some tense moments before I found out he got through OK—just a bit singed and a burned hat. Not a nice day.

God Bless,

Ray

Ventersdorp, August 26, 2014

TIMELINE

1652 The first settlers from Europe arrive at the Cape of Good Hope, Dutchmen who found a port here and a supply base for the merchant ships of the East India Company. They are soon joined by refugees from Europe, including French Huguenots and the German Protestants, victims of religious wars. With them comes the first of the Terre'Blanche family, Étienne. The settlers found Cape Town.

1806 Great Britain annexes the Cape Colony from the Dutch and establishes its own colony there. In 1820 the British government conducts the first settlement campaign in the colony. The first of the Boardman family, the pastor William, arrives in southern Africa.

1793–1835 The Dutch settlers, known as Boers (from the Dutch boer, meaning "farmer"), and British troops wage war on the Xhosa people, who inhabit the territory to the east of the Cape Colony.

1817–1828 The Zulu king Shaka routs other African tribes, and by waging numerous wars, builds a mighty kingdom from the Drakensberg Mountains to the shores of the Indian Ocean.

1836 Thousands of Boers, dissatisfied with British government in Cape Town, leave the Cape Colony and set off on the Great Trek deep inside the African continent. They establish their own republics, Transvaal, Natal, and the Orange Free State, which fight constant wars against the Zulus. In 1837, at the Battle of Blood River, a handful of Boers defeats a mighty Zulu army, killing more than three thousand warriors.

1879 British troops finally conquer the Zulu lands and incorporate them into their colony of Natal.

1886 In the Boer Transvaal Republic some of the world's richest deposits of diamonds and gold are discovered. Gold fever brings treasure hunters down to Transvaal and makes the Boers start to fear they will become a minority in their own land.

1899–1902 On the excuse of protecting the rights of English-speaking settlers in Transvaal, and in fact to subordinate the Boer republics and appropriate their wealth, Great Britain declares a new war on the Boers (the first, from 1880–1881, ended in victory for the Boers). After a long war, in which to break the Boer partisans the British employ concentration camps for the civilian population, the Boers capitulate, and their republics are incorporated into the colonial possessions of Great Britain.

1910 The British Cape Colony and Natal, and the formerly Boer republics of Orange Free State and the Transvaal are declared the Union of South Africa, in which Boer politicians conciliatory to Great Britain hold the power. Blacks have no civic or political rights in the Union.

1912 The South African Native National Congress is formed, from 1923 the African National Congress (ANC), the aim of which is to fight against racial discrimination.

1948 Afrikaner nationalists from the National Party win the election to parliament, take power in the country, and introduce the apartheid system, enforced racial segregation.

1960 The Sharpeville massacre. More than sixty blacks are killed by police bullets during a peaceful protest against the apartheid laws. The white authorities ban ANC activities. In view of the repression, the young ANC activists, led by Nelson Mandela, convince the old leadership that it's time to stop modeling themselves on Mahatma Gandhi and drop the idea of a nonviolent struggle. Mandela prepares to take on the role of black rebel leader.

1964 Mandela is sentenced to life imprisonment. Almost the entire leadership of the black liberation movement ends up in jail with him.

1976 In Soweto and other black townships anti-apartheid riots break out. More than five hundred people are killed in them, and almost two and a half thousand are injured. The brutally suppressed riots prompt international sanctions and ostracism for the racist white government.

1985 A new black uprising. The white government introduces a state of emergency.

1990 To avoid civil war, the last white president, F. W. de Klerk, declares an end to apartheid and releases Mandela from jail.

1994 The first free election, in which the blacks can vote too. The ANC takes power in South Africa and Nelson Mandela becomes the country's first black president. He is succeeded in 1999 by Thabo Mbeki, and in 2009 by Jacob Zuma.

2010 Afrikaner Resistance Movement founder Eugène Terre'Blanche is murdered at his farm by laborers. Two months later, South Africa hosts the FIFA World Cup.

2013 Nelson Mandela dies on December 5, aged ninety-five. His state funeral was attended by some ninety heads of government from around the world.

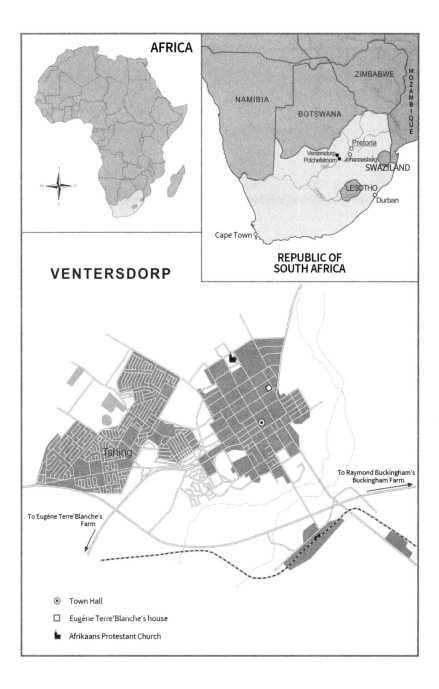

AFRICA

NAMIBIA

BOTSWANA

ZIMBABWE

MOZAMBIQUE

Pretoria

Ventersdorp
Potchefstroom
Vaal

Johannesburg

SWAZILAND

LESOTHO

Durban

Cape Town

REPUBLIC OF
SOUTH AFRICA

VENTERSDORP

Tshing

To Raymond Buckingham's
Buckingham Farm

To Eugène Terre'Blanche's
Farm

⊙　Town Hall

☐　Eugène Terre'Blanche's house

🔺　Afrikaans Protestant Church

AUTHOR'S NOTE

The identify of some characters has been changed to protect their privacy.